AF786976

The Girl Who Lived on Her Clothes

Studies in the History and Culture of Scotland

Volume 14

Valentina Bold, General Editor

PETER LANG
Oxford - Berlin - Bruxelles - Chennai - Lausanne - New York

The Girl Who Lived on Her Clothes

The People of Paisley and the New Poor Law, 1839–1876

Wendy M. Gordon

PETER LANG
Oxford - Berlin - Bruxelles - Chennai - Lausanne - New York

Bibliographic information published by the Deutsche Nationalbibliothek.
The German National Library lists this publication in the German National Bibliography; detailed bibliographic data is available on the Internet at http://dnb.d-nb.de.

A catalogue record for this book is available from the British Library.

Library of Congress Cataloging-in-Publication Data

Names: Gordon, Wendy (Lawyer), author.
Title: The girl who lived on her clothes : the people of Paisley and the new poor law, 1839-1876 / Wendy M. Gordon.
Description: Oxford ; New York : Peter Lang Publishing, 2024. | Series: Studies in the history and culture of scotland, 16616863 ; vol no 14 | Includes bibliographical references and index.
Identifiers: LCCN 2023054811 (print) | LCCN 2023054812 (ebook) | ISBN 9781800799905 (paperback) | ISBN 9781803744162 (ebook) | ISBN 9781803744179 (epub)
Subjects: LCSH: Poor laws—Scotland—History—19th century. | Public welfare—Law and legislation—Scotland—History—19th century. | Working class—Scotland—History—19th century. | Brown, James Shaw.
Classification: LCC KDC670 .G67 2024 (print) | LCC KDC670 (ebook) | DDC 364.1/4--dc23/eng/20231201
LC record available at https://lccn.loc.gov/2023054811
LC ebook record available at https://lccn.loc.gov/2023054812

Portions of Chapter Five previously published as "The Obligation to Support the Widow: Settlement, The New Poor Law and The Scottish Local State," *Journal of Scottish Historical Studies* 35.1 2015.

Cover design by Peter Lang Group AG

ISSN 1661-6863
ISBN 978-1-80079-990-5 (print)
ISBN 978-1-80374-416-2 (ePDF)
ISBN 978-1-80374-417-9 (ePub)
DOI 10.3726/b21617

Published by Peter Lang Ltd, Oxford, United Kingdom
info@peterlang.com - www.peterlang.com

This publication has been peer reviewed.

For 'Jean Watson', who deserved better than she got.

Contents

Tables and Illustrations

Tables and Illustrations

Acknowledgments

No project of this kind is the product of individual effort, and I have incurred significant debts in the two decades I have been rummaging through the poor law in Paisley. First, credit must go to Professor Sir Tom Devine, who pointed me toward Paisley in 1995 and set me on a track I've been following ever since. On that first visit to Paisley and every subsequent one I have been greeted and supported by the archival staff at The Heritage Centre @ OneRen (previously part of the Paisley Central Library), particularly David Weir. Through multiple relocations and refurbishments they have accommodated my needs for space and power. Mr Weir has been especially helpful in reading manuscripts at a number of stages and patiently correcting my Americanisms. I'm also extremely grateful to Cath Mitchell and Dan Coughlin at the Sma' Shot Cottages, who kindly gave me an extensive tour and conversation outside the normal season, enabling me to more effectively imagine the lives of Paisley's weavers. Any errors that remain in this text are my own alone.

This book builds on and extends numerous shorter projects regarding Paisley and the New Poor Law. Only one of those articles came substantially into the text, but the community of scholars working in Scottish, gender, and migration history have all contributed to my thinking and understanding as I have worked toward this monograph. A 2013 Conference on Singles in the Cities of North-West Europe, c. 1000–2000 hosted by the University of Antwerp was especially influential in shaping my thinking about people in and outside of families and their resulting relationships to the law, and also ways to tell the stories I was uncovering. Completing these projects has relied on a community of scholars whom I have never physically met, including editors and readers for the *Journal of Scottish Historical Studies* and Professor Kevin James at the Centre for Scottish Studies at the University of Guelph. With Professor James's support, the Society of Antiquarians of Scotland granted tangible support for my final research push in 2022. In addition, I had a remarkably good time with the

British Association for American Studies in Hull that Spring, when at last I knew the right questions to ask about local government in the nineteenth century and found an audience happy to answer them.

My students and colleagues at SUNY Plattsburgh in the History Department and across the campus have earned my appreciation in innumerable ways, from sabbatical funding to interlibrary loan to tolerant ears and probing questions that reassure me there really is an interesting story to tell about a seemingly arcane subject. Vincent Carey and Jeff Hornibrook have been especially supportive of my scholarship since the moment I set foot in Plattsburgh. The late Douglas Skopp and Kathy Lavoie were crucial cheerleaders, role models in balancing all the responsibilities of a career in public academia. Recognition is also due to United University Professions (especially Patty Bentley who pulled me into union work); I can't imagine completing this project without the stability a unionised university system provides.

At last to the family: I am immeasurably grateful to my parents for just about everything but most recently to my father Tom for his 'layman's eye' over the manuscript and commiseration over the woes of a historian. My mother, Patricia, passed away from multiple myeloma in 2020, and I am thankful every day for her legacy of grace, whimsy, and sharp editorial eye. Most fervent thanks and love go to the Guenther contingent of our GuenGord Conglomerate. Chet and Vivien have lived with this project their entire lives, and a couple of trips abroad seem like small repayment for the joy they have brought to my life. Ed, who does remember the before-Poor-Law time of my life, has been a constant source of support and distraction when I need it most, as well as a timely push to just get the job done. Thank you for being a part of everything.

Introduction: Inspector Brown and the New Poor Law for Scotland

James Shaw Brown devoted his life to the poor people of Paisley. From his first professional position as a teacher at Hutcheson Charity School to his death in 1876 he worked in daily contact with the people in Paisley who had no resources and nowhere else to turn. Whether sick, abandoned, profligate or unlucky, desperate people in Paisley relied on the poor law, colloquially called 'the parish', when their options narrowed to that or houselessness and hunger. From 1845, when he formally became Paisley's Inspector of the Poor, Brown's job was to determine who qualified for relief from the poor law, to manage the paperwork involved, and to keep the elected officials he served apprised of the situation. As Inspector, he stood at the centre of a relationship between the poor, the ratepayers, and the text of the law governing poor relief.

None of Inspector Brown's personal writings are known to survive, but it is hard to look at the records of his life and actions and not conclude he held a deep compassion for the poor people he served. Telling the story of the New Poor Law in Scotland as far as possible through his experiences emphasises the human interactions that were at the heart of caring for the poor in the nineteenth century (as they are today). Then as now, it was easy to generalise the poor as an undifferentiated mass of misery, lacking power and too numerous to help if one wanted. It was a poor law inspector's job to look past the misery and discover the human details that brought a person to desperate want. Through the records Paisley Burgh kept and husbanded for well over a century, that humanity can be revealed again today. Fundamentally this – as every discussion of poverty should be – is a book about people, the difficulties they faced and how they sought to help or be helped. Inspector Brown, quiet though he was, is an apt guide.

Poverty and Poor Relief in Scotland: Definitions

An Act for the Amendment and better Administration of the Laws relating to the Relief of the Poor in Scotland, more commonly called The Poor Law Amendment (Scotland) Act, the New Scottish Poor Law, or a similar variation, was broadly based in the idea that poverty was endemic to society, even divinely ordained, and that some poor people had a right to support from the church or civil government. A 'poor law' governed which poor people were entitled to formal relief and how the funds to pay relief would be raised, allocated, and distributed. In England, civil authorities took over the distribution in the late years of Elizabeth I's reign, and the law there was reformed in 1834. In Scotland, while there were laws governing vagrants (unemployed strangers) and mendicants (beggars) passed during the reign of James VI, the Kirk (Church of Scotland) took the leading role in collecting and distributing relief until 1845.

Poor relief in Scotland rested on two key philosophies: first, that only some kinds of poverty deserved to be relieved, and second, that individual communities were responsible for supporting their own poor. Vagrants, who came from outside a locality, and beggars, who defied the Kirk's gatekeeping over alms, violated this philosophy. The so-called 'deserving poor' were those who had no ability to support themselves, primarily envisioned as the elderly, orphaned, and severely disabled. In Scotland (more so than in England), an 'able-bodied' person was considered automatically disqualified from poor relief. Historians have argued over how absolute this prohibition was over time, and the poor relief community themselves argued this point well into the period of concern here.[1] Philosophically, however, the exclusion of able-bodied people from deserving relief was a key factor distinguishing the Scottish law from its English counterpart.

1 See, for example, R. Mitchison, 'The Creation of the Disablement Rule in the Scottish Poor Law', in *The Search for Wealth and Stability: Essays in Economic and Social History Presented to M.W. Flinn*, ed. T.C. Smout (London: Macmillan, 1979), 199–217; I. Levitt, *Poverty & Welfare in Scotland 1890–1948* (Edinburgh: Edinburgh University Press, 1988), 9–12; and also Chapter 4 of this book.

The official position that paupers were disabled led to relatively sympathetic treatment. There is no doubt that the amount of relief given was insufficient both before and after the passage of the New Poor Law in 1845, but the attitude that paupers must be punished or reformed of moral failing (as Charles Dickens extravagantly illustrated in *Oliver Twist*) was not endemic in Scotland. Poorhouses (not 'work houses') in Scotland were conceptualised as care facilities, and 'indoor relief' was granted to paupers who could not access or maintain their own housing. 'Outdoor relief', without incarceration, was far more common and more economical to give. In the period under study here, and particularly in Paisley, the Scottish poor law does not align with the broad-brush description derived from Dickens or many English histories.

The New Poor Law Act, subsequent amendments, associated legal cases and the bureaucracy that implemented them (broadly referred to in this text as the uncapitalised poor law) utilised additional specialised vocabulary that will appear in these pages. The basic administrative unit for the law was the *parish*, a civil division based on ecclesiastical boundaries within a county. The men who administered the law were given a range of specific and general titles, most commonly *managers* or *overseers* of the poor, and the New Poor Law organised them into a *parochial board* for each parish. When an individual or family applied for help from the poor law (*relief*), their information was recorded on a paper form that was referred to as a *schedule* or a *statement*. The individuals who were officially approved to receive relief were recognised *paupers*, which was a different legal status than being simply poor. A few technical terms were used to further define the paupers: *pupillarity* referred to young people who were past infancy but not yet self-supporting, and *nonage* indicated anyone considered too young for legal responsibility. When these young people did take jobs and leave their parents' homes, they were considered *forisfamiliated*. Paupers might receive relief either in money or in kind – a cash payment was also called an *aliment*. The funds to pay the aliment were raised through a local tax called a *poors' rate* or simply *rates*. Logically, the members of the community who were liable to pay (or to be *assessed*) this tax were usually called *ratepayers*. The ratepayers, who ranged from large landowners to simple *operatives* employed in the town's mills and factories, were enfranchised to elect the poor law managers, thus keeping daily control of the poor law a local affair.

Poor Law and the Local State

Scotland's separate control of poor relief was an important feature of the nation's agency and identity within the United Kingdom in the nineteenth century. Following Parliamentary Reform in 1832 and the subsequent reform of municipal governments, burgh-dwelling Scots took renewed control of community issues such as water supplies and road works. These projects were managed by town councils, police boards, and similar governing bodies that emerged in response to demand. The passage of the Poor Law (Scotland) Amendment Act in 1845 gave new local bodies, the parochial boards, responsibility for carrying out the national law at local scale. Unlike most other local concerns, the poor law required correspondence and negotiation between parishes and between the parochial boards and a national body, the Board of Supervision. Through these conversations across decades, the Scottish poor law was defined and shaped into a uniquely Scottish institution, a source of national pride for the men engaged in its management. Fully aware that the Poor Law (Scotland) Act and its amendments were passed by the UK Parliament where Scotland was a minority voice, managers of the poor were alert for evidence that English ideas and practices would be imposed on their Scottish concerns.

Scots were able to have such a strong voice in the interpretation of the poor law because of the peculiar structure of Scottish governance following the Union of Parliaments in 1707. Although Scotland retained its distinctive legal system and religious autonomy under the Union, there was no administrative structure for these institutions at the national level. Instead, towns, counties, and parishes managed areas that were left to Scottish control such as policing and education. Since the 1990s, historians of Scotland have adopted the idea of a 'local state' (which originated from sociologist Cynthia Cockburn in 1977) to describe the peculiar system of government for Scotland within the United Kingdom.[2] Graeme Morton wrapped such local oversight into the idea of a Victorian civil society that was managed primarily by voluntary organisations rather than national bureaucracies.[3] Relief for the poor, originally administered through the established churches in both Scotland and England, fell into the same category.[4]

Therefore, while the Parliament at Westminster passed the *Act for the Amendment and Better Administration of the Law Relating to the Relief of the Poor in Scotland* in 1845 for the whole of Scotland, it was implemented at the most-local level.[5] The newly-created parochial boards were to oversee relief, and day-to-day functions would be administered by newly-hired poor law inspectors. The Act encouraged combination of parishes that were physically proximate to reduce confusion, but that rarely occurred before the end of the century. The Edinburgh-based Board of Supervision at first neither claimed nor exercised strong central control.[6] For the first few decades, the board 'spent most of their time considering appeals against inadequate relief' rather than imposing a uniform interpretation of the law.[7] It was only in the early 1860s that the board began to require even

2 C. Cockburn, *The Local State: Management of Cities and People* (London: Pluto Press, 1977). A synopsis of the 'local state' in Scotland is provided by T.M. Devine, *The Scottish Nation: A History 1700–2000* (New York: Viking-Penguin, 1999), 287–9.

3 G. Morton, 'Civil Society, Municipal Government and the State: Enshrinement, empowerment and legitimacy. Scotland, 1800–1929', *Urban History* 25:3 (1998): 348–67. Similarly, see J.D. Myers, 'Scottish Nationalism and the Antecedents of the 1872 Education Act', *Scottish Educational Studies* 4:2 (1972): 73–92; A. Bain, 'The Beginnings of Democratic Control of Local Education in Scotland', *Scottish Economic and Social History* 23:1 (2003): 7–25; D.G. Barrie, 'Anglicization and Autonomy: Scottish Policing, Governance and the State, 1833 to 1885', *Law and History Review* 30:2 (May 2012): 449–94.

4 Morton mentions 'the … independence of the burgh, particularly in the relief of the poor', 365, a point reiterated by Devine, 288.

5 A. Paterson, 'The Poor Law in Nineteenth-Century Scotland', in *The New Poor Law in the Nineteenth Century*, ed. D. Fraser (New York: St. Martin's Press, 1976), 174–6.

6 Paterson, 'Poor Law in Nineteenth-Century Scotland', 176.

7 M.A. Crowther, 'Poverty, Health and Welfare', in *People and Society in Scotland 1830–1914*, ed. W. Hamish Fraser and R.J. Morris (Edinburgh: John Donald, 1990), 273.

standardised record-keeping from the parishes.[8] The implementation of the New Poor Law, then, first came at the parish level, where it was subject to a wide variety of interpretation by the various inspectors, who were either new to the job or familiar with whatever older system of relief had been in place in their parish before 1845. Details of how the poor law was enacted – who received relief, from what source, how it was funded and how transactions were recorded were worked out first at the parish level and then through dialogue among the parishes. When parish-level interpretations came into conflict, they were resolved in the courts or through extra-judicial consultations with Sheriffs or other knowledgeable arbitrators. Particularly difficult questions in the courts moved upward from the Sheriffs' Courts through appeals to the Courts of Session, the Scottish Supreme Court, and in occasional cases to the House of Lords. Court decisions then flowed downward to influence the extra-judicial arbitrations and discussions among the inspectors. In this way, although the law itself came from the Parliament of the United Kingdom, interpretation and implementation of the New Poor Law for Scotland was an organic expression of Scottish values from the local level.

Scotland's New Poor Law

The Poor Law Amendment (Scotland) Act and its effects has received far less scholarly attention than its counterpart passed for England in 1834. In part, this is attributable to the general conflation of Scottish history with British history, strongly favoring the southern partner after the Union of 1707 and the conclusion of the Jacobite movement in 1745. Only since the revival of a strong movement for Scottish independence in the 1990s has separate study of the Scottish experience in the post-Union period and later become common, expanding and redefining the idea of nation as it grapples with Scotland's relationship to the United Kingdom

8 Heritage Centre, Paisley @OneRen [hereafter HCP] Parochial Board Minutes, vol. 7–19, 11 Dec. 1861.

and empire.[9] Academic interest in Scotland's poor law has also been limited by the undeniable fact the Poor Law Amendment (Scotland) Act strongly reflected the preferences and prejudices of the English-dominated Parliament in Westminster that passed it. In broad strokes, the parsimonious, judgmental image of a Dickensian poor law can be applied across the United Kingdom with some accuracy. Narrowing the focus even slightly to Scotland's experience, however, reveals important differences between the nations.

England's early experience with their New Poor Law was an experiment in consolidation and centralised control. The initial period of forceful combination was brief – half a decade or so, according to Anthony Brundage – before some degree of local flexibility was allowed, but significant.[10] The unions created by merging parishes and centralised interpretations of the law from the Poor Law Commission imposed uniformity and cooperation on the English Poor Law experience from the outset, with a strong central body poised to enforce compliance until local institutions were sufficiently established.

In Scotland, by contrast, the Board of Supervision (the Scottish equivalent to the Poor Law Commission) had no powers of enforcement and until the mid-1860s they offered advice rather than dictates.[11] As Ian Levitt observed and is described in the next chapter, the impulse to reform the poor law in Scotland came from the traumatic experience of devastating want due to economic collapse in the 1840s. In the initial decades of the law's implementation, administrative concern was centred on providing appropriate

9 G. Morton and T. Griffiths, 'Closing the door on Modern Scotland's Gilded Cage', *The Scottish Historical Review* 92:234 (April 2013): 49–69. See also R.J. Morris and G. Morton, 'Where Was Nineteenth-Century Scotland?', *The Scottish Historical Review* LXXIII:195 (April 1994): 89–99; J. Stevenson, 'Writing Scotland's History in the Twentieth Century: Thoughts from across the Border', *The Scottish Historical Review* 76:201 (April 1997): 103–14; and A. Raffe, '1707, 2007, and the Unionist Turn in Scottish History', *The Historical Journal* 53:4 (Dec. 2010): 1071–83.

10 A. Brundage, *The Making of the New Poor Law: The Politics of Inquiry, Enactment, and Implementation, 1832–9* (New Brunswick, NJ: Rutgers UP, 1978), 178–9.

11 Paterson, 'Poor Law', 176.

and adequate support rather than minimising expense or enacting moral reform.[12] When uniform interpretations and requirements eventually came into force, they arose from decades of local experience and debate rather than from a top-down fiat regarding the meaning of the law. This book, through a close examination of poor relief as it was administered in Paisley through the forty years of James Shaw Brown's career, illustrates this process of bottom-up consensus-building that created the poor law in Scotland in its mature form.

Poor Relief in the Community

Poor relief was experienced most profoundly at the individual level. It was irrelevant to a pauper how a court decided, until that decision resulted in the approval or denial of an aliment by the local poor law inspector. Poverty and poor relief were familiar elements of society in nineteenth-century Scotland. Even when linked to England and the British Empire the economy left significant numbers of Scots vulnerable to hunger. Both rural and urban inhabitants faced economic challenges; throughout the century opportunities for agricultural labor and self-sufficiency declined, and wide fluctuations in the industrial economy undercut the security of those who relied on factory labor or trades. Workers and families in these vulnerable strata employed what scholars have termed the 'economy of makeshift', piecing together waged labor, scavenging, charity, theft, and even less savory activities to secure the means of survival.[13] Formal poor relief was an important if sometimes elusive resource in this portfolio of options. The people who applied for relief left traces of their lives and struggles behind, humanising caricatures and horrifying portrayals of

12 Levitt, *Poverty & Welfare*, 15–18.

13 S. King and A. Tomkins, eds, *The Poor in England 1700–1850: An Economy of Makeshift* (Manchester: Manchester University Press, 2003); S. Williams, 'Earnings, Poor Relief and the Economy of Makeshifts: Bedfordshire in the Early Years of the New Poor Law', *Rural History* 16:1 (2005): 21–52.

the poor. To balance the thrill-seeking, disgust and shock journalism of Charles Dickens, Henry Mayhew, and their ilk, this study endeavors to place the paupers in their own context without undue emphasis on the physical conditions of their experiences. What I have struggled to recover are the human connections, assuming that the same range of emotions and needs affected individuals' actions then as they do today.

In addition to recipients of relief, significant numbers of more economically secure Scots participated in the governance and administration of poor relief. Relief was self-funded by each parish, through either voluntary or (increasingly across this period) mandatory contributions from householders, which gave ratepayers a vested interest in the poor law, its effectiveness and its efficiency. By virtue of paying rates, the payers gained the right to directly elect up to thirty members of their parochial board, which directed and controlled the administration of the poor laws in their parish. (Thirty was a maximum set by the Act. One of the few powers given to the Board of Supervision was to determine the actual number of members to be elected to the board for each parish. In Paisley Burgh Parish, the number was fifteen, with an additional four members selected by the town council and up to four by the kirk session.[14]) The parochial boards and administrative staff each parish employed, multiplied by the eight-hundred-eighty parishes in Scotland, meant that thousands of men in various levels of the middle class were intimately engaged with the business of relief. Some were active for only a year or two to effect some desired reform while others, like James Shaw Brown, made it their life's work. The Inspectors of the Poor and their clerks spent endless hours in interviews and correspondence attempting to determine to which parish paupers rightly belonged. They parsed the nuances of the law and previous cases, debated the precise moment of forisfamiliation, what could be construed as migration and what was simply a temporary absence from home, what constituted a legal marriage, and drew out logical conclusions from expedient interpretations.

14 *An Act for the Amendment and Better Administration of the Laws relating to the Relief of the Poor in Scotland*, [hereafter *Poor Law (Scotland)*], 1845, Section 17.

Faced with a complex problem and a lack of centralised guidance except through the courts, the administrators of the poor law reacted with a method familiar in nineteenth-century Britain – they formed a society. In the mid-1850s, poor law inspectors began to consolidate themselves into first regional and then a national Society of Poor Law Inspectors of Scotland. After 1855, contested cases that might previously have ended in court were debated among a group of inspectors at quarterly Society meetings or were agreed to be brought to arbitrators rather than to a court. The Society began to publish a journal, *The Poor Law Magazine for Scotland*, in 1858, and to include in it not only synopses of court cases but also records of the arbitrations and debates it believed would interest its members.

In 1861 an editor of the *Poor Law Magazine* recalled the difficult days after the new law's passage, when tensions were high between old managers of the poor and the new crop of inspectors, and several parochial boards were so frequently engaged in litigation that they retained law agents on salary. He cheerfully reported that since the establishment of the societies, 'the jealous feeling which used to prevail, is now almost wholly eradicated'. Instead of 'the asperity which used to have a permanent place in the correspondence of Inspectors', the men met 'each other openly, and as equals … and whilst they still differ[ed] they [did] so with a full regard to each other's honesty of purpose'.[15] This optimistic synopsis underscores the humanity of all those involved in the poor law at this time and the importance of individual interactions to the process of implementing the New Poor Law across the nation.

The Girl Who Lived on Her Clothes

This book explores key moments in the development of this institution, focusing on the people and experiences in the Paisley Burgh Parish. The first two chapters describe how the Poor Law Amendment was passed, first describing Paisley's efforts to provide for the poor under the Old

15 *The Poor Law Magazine for Scotland*, 4 (Oct. 1861), 82–4.

Poor Law from the 1830s until the terrible economic collapse of the 1840s. Chapter 2 traces what happened after the crisis as Paisley's leaders determined how to carry the new legislation into practice. Chapter 3 examines who applied for relief and who managed it, exploring the poor law as a framework to mediate between the destitute and charitable classes in Paisley.

The second half of the book covers specific issues that emerged from interpreting the New Poor Law and how those issues developed through local and national conversations. Support for the able-bodied unemployed during periods of economic distress was the greatest difference between the Scottish law and the English one, and as described in Chapter 4 Paisley voices fought valiantly but ultimately unsuccessfully to carve out an exception to the Law's able-bodied rule. A more successful though more narrowly applicable argument is the focus of Chapter 5, the question of when and in what circumstances a woman had control of her own poor law settlement. Victorian Scotland has already been recognised as less bound to rigid gender roles than previously believed.[16] This chapter suggests that middle-class ideas about women's autonomy were also applied by them to the poor.[17] Finally, Chapter 6 demonstrates the strategies and the limits of local control over relief. In 1857 a new Lunacy Act for Scotland created a national governing body to oversee treatment of all mentally ill and intellectually disabled people in Scotland, including those who were also paupers. The Scottish General Lunacy Board, unlike the Board of Supervision, had enforceable powers. When they decreed that Paisley must reform its provisions for pauper lunatics, the parochial board used every tool at their disposal to assert local autonomy but ultimately had to accept the mandate from centralised power. This defeat was emblematic of the progress of poor relief more generally. By the mid-1870s the messy

16 E. Gordon and G. Nair, *Public Lives: Women, Family, and Society in Victorian Britain* (New Haven: Yale University Press, 2003); M. Smitley, *The Feminine Public Sphere: Middle-Class Women in Civic Life in Scotland, c. 1870–1914* (Manchester: Manchester University Press, 2009).

17 Segments of Chapter 5 were previously published as 'The Obligation to Support the Widow: Settlement, the New Poor Law and the Scottish Local State', *Journal of Scottish Historical Studies* 3:1 (2015): 45–69.

process of implementation through local boards and national guidance resulted in largely uniform practices around the nation.

Four decades before Paisley Burgh bowed to pressure and opened their new asylum, a young James Shaw Brown, teacher, submitted his application for the advertised position as Master of the Town Hospital. He may have seen the post as a temporary stop on his way to a career as a solicitor or writer, but instead it was the first step in devoting his entire professional career to poor relief. He became the most knowledgeable figure administering the poor law in a parish that was central to the passage of the New Poor Law Act itself. His was a confident, if quiet, influential voice threaded through the implementation of the Act in Scotland. He is not in any way a 'father' or creator of the Law as it came to be. Instead, he is a stand-in for the thousands of dedicated officials and bureaucrats in Scotland who worked together to create and manage a law that would suit all Scots.

A Note About Sources and Method

Personal details in this book are drawn from primary source material, with the exception of occasional scene-setting details. We cannot really know if a mother dandled her baby or if a man wept, or a House matron's mood when she requested new carpet for her quarters. Where used, these descriptions were inferred from context. The foundation of this book is the astonishing collection of poor law records held by the Scottish National Archive and housed at the Paisley Heritage Centre. Of first importance are the Statements of Cases, the individual case records of nearly every person who applied for relief in Paisley from 1839 past the end of the century. Nearly as important and certainly indispensable are the minute books that recorded meetings of the town council, the Town Hospital Board, the Parochial Board, and its several committees for the same long period. Minutes are of course only minutes, rarely recording personalities or intimate details, but they are a critical source for understanding how Paisley's governing class perceived and treated the poor in the town. In citing from these records I have mostly modernised punctuation, capitalisation and some spelling for ease of reading, without altering the substance.

These two collections are fleshed out with the near-miraculous (to a gen-x historian) digitisation of vital and other personal records through the *Scotland'sPeople* database crafted and maintained by the National Record Office.[18] Although intended primarily for genealogy, it was invaluable for this research. The last major source used was the decennial census enumerators' books of 1851, 1861, and 1871, in both microform and digitised. I used the census for record-matching, and also made some use of the 10 percent sample of adults in Paisley that I drew for my first book.[19] To complement the census years, I focused my work with the Statements of Cases on the same years, because to look at the entire run of cases would be fascinating but unfeasible. There are some cases that fall outside these years, but the vast majority of individuals described in this book first applied for relief in one of the census years.

Every one of these sources needs to be addressed with a critical eye. It was evident early on, when I first began record-matching, that untruths both inadvertent and purposeful permeated every source.[20] My own experience as a committee recording secretary leads me to a healthy skepticism of even the minute books. My solution to the discrepancies has been a shrug and a commitment to make the uncertainties transparent. Personally, it may have mattered a great deal if a woman was named Helen or Elin, and if her child was 7 months or 1 year old.[21] Historically, for the purposes of the story I am telling, it does not. What matters is that they lived, and their existence deserves to be recalled as much as that of the illustrious twice-Provost David Murray, who also graces these pages.

18 *ScotlandsPeople* scotlandspeople.gov.uk.

19 W. Gordon, *Mill Girls and Strangers: Single Women's Independent Migration in England, Scotland, and the United States, 1850–81* (Albany: State University of New York Press, 2002).

20 The fluidity of facts is particularly evident in W. Gordon, 'Destitute in December: Unmarried Scots Navigating Poverty in Paisley, 1861', in *Single Life and the City 1200–1900*, ed. J. De Groot, I. Devos and A. Schmidt (New York: Palgrave Macmillan, 2015), 93–113.

21 HCP Statements of Cases, vol. 11–6, Statement 4641; ScotlandsPeople Census 1851 573/1/15. Leitch, Daniel.

CHAPTER 1

The Case of the Unemployed and Destitute Inhabitants: Managing Poverty in Paisley before the New Poor Law: 1834–42

Paisley and the Old Poor Law

Around 1814, blacksmith David Brown decided to try his luck in Paisley. Brown and his wife, Euphemia Sellars, lived in rural Ayrshire with a daughter Euphemia and toddler son James Shaw. A second son, named for his father, died before his second birthday. Shortly after his death, the family decided to make the move.[1] Paisley was a booming town in which to find a fresh start. The town's history stretched back to at least the twelfth century, centred around its eponymous Abbey. Aside from a suggested connection to William Wallace and the acquisition of burgh status under James IV there was little to note in the town's history until the start of the eighteenth century, when, one historian noted, 'Never was there a more fortunate occurrence for Paisley than the Union of Parliaments of England and Scotland which took place in 1707.'[2]

1 James Shaw was – for reasons lost to time – baptised as Robert. Euphemia's age is uncertain. She was usually listed first among the sisters but no birth record has survived and the ages given for census and her death record varied by as much as 10 years. Brown, Robert; Brown, David, Old Parish Registers Births 584/Craigie; Brown, Ann; Brown David; Brown, Janet; Brown John, Old Parish Registers Births 573/2 Paisley Middle, *ScotlandsPeople*.

2 J.W.C., *The Town of Paisley: Historical Sketch* (Paisley: Dailey Express, 1878), i, vi–viii.

After the Union the manufacture of linen thread (introduced in 1722), silk gauze (first manufactured in 1759), and then cotton (1782) were established in the town. The population rose from fewer than 4,000 in 1744 to 17,560 forty years later. At the first official census in 1801, Paisley Burgh had a population of more than 24,000.[3] The town found its true niche in 1805 when 'both manufactures and weavers had a great desire to engage in the imitation of Indian shawls'.[4] The next three decades were marked by booming industry, phenomenal population growth and repeated collapses in the fickle fashion trade that required extraordinary intervention.

David Brown secured an establishment on Back Sneddon Street, which was then the growing edge of the town, while Euphemia presided over a growing family. Little sisters Margaret Weir, Ann, another David who did not survive, then Janet and finally a baby brother John arrived by the end of 1823. Brown's smithy was successful enough that he could engage in a side-line lending small sums to other tradesmen and merchants in the town.[5] The children attended school. In 1824 James Shaw had exhausted the schooling Paisley had to offer and enrolled at University of Glasgow, pursuing courses in the Faculty of Arts. Although he was praised by his instructors and there were opportunities across the Empire for talented young men, James Shaw was not inclined to travel any further from home. At age 20 in 1831 he accepted a position as the teacher at Hutcheson's Charity School, which was under a thousand yards (1 km) from his parents' home. His sisters trained in needlework, and John ultimately followed his brother to Glasgow University, where he studied medicine.

When David died in 1837 he left property totaling more than £700. After his death the family built or acquired a building at 3 Back Sneddon, where the street made a triangle of land at the intersection of St James's Place and Old Sneddon Street. 'The Sneddon' was a district of institutions; just across Old Sneddon stood the new county buildings and jail, and up New Sneddon Street was the Town Hospital that housed Paisley's disabled

3 J.W.C. *Town of Paisley*, l–lxiii.

4 J.W.C., *The Town of Paisley*, lxiii; John Parkhill, *The History of Paisley* (Paisley: Robert Stewart, 1857), 38.

5 David Brown Testament, 11 Nov. 1837, SC58/42/10 Paisley Sheriff Court, *ScotlandsPeople*.

poor.[6] Around these imposing structures, along all the 'Sneddons', Hospital Lane, and surrounding streets stood crowded, cheap tenements. Residents lived among the stench and noise of the Sneddon Quay on the White Cart Water and the looming presence of poverty and prison. Although the Browns were reasonably prosperous, they were also adjacent to poverty and chose to stay there even when conditions would have allowed them to move elsewhere. The building at 3 Back Sneddon (which included at least five individual houses) provided a home and income for members of the Brown family into the twentieth century.[7]

The growing Brown family, especially the older children, must have been aware of Paisley's radical politics in the late eighteen-teens. In 1819 and 1820, during the widespread unrest that gave rise to the infamous Peterloo Massacre in England, Paisley unions were leading a movement for armed revolt against inequities of capitalism.[8] The incipient rising was quelled by the arrival of British troops and the ringleaders either escaped to America or were captured and taken to trial. The jury in this trial, however, refused to render a guilty verdict.[9] The town did not verge on armed rebellion again, but the workers maintained a political voice and a propensity for public meetings. Nearly two hundred years later Paisley (along with Glasgow) was remembered as an exception to the rule that Scottish burghs were 'relatively stable, orderly places'.[10] Whenever trade fell and unemployed operatives grew hungry, town leaders remembered the workers' volatile past.

Textile production grew steadily throughout the eighteenth century, so that in 1820 there were 7,000 working handlooms in the town, nearly

6 J. Wood, *Paisley, 1828* (map), National Library of Scotland maps.nls.uk/view/74400051; 'A Unique view of the Paisley Prison', *Paisley on the Web*, paisley.org.uk.

7 Prior to the Brown family's residence at 3 Back Sneddon, the address does not appear in town directories. The smithy was slightly north, at 7 Back Sneddon. *Fowler's New Commercial Directory of the Principal Towns and Villages in the upper Ward of Renfrewshire, for 1829–30* (Paisley: G. Fowler, 1829), 18.

8 A. Dickson and W. Speirs, 'Changes in Class Structure in Paisley, 1750–1845', *Scottish Historical Review* 59:167 part 1 (April 1980): 67–8.

9 J. Parkhill, *The History of Paisley* (Paisley: Robert Stewart, 1857), 46–70.

10 B. Harris and C. McKean, *The Scottish Town in the Age of the Enlightenment 1740–1820* (Edinburgh: Edinburgh University Press, 2014), 428.

9 percent of all the handlooms in the nation.[11] By that time the craft had gone largely to making the lucrative imitations of Kashmiri shawls, woven in the fancy, colorful patterns that took on the name of the town itself and could not yet be duplicated on a power loom. The shawls were a fashion necessity in a period when women's silhouettes did not lend themselves to more fitted outerwear. In the 1830s, the Paisley Shawl became the 'universal bridal present'.[12] Each shawl-weaving harness loom employed a skilled weaver and at least one draw boy or girl (who performed the mechanical operation of shifting the colors picked up by the weft). The jacquard loom, which replaced the human assistant with punch cards, was only slowly adopted over the course of the first half of the century.[13] One or more female winders wound the yarn to be woven from loose hanks onto spools or pirns that would be sent through the loom. In addition to the workers actively involved in weaving, there were specialists to prepare the web and set up the loom (including beamers, warpers, enterers and flower lashers) and others that finished the shawls (such as clippers and fringers) when the web was complete. When the shawl trade was slack, this whole community of workers was idle.[14]

Sewing thread production was also a crucial if less colorful element of Paisley's economy. Corporate giants Clark and Coats were established in 1812 and 1826, respectively. The sale of sewing thread on spools rather than in loose hanks was pioneered in 1814.[15] A Parliamentary report on handloom weavers in 1839 noted that when the shawl trade was stagnant, the thread factories were an important source of employment for the women and children in weavers' families.[16] That pattern maintained for decades;

11 M. Blair, *The Paisley Shawl and the Men Who Produced It: A Record of an Interesting Epoch in the History of the Town* (Paisley: Alexander Gardner, 1904), 2; C. A. Whatley, *The Industrial Revolution in Scotland* (Cambridge: Cambridge University Press, 1997), 26.

12 Blair, 25.

13 Blair, 43.

14 S. Clark, *Paisley: A History* (Edinburgh: Mainstream Publishing, 1988), 30.

15 W.W. Knox, *Hanging by a Thread: The Scottish Cotton Industry, c. 1850–1914* (Preston: Carnegie Publishing, 1995), 78.

16 'Reports from Assistant Hand-Loom Weavers' Commissioners', 1839, 34. Unless otherwise noted, all Parliamentary Papers retrieved via *House of*

when other textiles faltered, thread mills remained major employers in the district well into the next century. In spite of sharp economic fluctuations and the danger of too much specialisation, Paisley thrived in the early years of industrialisation and migrants arrived by the thousand.

Paisley's population more than doubled from 1801 to 1840, topping out at nearly 49,000. The first migrants, like the Brown family, came from neighboring Ayrshire, but as the boom continued Highlanders and Irish immigrants joined the flood.[17] After that peak, Paisley's population remained flat. Irish immigrants and their descendants remained a significant part of the community, but they were an aging population. Even the waves of Irish immigrants that accompanied the potato famine of the 1840s and 1850s largely bypassed Paisley in favor of the more dependable economies of Glasgow or Liverpool.

With the growth of the town came increased poverty. Even if the proportion of the poor in the new cities of Scotland was the same as in the rural parishes, the concentrated volume of humanity would mean a rising real volume of want in Paisley. Poverty was not, of course, proportionally distributed around the nation. The opportunities in Scotland's growing towns drew migrants, people often on the move because they were already economically disadvantaged through a loss of agricultural employment.[18] Young people sought the opportunities in towns, and aging parents frequently followed. The Town Hospital was founded in 1752 to house the 'destitute and infirm', funded by contributions from Paisley's trade societies and individuals.[19]

Commons Parliamentary Papers Online (ProQuest Information and Learning Company, 2006).

17 Parkhill, *History of Paisley*, 32; W. Gordon, 'The Demographics of Scottish Poverty: Paisley's Applications for Relief, 1861–71', *Journal of Scottish Historical Studies* 30:1 (2010): 30.

18 C. Whatley, *Industrial Revolution in Scotland* (Cambridge: Cambridge University Press, 1997), 66, 79.

19 R. Brown, *The History of Paisley from the Roman Period Down to 1884*, vol. II (Paisley: J. & J. Cook, 1886), 17–18.

Contemporaries estimated that around 3 percent of Scotland's population received formal poor relief,[20] but many more lived in an 'economy of makeshift' that combined paid labour, personal connections, informal charity, pawnshops and extra-legal activities to piece together a living.[21] The 1841 census (the earliest to record occupations) found 580 people in Paisley classified as 'Almspeople, Pensioners, Paupers and Beggars', making just under 1 percent of the population. In the same year, Paisley Burgh Parish reported 930 'impotent persons …. legally entitled to relief', who likely had some overlap with the census category.[22] However, there were also 716 men whose primary occupation was 'Labourer', the lowest class of regular employment, and 513 adult men categorised as 'residue of population' – a grouping that also included more than 30,000 children and women who were not in the paid workforce.[23] These numbers give the roughest possible minimum – in the neighborhood of one to two thousand or as much as 4 percent of the population – of how many families and individuals were eking out survival with casual labour, casual charity, and turning to formal relief when they could. However, the tremendous dominance of textile production in Paisley's economy was even more ominous for the town than this economically tenuous population.

Taking only the largest categories in 1841, 'cotton manufacturing' employed 7,429 in Paisley Town and Parish, 'silk manufacture' 1,572, and 'weaver' (both hand and power) 1,199. Thread, woolen, and worsted manufacturing each employed another few hundred workers. Only domestic service (for women) and agricultural labor rivaled the numbers in these occupations.[24] Altogether, employees in these textile categories were more

20 House of Commons, 'Return of Population; Annual Value of Property rated to Poor; Expenditure for Relief of Poor; and Number of Paupers relieved in Scotland, 1851–2'; 'First Annual Report of the Board of Supervision for the Relief of the Poor in Scotland', 1847, xxiii.

21 S. King and A. Tomkins, eds, *The Poor in England 1700–1850: An Economy of Makeshift* (Manchester: Manchester University Press, 2003).

22 House of Commons, 'Return of the Population in Scotland at the Last Census, and of the Management and Support of the Poor from 1836 to 1841', 1843, 32.

23 House of Commons, 'Occupations of the People', *Abstract of Answers and Returns under the Population Act, 3 & 4 Vic. C. 99*, 1841.

24 'Occupations of the People'.

than 40 percent of all employed people in Paisley. A Parliamentary commissioner reported in 1839 that Paisley had more than 5,500 handlooms, most of them the complex harness looms needed to weave the namesake patterns. The report detailed years of declining income for the weavers; even the highest-earning weavers in Paisley earned half as much in 1838 as they had in 1815.[25] To compensate for falling income and inevitable slack times, women and children in weaving families worked in warehouses and thread factories, and the weavers themselves took whatever temporary labor they could find.[26] Even in good times, weaving families struggled. When trade in textiles was weak, a huge proportion of the town was threatened with destitution. Paisley, like many parts of Britain, had a poverty problem even when their economy was booming; when the economy collapsed, it became disastrous. In the rugged laissez faire economic policy of nineteenth-century Britain, such a disaster was considered purely a local problem.

The Union established a united Parliament but weakened direct national government in Scotland, with the result that Scottish towns in the second half of the eighteenth century 'nurtured a very strong and independent sense of civic identity'.[27] Rapid urbanisation and social change strained the old civic order, but with little in the way of a national government to exert a new regime, individual communities in Scotland struggled to find local solutions to their increasingly interconnected problems. It was a small comfort that Paisley Burgh had been largely spared from the economic disorder that self-elected town councils could inflict in the first part of the century, before Scotland's local governments were reformed.[28] Following the Municipal Government Reform in 1833 the Paisley Town Council (made up by the Provost, four Baillies, and ten Councilors, elected

25 House of Commons, 'Reports from Assistant Hand-Loom Weavers' Commissioners', 1839: 3, 15.

26 'Assistant Hand-Loom Weavers'', 34.

27 Harris & McKean, *Scottish Town*, 433.

28 J.C. Murray, *Memoir of David Murray, Late Provost of Paisley, with Sketches of Local history in his Time* (Paisley: Alexander Gardner, 1881), 55–7. In contrast to Murray's grudgingly positive assessment, see F. McKichan, 'A Burgh's Response to the Problems of Urban Grown: Stirling, 1780–1880', *The Scottish Historical Review* 57:163 part 1 (April 1978), 72.

by the same population newly enfranchised with the Parliamentary vote) worked with diligence and notable civic pride to sustain and improve the community.[29] One of the town council's first acts of fiscal housecleaning was to provide for the election of the managers of the poor by the burgh's ratepayers.[30]

Paisley's poor relief system in the 1830s was a patchwork, as it was across Scotland.[31] Beginning in 1828 care of the 'deserving poor' in Paisley was shared by the kirk session and the Town Hospital. Barring the occasional legacy, funding for relief came from a combination of voluntary kirk-door collections and mandatory poor rates assessed on landowners. Half of the contributions from the congregations went to support the 'kirk poor', who were members of a Church of Scotland congregation and received the aliment while staying in their own homes. The other half of the collections were combined with the rates for the support of the hospital. This institution, founded in 1752, was nestled in the corner of Hospital Lane and New Sneddon Street, with a large expanse of town-owned land to the West extending to Back Sneddon and abutted by unrelated buildings to the North up to Middle Lane (see Illustration 1). While kirk elders managed the kirk poor, the hospital was managed by an elected board of fifteen men and a corps of sixty-three overseers who distributed the relief.[32] In addition to the actual inmates of the hospital, the hospital board maintained a list of individuals who were not members of a kirk session but were entitled to outdoor relief from the hospital funds.[33] There was also a team of district surgeons that provided medical care to the town's poor.

29 T. Keith, 'Municipal Elections in the Royal Burghs of Scotland: II. From the Union to the Passing of the Scottish Burgh Reform Bill in 1833', *The Scottish historical Review* 1:51 (1916): 278; *Fowler's Paisley Commercial Directory for 1838–9* (Paisley: G. Fowler, 1838), 93.

30 Brown, *A History of Paisley*, 266.

31 Rosalind Mitchison, *The Old Poor Law in Scotland: The Experience of Poverty, 1574–1845* (Edinburgh: Edinburgh University Press, 2000), 7–19.

32 HCP Town Council, vol. 1–28, 19 June 1839.

33 House of Commons, 'Poor Law Inquiry (Scotland.) Appendix, Part I, Containing Minutes of Evidence Taken at Edinburgh, Glasgow, Greenock, Paisley, Ayr and Kilmarnock', 1844. 572.

The town council's interest in making the managers of the poor answerable to the electorate was at least in part a response to surging expenses. From 1824 to 1829, the Kirk Session spent just £730 on outdoor poor. After the implementation of the assessment and creation of the hospital overseers, five-year expenditures rose to more than £1,240. One explanation for the increase may have been that the men charged with directing relief had close ties to the industrial heart of Paisley, and had to be aware of the hardships workers faced. Not all of the overseers can be traced in the town directories, but those who can be included tradesmen, merchants and manufacturers, who lived cheek-by-jowl with the people they cared for.[34] More than sixty men empowered to authorise relief meant there was ample opportunity for potential paupers to seek out a sympathetic ear or to secure payment more than once.[35]

Reorganisation of Paisley's Care for Their Poor

A first step that had long repercussions came in 1834, when the hospital board appointed a new Master of the Hospital. Out of the 'considerable number' of applicants, the board unanimously selected James Shaw Brown, then in his third or fourth year as the teacher at Hutcheson's School.[36] One of his responsibilities as teacher was to act a clerk to the directors of the school, a board that included the prior Hospital Governor, so he must have been to some extent a known quantity to the overseers.[37] It was a short move for him from the family home on Back Sneddon to the governor's apartments in the hospital. Brown's charge included a general oversight of all the poor for whom the burgh was responsible, but he first took on improving conditions in the increasingly crowded hospital itself.

34 *Fowler's 1838–9*, 131 and *passim*.
35 HCP Hospital, vol. 6–3, 29 March 1839.
36 HCP Hospital, vol. 6–3, 15 Sept. 1834.
37 Brown, *History of Paisley*, 102.

As Paisley's economy lurched from boom to bust in the later 1830s, more and more of the town's inhabitants fell to residential care. From 1837 to 1839 there was an average of 245 inmates in a facility built to house 190, including nearly one hundred children, whom Brown was particularly charged to teach. Unlike the adults in the hospital, who were unable to support themselves due to physical or mental disability, the children – foundlings or orphans or from families so destitute they could not care for them – were as healthy as any in Paisley; or at least they could be with adequate food and if released from the confines of the institution. However,

> The confused and crowded state of the wards not only rendered it extremely difficult to maintain the order necessary in such an Establishment but … it diminishes greatly the enjoyments of the inmates … For some of the wards there were from 30 to 50 persons assembled together necessarily breathing an unwholesome and foetid atmosphere, always unfavourable to health and particularly to the young when tender lungs are easily injured so as to produce general debility of the whole constitution.[38]

As a result, children in the hospital experienced a shocking mortality rate. A report from the attending doctor to the hospital directors noted that from 1835 to 1839 there was an average number of ninety-two children among the inmates, and least fifty-two children had died while in the institution. The children arrived in the hospital in a malnourished, unhealthy state, 'but their admission to the Hospital … seldom if ever improves their health but generally the very reverse. Indeed few, very few of those who are admitted young survive to adult age and still fewer become robust.' The report confirmed that the hospital matron was scrupulous in her attention to cleanliness, but that nothing could overcome the 'confined condition and … crowded state of their sleeping apartments'.[39] In addition to health concerns, the directors feared for the moral condition of their young inmates. The institution was too small to permit separation of the young people,

> and the young have in consequence been introduced into the society of the adults, many of whom are people of improvident character and not a few of them have been under the necessity of becoming inmates chiefly on account … of former indulgence

38 HCP Hospital, vol. 6–3, 7 June 1839.

39 HCP Hospital, vol. 6–3, 7 June 1839.

> in vicious propensities. … The presence of such bad examples pollutes the minds of the young and … blunts their moral sensibilities.[40]

As early as 1819 some parishes in Western Scotland were experimenting with fostering urban poor children instead of institutionalising them.[41] The directors' attention in 1839 was particularly drawn to the fact Glasgow City parish boarded out all of their children, and that the system had also been adopted by one of the London workhouses.[42] After a successful experimental phase in 1838, boarding out became the ordinary means of caring for pauper children in Paisley and not incidentally reducing the population in the hospital.[43] Almost forty years later, James Shaw Brown's obituary gave him credit for this development. 'Much of his attention', it recalled, 'was always devoted to the development and application of the plan of boarding out orphan and deserted children with private families'.[44]

While Brown was transforming the care given to pauper children, the hospital board was working on bringing efficiency to its own processes. The first step the elected managers took in coming to grips with the poor in their streets and the real increase in costs associated with their support was to catalog and count the paupers. Paisley was not alone in this agenda. The entire British nation was swept into a passion for statistics and management in the first half of the nineteenth century, prompted by the social changes arising from industrialisation and the professionalisation of the civil service.[45] Since the seventeenth century there had been sporadic and

40 HCP Hospital, vol. 6–3, 7 June 1839.

41 H.J. MacDonald, 'Boarding-Out and the Scottish Poor law, 1845–1914', *The Scottish Historical Review* 75:2, no. 200 (1996): 199.

42 HCP Hospital, vol. 6–3, 7 June 1839.

43 HCP Hospital, vol. 6–3, 7 June 1839.

44 'The Late Mr J.S. Brown', *Poor Law Magazine and Parochial Journal* (second series) IV (March 1876): 240.

45 D. E. Marion, 'The British Civil Service: A Political Excavation and Review', *Administration & Society* 24:4 (Feb. 1993): 470–87; C. R. Middleton, 'The Emergence of Constitutional Bureaucracy in the British Foreign Office, 1782–1841', *Public Administration* 53:4 (Winter 1975): 365–81. E. Evans, *The Forging of the Modern State: Early Industrial Britain 1783–1870*, 3rd edn (London & New York: Longmans, 2001), 361–4.

often individual attempts to direct government policies through data analysis, a trend that gained significant traction in the early nineteenth century with the introduction of the decennial census. Scotland's famous Statistical Account and New Statistical Account are examples of this trend, unique in their broad scope but not in purpose.[46] In the 1830s non-governmental statistical societies were founded across Britain, including at least one in Glasgow. Statistics became a new currency in coping with social disorder, including relieving the poor.[47]

While statistical societies responded to Malthusian theories and the possibilities raised by the national census, the nation's political class was paying more attention to the system of government itself, particularly in the face of George III's illness followed by 'the reign of his inept and profligate son, George IV'.[48] The Great Reform of 1832 (when Paisley gained Parliamentary representation for the first time) cracked open the Constitution and pushed Britain toward a modern democracy.[49] While the most significant bureaucratic reforms would be codified with the Northcote-Trevelyan report in 1854, the urge to regularise government processes ran throughout the century.[50] The combination of information and regulation seemed like a clear route to an improved world. Scottish burghs already had a strong tradition of self-government and 'a very strong and independent sense of civic identity. … Magistrates regard[ed] themselves as the embodiment of the burgh and as the protectors of its privileges'.[51] As the Scottish Kirk, the magistrates' traditional partner in the civil society, faltered through repeated schism on its way to the 1843 Disruption, and the industrial burghs' populations continued to swell, governing became more and more complex.

46 'Statistical Account: Surveying the Nation', National Library of Scotland digital. nls.uk/learning/scottish-enlightenment/statistical-account/.

47 M.J. Cullen, *The Statistical Movement in Early Victorian Britain: The Foundations of Empirical Social Research* (New York: Barnes & Noble Books, 1975), 8–16.

48 Middleton, 'Emergence of Constitutional Bureaucracy', 367.

49 Evans, *Forging of the Modern State*, 266.

50 Marion, 'Civil Service'.

51 Harris and McKean, *Scottish Town*, 433.

In this context, the consideration of how poor relief was granted and paupers cared for was just one element in a larger process of developing local government in the 1830s. Nevertheless, 1839 was a crucial turning point for Paisley's care for the poor. The town's textile-based economy was vibrant, buoyed by new transportation infrastructure via the Cart Water and a new railway line under construction, but it was also volatile. Periods of economic distress that had been met by public subscriptions and support to individuals throughout the 1820s were met by soup kitchens beginning in 1832.[52] 1837 was recorded as a year 'of very bad trade' in which at least a thousand fancy textile workers were out of work and upwards of £13,000 was spent on relief.[53] The town's reliance on specialty textiles exaggerated the boom-and-bust cycle already typical of industrialising Britain. Repeated crises drained the ability of the capitalist class to perform their traditional role of charitable support, and as the population of workers grew the landed classes shifted their residences out of the burgh. By the last years of the decade it was clear the old system of relief was not sufficient for the need.

In the middle of 1839 a joint committee representing the town council, Kirk Sessions and hospital directors set about introducing new efficiency to the system. Like the plan to board out the hospital's children, this organisation was adapted from schemes already in place in the Glasgow parishes of Barony and Gorbals.[54] The plan re-assigned the duties of accepting and alimenting (i.e., paying relief to) applicants from the voluntary, appointed Directors of the Hospital to a professional Supervisor of the Poor, and the number of overseers was reduced from an unwieldy sixty-three to eighteen, who would simultaneously serve as the hospital's Board of Directors. It gave the Superintendent the particular charge to investigate petitioners for aid, 'in particular to prepare an accurate report of the condition and circumstances of such applicants as the Directors shall think proper to supply with schedules'.[55] He was further required to regularly visit the poor on the permanent rolls, to personally ensure that children on the poor roll

52 J.W.C., *Town of Paisley*, xv.
53 J.W.C., *Town of Paisley*, xvii.
54 HCP Hospital, vol. 6–3, 5 July 1839.
55 HCP Town Council, vol. 1–28, 19 June 1839.

'have the benefit of obtaining the elements of an ordinary education', and report regularly on the matter.[56] The council summarised the changes as,

> productive of considerable advantage in every department. It will establish a uniform system throughout all the districts of the Town, and it will bring the whole administration of the Poors matters under the immediate control of the General Board. It will prevent all complaint and inconvenience arising from the poor of one ward being dealt with in a different manner from the poor of another. And it will afford the means of preserving for important purposes, a regular register of payments made to every recipient of the poors funds.[57]

Their ultimate hope was to eliminate waste and reduce the cost of poor relief overall, while also 'securing to the really destitute a more liberal maintenance than they at present enjoy'.[58]

When the hospital overseers received the final report from the council, they moved quickly to implement the changes suggested. James Shaw Brown was appointed on 5 July 1839 to act as interim Superintendent in addition to his duties as Governor, and committees were formed to enact the alterations.[59] By the middle of July the necessary books and forms for the new system were prepared and plans were underway for refitting a room in the hospital itself for the directors' meetings.[60] In the midst of those changes, the much-praised hospital matron resigned her position for one at the Glasgow jail, so among their other preparations the directors reviewed applications and hired Miss Elizabeth Baird, aged 25, the Paisley-born daughter of a shawl weaver.[61] Miss Baird, upon moving into her quarters, suggested that the room was in need of freshening up. The directors agreed to provide new curtains and 'orders were also given to the Repair Committee to examine the walls [of her room] and to cover them with paper if deemed expedient'.[62]

56 HCP Town Council, vol. 1–28, 19 June 1839.
57 HCP Town Council, vol. 1–28, 19 June 1839.
58 HCP Town Council, vol. 1–28, 19 June 1839.
59 HCP Hospital, vol. 6–3, 5 July 1839.
60 HCP Hospital, vol. 6–3, 10 July, 26 Aug. 1839.
61 HCP Hospital, vol. 6–3, 19 Aug. 1839, Elizabeth Brown, Statutory Registers Deaths 573/867, 1872, *ScotlandsPeople*.
62 HCP Hospital, vol. 6–4, 18 Sept. 1839.

The new matron undoubtedly caught 28-year-old James Shaw Brown's attention, but he had little time to devote to any courtship. In his new role as Superintendent of the Poor, Brown had general oversight of all paupers and their relief (except for those relieved separately by the Kirk Session). The directors of the hospital (two for each of the nine police wards) could supply paper schedules to those in need of aid in their area of responsibility. When the applicants brought the schedules to the superintendent he would research their situations and prepare a recommendation. While he could – with a single director's approval – provide immediate aid to an applicant, the usual process would be for the superintendent to present the list of applicants to a general meeting of the directors for approval before any aid was granted. The superintendent was then responsible for visiting every pauper on the roll once every three months, to determine that they were still in need and to adjust their aliment if needed. In addition to cataloging the poor people, the superintendent also kept the monetary books, a separate account for each ward, supervised the education of pauper children, and pursued men who deserted their families. He was to be available at the hospital from 10 – noon and 6–7 on 'every lawful day' to receive applications and correspond with the directors.[63] Finally, the role of clerk to the general meetings of the directors was added to Mr Brown's responsibilities.[64] Although he had no official management role, every element of poor relief ran through his fingers.

With all of these changes enacted, September 1839 was a new era for poor relief in Paisley. Bound volumes of statements run from the first of the month through 1942 when local control over poor relief ended.[65] For a few months, the hospital supported their poor and supervised their boarded-out children, satisfied with their new process. Meanwhile, unemployment in Paisley was surging once again.

63 HCP Hospital, vol. 6–3, 17 July 1839.

64 HCP Hospital, vol. 6–3, 26 Aug. 1839.

65 I. Levitt, *Poverty & Welfare in Scotland 1890–1948* (Edinburgh: Edinburgh University Press, 1988), 204.

Distress in Paisley

The new emphasis on centralised poor relief, as well as the exhaustion of the benevolent class, was evident in November 1839, when a newly formed Relief Committee responded to rising unemployment by deciding against attempting another general subscription. Instead, they determined that the established managers of the poor in Paisley and neighboring Abbey Parish should 'take charge of and relieve the most [urgent] cases of distress'.[66] In response, the hospital managers held an emergency meeting a few days later and resolved, 'the Overseers shall interpret the poor law as liberally as possible, and shall extend relief to such persons as from age and distress are proper objects of parochial relief'.[67] This was a resolution for public consumption; as will be discussed in a later chapter there was a great deal of overlap between the overseers, the hospital directors, and the town council, so purely private managerial matters could be handled quietly if desired. Formal communications between these bodies always carried some element of performance. The resolution made it clear the burgh would give some aid to unemployed operatives' families when their resources were exhausted, while still denying direct aid to any man who was fit and happened to be out of work. The assurance of liberal interpretation might ease the potential for political unrest as healthy men watched their families suffer.

The town council wanted the hospital and overseers to do more.[68] The council received a petition on behalf of unemployed operatives with about 1,500 signatures on 17 December 1839 and assured the petitioners that they had, in conjunction with the Managers of the Poor, agreed to raise a public subscription for relief of the unemployed. The hospital directors

66 HCP Hospital, vol. 6–4, 26 Nov. 1839.

67 HCP Hospital, vol. 6–4, 29 Nov. 1839. After the new system went into effect in September, twelve of the twenty-three Hospital Directors were also Overseers of the Poor, and two or three were members of the Town Council. By 1845 there was complete overlap; every one of the burgh's Overseers of the Poor was also a Director on the Hospital Board. *Fowler's 1838–9*, 107, 131–2; *Fowler's 1841–41*, 111, 139.

68 *Fowler's 1838–9*, 93, 107.

were accordingly invited to a meeting the next day with the town council to discuss the issue. However, when the directors arrived at the council chambers there were no councilors present. The directors returned to their regular business with no plans to raise any additional funds for the able-bodied men.[69] Supervisor Brown was charged again to 'interpret the Poor Law as liberally as possible', while also ensuring that aid would go only to 'such persons as from age or disease were proper objects of parochial relief'.[70]

Throughout the 1820s and 1830s, Paisley's economy had rebounded from its repeated collapses within a few months. But in 1840, fashion was shifting away from patterned shawls, and all the management efficiency in the nation could not make up for the loss of trade. By mid-1840, distress in the town was severe. In April, the First Paisley Emigration Society petitioned the town council for aid to support the emigration of unemployed applicants to Canada. In June, the council submitted a 'memorial relative to the Poor' to the government in London, describing the destitution and pleading for relief, while themselves receiving petitions from 'a number of the Inhabitants' for a public meeting to raise relief funds.[71] The council also volunteered to provide their new collection of statistical information to the Home Secretary 'as to the destitute state of the working classes of Paisley'.[72] In July, a politically radical Paisley minister, Patrick Brewster, wrote personally to the hospital regarding 'the destitute condition of the unemployed operatives of the town'.[73] Making matters worse for Paisley, Parliament (while retaining the hated corn laws that kept bread costs high) had dramatically reduced the duty charged for importing Indian silks, further weakening the market for figured shawls.[74] While the hospital directors were sympathetic and well aware of the potential consequences of masses of unemployed men, they felt helpless against the problem and

69 HCP Town Council, vol. 1–28, 17 Dec. 1839; HCP Hospital, vol. 6–4, 18 Dec. 1839.

70 HCP Hospital, vol. 6–4, 22 June 1840.

71 HCP Town Council, vol. 1–28, 3 June; 18 June; 23 June 1840.

72 HCP Town Council, vol. 1–28, 14 April 1840.

73 HCP Hospital, vol. 6–4, 19 June 1840; J. McKay, *The Kirk and the Kingdom: A Century of Tension in Scottish Social Theology, 1830–1929* (Edinburgh: Edinburgh University Press, 2012), 18.

74 HCP Town Council, vol. 1–28, 7 July 1840.

replied to Brewster as they had six months earlier to the town council, that all they could do was interpret the law as liberally as possible.[75] The next day the town council, for the second year in a row, authorised a poor rate assessment of £3,500, nearly £2,000 above the average expenditure from the past five years.[76]

The need exceeded what the town could relieve on their own, yet the Government (in the person of the Marquess of Normanby, the Home Secretary) stood by its free market ideology. Normanby replied to the town council's plea for aid that while he 'deeply regret[ed] to learn the state of destitution. … His lordship fear[ed] that the Government cannot interfere, but recommend[ed] that every attempt should be made to call forth private benevolence.'[77] In a comparatively more private context Normanby implied the government was not interested in providing legislative help to Paisley or any similar community in Scotland. Although Parliament had undertaken a survey of the living and health conditions of workers in Scotland, known informally as the Sanitary Inquiry,[78] when challenged in the House of Lords regarding the Inquiry, the Home Secretary replied, 'On one point he could readily dispel the apprehensions of his noble Friend. It was not intended that the inquiry should be at all connected with the Poor-law system in Scotland.'[79]

Normanby's assurance to his noble colleague was contradicted by demands from Paisley. By the end of 1840, the managers of the poor began to argue that the unreformed poor law in Scotland was inadequate to meet the town's need. Dr John Brown (no known relation to James Shaw), who served on both the town council and as a hospital director, announced that he intended to 'bring under the consideration of the council the subject of the poor law of Scotland'. The hospital board saw an opportunity in the Sanitary Inquiry and petitioned Her Majesty's government 'to extend the investigation now going on as to the sanitary condition of the labouring

75 HCP Hospital, vol. 6–4, 7 July 1840.
76 HCP Town Council, vol. 1–28, 8 July 1840.
77 HCP Town Council, vol. 1–28, 8 July 1840.
78 House of Commons, 'Sanitary Inquiry: Scotland', 1842.
79 Lords Sitting of Friday, July 3, 1840, *19th Century House of Lords Hansard Sessional Papers,* Third Series, vol. 55.

classes in Scotland, so as to include the condition generally of the poor in Scotland particularly in cities and large towns with a view to an early and complete alteration of the existing Poor Laws'.[80] The Sanitary Inquiry Report did not ultimately include information from Paisley, but it did include repeated descriptions of how the examined towns supported their paupers, as well as summaries of crowded, barely habitable houses and closes (alleyways) overwhelmed with miasmic fumes.

In January 1841 the council appointed Dr Brown to convene a committee 'to enquire and report as to the best means of remedying the existing evils of the Poor Laws', empowered to correspond with similar committees around Scotland and bring the question to Parliament's attention.[81] Again in February 1841 the Paisley Town Council begged Normanby for aid, noting 'with deep concern the alarming increase in numbers and destitution of the poor in this part of the Country' and adding the new request for 'an immediate and searching enquiry' into the state of Scotland's poor, arguing that the fault was not Paisley's but in the structure of the poor law itself.[82]

The normal Spring improvement in trade did not arrive, and the town's economic condition spiraled out of control. The *Paisley Daily Express* recorded, 'The years 1841, '42 and '43 were a time of very great distress in Paisley. About 150 of the leading businessmen in town failed; and the banks in town lost about £100,000. The liabilities of the insolvents reached £650,000. … There was no work for the operatives – subscriptions were raised and soup kitchens erected.'[83] Throughout 1841 the town council received memorials from unemployed operatives seeking work or relief.[84] The council and hospital directors attempted to aid them through providing rocks to be broken for pay, enacting a new compulsory assessment, memorialising the government again, and sinking deeper into debt as they funded soup kitchens and other forms of outdoor relief.[85] On December

80 HCP Hospital, vol. 6–4, 16 Dec. 1840.
81 HCP Town Council, vol. 1–28, 20 Dec. 1840; 20 Jan. 1841.
82 HCP Town Council, vol. 1–28, 9 Feb. 1841.
83 J.W.C. *Town of Paisley*, xix.
84 HCP Town Council, vol. 1–28, 22 June; 13 July; 20 July; 7 Dec. 1841.
85 HCP Town Council, vol. 1–28, 7 July; 20 July; 14 Sept.; 28 Sept. 1841.

27, after a closed-door meeting, the Town ceased making any payments on their debts at all.[86] Only then, when Paisley Burgh was bankrupt with its attempt to support their poor, did aid from London arrive.

86 HCP Town Council, vol. 1–28, 27 Dec. 1841.

CHAPTER 2

The Case of the Distant Legislature: How the New Poor Law Came to Paisley: 1842–6

Parliamentary Notice

Although the council and hospital directors may have felt quite abandoned by the Government, their concerns were not going unheard. After Paisley's bankruptcy in December, the issue of the distress in Paisley was finally brought to the floor of the House of Commons in February 1842. Several MPs called for an inquiry into the distress, offered explanation for the collapse due to Paisley's reliance on the fickle fashion trade, and suggested remedies such as direct government relief, assisted emigration, and repeal of the Corn Laws. While the new Home Secretary, James Graham, Baronet, maintained there was no need for an inquiry into a distress that they all knew already existed, Paisley's own MP, Mr Archibald Hastie, made a plea tinged with the threat of civil disturbance as he compared the 17,000 people in need of relief with the mere £1,500 available for their relief. 'He threw out these hints that the House might take them into consideration before despair should seize on the unhappy sufferers of Paisley.'[1] Everyone in the chamber knew that despair in the town could quickly lead to violence, as it had just twenty years earlier.[2]

Minutes later MP Mr Wakley, a Whig representing a district in Central London, declared his deep sympathy for the inhabitants of Paisley, but also

1 'Commons Sitting of Tuesday, 8 February 1842', *19th Century House of Commons Hansard Sessional Papers*, Third Series, vol. 60.

2 House of Commons, 'Papers relative to Internal State of the Country', Nov. 1819, 38–39.

his skepticism that the House of Commons was the proper place to beg more relief. He continued,

> His object in rising was to ask those Gentlemen who were acquainted with the law of Scotland what was the nature of the Poor-law in that country, and why the property of Scotland was not applicable as well as that of England to relieving the distress of the poor? He saw the Lord Advocate in his place, and he would ask him was there a poor-law in Scotland? He understood that there was. And next, because it was no use for Scottish Gentlemen to come here and make application for the relief of that distress for which, perhaps, the existing law of Scotland might provide, what was the state of the administration of that law? … Considering what were now the sufferings of so many human beings in that country … he thought it would be a satisfaction to the House and to the country to know precisely and distinctly what was the nature of the poor-law of Scotland, and how it was carried into effect; for if it was not effectual for relieving the distresses of the poor of that country, he was confident that an effectual law would be speedily adopted.[3]

The Lord Advocate, Sir William Rae, quickly assured Mr Wakley,

> There were Poor-laws existing throughout Scotland, but in many parishes it was not found necessary to put them into execution. … He could assure the House that relief had not been found wanting in the grievous distress of the people of Paisley. A sum to the amount of ten thousand pounds had, in one form or another, been bestowed on the suffering poor of that place. It was a great and important question, whether a workhouse system was a better system; but into such a question the House could not now expect him to enter.[4]

While Parliament debated, the distress in Paisley persisted, with thousands out of work and large public meetings calling for action and relief. As early as October 1841 and publicly acknowledged by May 1842, representatives of the Government were in Paisley, examining the methods of providing relief and the local funds available, leaving hazy the question of whether any tangible relief had been offered.[5] The conversation about

3 'Commons Sitting of Tuesday, 8 February 1842.'

4 Commons Sitting of Tuesday, 8 Feb. 1842.

5 Hansards 'Commons sitting of Friday, May 27 1842', *19th Century House of Commons Hansard Sessional Papers*, Third Series, vol. 53. For more on Government intervention in Paisley during the crisis, see T.C. Smout, 'The Strange Intervention of Edward Twistleton: Paisley in Depression, 1841–3', in *The Search for Wealth and*

relieving distress in Paisley became, over the course of the year, an inquiry into the whole of the poor law in Scotland. While the early 1840s saw economic distress right across Britain, the extreme degree of want in Paisley and the town's bankruptcy made it a common reference point in the Parliamentary discussions that followed.[6] In early 1843, the Government's insistence that the Scottish poor laws were adequate to purpose gave way to a royal commission charged with examining the 'Administration and Practical Operation of the Poor Laws in Scotland'. Paisley figured prominently in the inquiry.

While Paisley suffered and Parliament debated, the British press also articulated the conflict over how poverty in Scotland should be relieved, bringing the debate freshly into the public intellectual sphere. The Whig *Edinburgh Review*, the Tory *Quarterly Review* and the ostensibly non-partisan *Westminster Review* all summarised and commented on the major reports and commentaries of the day. England's passage of their own amended Poor Law in 1834 inevitably framed the media conversation. The English law did provide relief to the unemployed, but forbade outdoor relief (on paper, at least; there is significant evidence that the ban was irregularly enforced).[7] The result was a surge in workhouses and the 'workhouse test' to discourage or incarcerate paupers. To cope with the cost of workhouses and the frequent migration of labourers, English parishes were grouped into new Unions and overseen by a powerful Poor Law Commission that was responsible for writing, observing and enforcing regulations under the Law.[8] Assistant Commissioners were dispatched across England to wrestle

Stability: Essays in Economic and Social History Presented to M.W. Finn, ed. T.C. Smout (London: MacMillan, 1979), 218–42.

6 Hansards, 'Lords Sitting of Thursday, June 2, 1842', *19th Century House of Lords Sessional Papers*, Third Series, vol. 63; 'Commons Sitting of Friday, July 1, 1842', *19th Century House of Commons Sessional Papers*, Third Series, vol. 64.

7 N. Goose, 'Workhouse Populations in the Mid-Nineteenth Century: The case of Hertfordshire', *Local Population Studies* 62 (1999): 52–67; A. Hinde, 'The Population of Two Hampshire Workhouses, 1851–61', *Local Population Studies* 61 (1998): 38–53; and M. MacKinnon, 'English Poor Law Policy and the Crusade Against Outrelief', *Journal of Economic History* 47:3 (1987): 603–25.

8 *An Act for the Amendment and better Administration of the Laws relating to the poor in England and Wales* (London: 1834).

the New Poor Law into existence, imposing a cruel severity most famously memorialised in *Oliver Twist*.

There had been no perceived need to overhaul the Scottish law in 1834. The Reverend Thomas Chalmers, who later became famous leading the 1843 exodus from the Church of Scotland known as the Disruption, was an overseer of the poor in St. Johns Parish, Glasgow from 1819 to 1823. He emerged as an important public figure in the poor law debate from the 1820s, promoting his own system of close observation and control of paupers to guard against immorality and waste. He maintained that Scotland was well served by the law that dated back to 1579, arguing that the traditional ban against giving relief to the able-bodied poor helped to keep costs down and opportunistic migrants away. Any guarantee of relief, such as had been given in Barony early in the century, he insisted, would disrupt the recipients' ability to work for their own support because it 'unsettled their habits of economy and foresight; and cruellest of all impositions, … misled them … from the only true source of a person's comfort and independence'.[9] The system of close record keeping and supervision that Chalmers introduced in St. Johns was similar to the model Paisley had adopted in 1828, with sixty-three overseers who could gain intimate acquaintance with the inhabitants of their wards. In addition to Chalmers himself (whose 1821 book was reissued and updated in 1840), David Monypenny wrote an influential book on the Scottish poor law in 1834, reiterating that it need only be properly administered, not revised.[10] The fear of ingrained pauperism Chalmers and Monypenny articulated recurred frequently throughout the century and is not unfamiliar today.

In just a few years sentiment about the need to revise the Scottish law shifted. In spite of the close attendance of the overseers, costs had gone up dramatically; even when the number of administrators was reduced Paisley operatives resorted to demonstrating and starving in the streets. Paisley, meanwhile, was acknowledged to be only the worst of a widespread problem. Commentators began to argue the inadequacy of the

9 T. Chalmers, *Christian and Economic Polity of a Nation with Special Reference to Large Towns* (Edinburgh: T. Constable, 1854), 324.

10 D. Monypenny, *Remarks on the Poor Laws and on the Method of Providing for the Poor in Scotland* (Edinburgh: T. Clark, 1834).

Scottish system. An Edinburgh physician, William Alison, made a direct connection between urban poverty and the fever epidemics that swept the cities.[11] Both the *Westminster Review* (in 1841) and the *Quarterly Review* (in 1844) published articles advocating a reform of the Scottish law along the same model as the recent reforms to the English law.[12] They maintained that the hundreds of individual Scottish parishes must be consolidated into unions that would give a larger pool of funds from a universal and compulsory assessment to be administered by professionals, not the voluntary donations meted out by kirk elders.[13] The able-bodied poor so evident in the early 1840s must be relieved, the commentators argued, and given work both to maintain their dignity and to ensure against abuse. Under Alison's influence, an Edinburgh society, 'The Association for obtaining an Official Inquiry into the Pauperism of Scotland', collected evidence and circulated reports to urge Parliament to official action.[14]

Meanwhile, Paisley Burgh's bankruptcy at last drew substantial aid from outside, though not overtly from the Government. The London-based Manufacturer's Relief Society provided a bolus of £500 in May 1842, with an intention of giving a total of £10,000 if it was needed. A Queen's Letter, making a special, nation-wide request for additional funds from the public through church collections, was issued in the same month.[15] These charitable funds came with strings attached. The English donors (who included well-known but unnamed government figures) insisted that their money be husbanded through the administration of relief only in kind, not in cash tickets that could be redeemed for such luxuries as a dram or

11 W.P. Alison, *Illustrations of the Scottish System of Management of the Poor* (Edinburgh, 1840).

12 A.W. Coats, ed., *Poverty in the Victorian Age. Vol. IV, Scottish Poor Laws 1815–70* (Westmead, Hants: Gregg International Publishers, 1973).

13 'Poor Laws for Scotland', *Quarterly Review* 75 (1844): 146, reprinted in Coats, *Poverty in the Victorian Age*, vol. IV.

14 *London Quarterly Review*, LXXIII (March and June 1844): 69 reprinted in Coats, *Poverty in the Victorian Age*, vol. IV.

15 House of Commons, 'Report from the Select Committee on Distress (Paisley): Together with the Minutes of Evidence', 1843, 4; 'Letter to Archbishop of Canterbury, May 1842, for Collection in Aid of Subscription for Relief of Working Classes in England and Scotland', 1842.

recovering pawned goods.[16] The shortage of relief funds also forced difficult conversations about who was entitled to relief. During the worst of the crisis in the winter of 1841–2, relief was offered to the able-bodied unemployed, ostensibly without further distinction. Some were given work, especially weavers and the literate, who were sometimes employed as clerks to administer relief to others. Yet there was simply not enough to go around. By September 1842 single men under 40 years old were struck off the relief list, men with families were provided only with cooked food (if found deserving), and all Irish applicants who had lived in Paisley less than ten years were refused relief entirely.[17] In January 1843, destitute heads of sixty families in Paisley were turned off the roll due to the lack of funds and were given permission to seek aid from individuals in the town – in other words, certificates for public begging.[18]

That same month, faced with starvation in Scottish streets, pressure from the press and direct petitions from local government, the House of Commons moved to impanel a Committee to Inquire into the Administration and Practical Implication of the Poor Laws in Scotland. Although they were addressing the law for all of Scotland, they gave particular attention to the urban areas that had been struck by the recent distress. In addition to the cities of Glasgow and Edinburgh, four towns in the West (Paisley, Ayr, Kilmarnock and Greenock) were singled out for special examination. Less than a fortnight after the Poor Law Committee was empaneled, a second committee was appointed to report specifically on the circumstances surrounding the distress in Paisley. In particular, this committee was to examine 'the treatment of the unemployed and destitute inhabitants of Paisley'.[19] The report from this second committee was produced in March 1843, when the Poor Law Inquiry had barely begun its work. It reported with relief that there was no significant fraud or

16 'Select Committee on Distress', 'Report from the Select Committee on Distress (Paisley): Together with the Minutes of Evidence', 10; Smout identifies the donors as including Queen Victoria and Robert Peel, among others. Smout, 'Strange Intervention', 232.

17 'Select Committee on Distress', 39.

18 'Select Committee on Distress', 40.

19 'Select Committee on Distress', ii.

mismanagement in the town and that the people of Paisley had borne up admirably well in their trouble.[20] The report and attendant evidence were, however, a clear example of the shortcomings of the Old Poor Law in Scotland.

From 29 April until 3 May the Poor Law Inquiry Committee examined witnesses from Paisley Burgh and Abbey Parishes, including a wide range of men with experience relieving the town's poor both before and during the economic collapse.[21] Reverend Robert Burns, William Mellis, Chair of the Hospital Board, Supervisor James Shaw Brown, and Provost Henderson, along with other ministers and treasurers of various funds all told much the same tale. Every man interviewed believed that the amount of aliment paid to the poor was too small, and that the system for assessing the poor rates was deeply flawed. There was not sufficient capital in the burgh to support the population of poor people, a situation that was exacerbated by a rule that only property owners who resided in the burgh could be assessed. Landlords and capitalists who lived outside the burgh were not liable for assessment even on their property within the town. These witnesses proposed a two-fold fix to the poor law in Scotland. First, to institute a national or at least regional system of assessment, so that an already impoverished town would not be forced to support a large population from a small tax base. Second, they universally proposed an increased period before a migrant gained a settlement in a new parish. In the 1840s, it took only three years of residence to gain a settlement (and thus a right to relief from the local parish), and it was widely believed that elderly Irishmen and women would immigrate to Scotland with a view to claiming poor relief as soon as they were qualified.[22]

Paisley's distress was a particular concern for the inquiry, and some witnesses from outside Paisley were asked their opinions of the reasons for the Paisley crisis. Thomas Chalmers maintained that his own system of close, individual supervision of paupers would have prevented the extent

20 'Select Committee on Distress', x.

21 Blair, *The Paisley Shawl*, 78.

22 House of Commons, 'Report from Her Majesty's Commissioners for Inquiring into the Administration and practical operation of the Poor Laws in Scotland', [Poor Law Inquiry (Scotland)], 1844, xxxix.

of want in the neighbouring burgh and that the problem in Paisley was simply one of inappropriate scale (not apparently aware the parish had implemented – then discarded – a system similar to what he advocated). He testified,

> If there had been a thorough parochial system in Paisley, and the amount of distress had been divided among parishes each having separate and independent management of its own, then each, with the small fraction of cases which might have fallen to its share, would have found ways and means of more easily providing for those cases. I feel, that if the mass of distress in Paisley, instead of being like a spectacle of such magnitude obtruded on the public eye, had been cut down into fragments, each of these fragments would have been found much more manageable than the accumulated distress.[23]

Chalmers made no suggestion of how this division of labour would have created either more jobs or more funds to relieve Paisley's poor.

In the Edinburgh evidence, William Muir, who had been secretary to the Relief Committee distributing funds in response to the Queen's letter in 1842, maintained that the authorities in Paisley had 'commenced giving relief too early' and compounded their error by declaiming 'in public meetings … on the people's right to support'.[24] The town council, Muir suggested, was at fault for attempting to support their hungry operatives. Then, rather than encouraging 'eleemosynary aid', discouraging applicants for relief or inducing them to leave the town, the Provost of Paisley himself told Muir, 'that government was bound to support them, and that they must be supported'.[25] This approach to relief in Paisley, at odds with many of their countrymen, spoke both to the history of radical activism in the town and its position as a small, specialised economy. The men who administered the poor law were intimately familiar with the conditions that created the unemployed poor, from the perspective of industrial management and local tradesmen as well as hospital managers, and some in

23 'Poor Law Inquiry (Scotland) Appendix Part I', 1843, 269.

24 'Poor Law Inquiry (Scotland) Appendix', 158.

25 'Poor Law Inquiry (Scotland) Appendix', 158. Eleemosynary aid was charitable aid freely given by individuals, not acquired through taxation.

Paisley, including the Provost, were openly critical of the Government's approach to relief.[26]

Although many of Paisley's social and political leaders voiced a humanitarian desire to provide adequate support to the unemployed and other poor in the town, the Poor Law Inquiry showed they were handicapped by the chaotic nature of relief in the town, even after the hospital's management reforms. In addition to representatives from the established Kirk Session and the Town Hospital, which shared responsibility for the 'ordinary' poor, the Commission interviewed representatives from the Manufacturer's Relief Association and a County Labour Committee that had provided the bulk of relief to the able-bodied unemployed in the recent distress. Compounding confusion, there were also charitable institutions such as the House of Refuge and the Town Infirmary. Finally, the town of Paisley was actually split between two parishes. Paisley Burgh Parish encompassed the bulk of the community, but the burghal boundary spilled over into neighboring Abbey Parish. Except for the residential streets around the Abbey itself, Abbey parish was predominantly rural and their relief accounts had reportedly been mismanaged for years. James Shaw Brown, when interrogated by the committee, had nothing to say about Abbey's reported mismanagement, but did suggest that the average support given to paupers there was among the highest in Scotland.[27] The committee recommended resolving such complexity through unions similar to those imposed in England, which would create 'a concentration of management, and an uniformity in the treatment of the poor, which could not otherwise be obtained except under the control of some general superintending authority'.[28]

With this and numerous other suggestions, and as the Paisley Town Council and others across Scotland had suggested, the committee concluded that a significant revision of the poor laws for all of Scotland was necessary, but must be carefully undertaken. Some elements of the old

26 'Select Committee on Distress', 80.

27 'Poor Law Inquiry (Scotland) Appendix', 622, 572.

28 'Poor Law Inquiry (Scotland)', xxii.

law – the able-bodied restriction prime among them – should be retained. All in all, they warned,

> It would be easy to produce an immediate effect by additional expenditure in the management of the poor, but the greatest caution is necessary in dealing with a subject so perplexing and so important, and where there is so much risk of aggravating the very evils which it is our object to alleviate. The suggestions, which we have made, we believe to be both safe and salutary, and at the same time calculated to relieve much of the wretchedness which has been brought under our notice.[29]

Following the presentation of the committee report in July 1844, the Home Secretary declined to take any immediate action, citing the great length of the report.[30] Paisley had finally emerged from its long emergency, somewhat helped Queen Victoria's notorious purchase of seventeen shawls to promote the industry.[31] The Parliamentary session adjourned with no further action to resolve the problem of Scotland's poor.

The next session of Parliament opened on 4 February 1845. Only a week later the MP for Stirling, Lord Dalmeny, rose to express the 'universal feeling of astonishment and horror at the distress' reported by the Inquiry and repeated the question of whether the government intended to 'introduce any measure for the alteration and amendment of the Poor Law in Scotland'.[32] This time, Graham acknowledged his opinion that some legislative fix would be necessary, but, hedging that 'to touch such a law … requires the utmost caution', he refused to provide a timeline or to commit to enacting all (or indeed any) recommendations of the committee.[33] After another month's delay, the bill was first moved in Parliament in April, and received a second reading in June.[34]

29 'Poor Law Inquiry (Scotland)', lxv.

30 'Commons Sitting of Wednesday, July 31, 1844', *19th Century House of Commons Sessional Papers*, Third Series, vol. 76.

31 Blair, *Paisley Shawl*, 26.

32 Hansards, 'Commons Sitting of Tuesday, February 11, 1845', *19th Century House of Commons Sessional Papers*, Third Series, vol. 77.

33 'Commons Sitting of Tuesday, February 11, 1845'.

34 Hansards, 'Commons Sitting of Wednesday April 2, 1845'; 'Commons Sitting of Tuesday June 12, 1845', *19th Century House of Commons Sessional Papers*, Third Series, vol. 81.

The bill being debated reflected the Report's recommendation that traditional structures of the Scottish poor law should not be changed where they were functional and sufficient.[35] The New Scottish Poor Law would not copy the English law, in spite of many men's conviction that the English system was superior. Parishes would not be forced into unions, the prohibition against able-bodied relief was maintained, and local autonomy would be retained to set the level and system of assessment. The most significant changes imposed were bureaucratic and aimed toward regularisation of governance and administration. Each parish was required to establish a new governing entity, a parochial board, made up of men elected from the ratepayers and members appointed by the local magistrates and Kirk sessions. Resolving the chaos of multiple providers, 'the whole Administration of the Laws for the Relief of the Poor [would] be under the Direction and Control of such Parochial Board[s]', including ensuring that any 'insane or fatuous persons chargeable as paupers' received appropriate care.[36] An Edinburgh-based Board of Supervision would oversee the whole system. The only major change to the rules for receiving poor relief – as opposed to the management of the system – was to set the period of residency required to gain a settlement at five years. In July, the House of Commons resolved itself into a committee of the whole to engage in discussion of the bill. It finally passed the House of Commons on 23 July and the House of Lords on 29 July 1845.

Having passed, the new Act was to take effect almost immediately. Each parish had to elect their new parochial board in a matter of weeks, on a timetable to be determined by the (equally new) Board of Supervision. By the latest, the parochial boards had to be in place by the third Tuesday of September to begin their work.[37] They then had to begin administering relief and collecting poor rates under the new system, regardless of whether or not the Board of Supervision had issued instructions at that point.

35 'Poor Law Inquiry (Scotland)', xiv.

36 *An Act for the Amendment and Better Administration of the Laws relating to the Relief of the Poor in Scotland*, [*Poor Law (Scotland)*], 1845, Section 17, 59.

37 *Poor Law (Scotland)*, Sec. 33.

Implementing the New Poor Law in Paisley

Paisley's managers met the New Poor Law with dismay. In spite of their role in spurring its creation, it did not address their most pressing needs. The burgh's own MP Hastie argued against its passage and then avoided casting a vote on the bill by serving as a teller.[38] Paisley's town council, upon learning that the bill had passed the House of Commons, immediately petitioned the House of Lords to alter the bill or delay its passage so that the people of Scotland could have more time to deliberate on the measure.[39] Their protests were futile. The amended law left the responsibility for funding poor relief to the individual parishes, not a larger geographic combination, it left compulsory assessment at the discretion of the parishes, and while it did lengthen the amount of time required to gain a settlement it was only to five years, half of what some had desired. The reiteration in the law that no able-bodied poor would have a right to relief was little compensation for the fact that Paisley would have no broader scope to raise funds for relief and only a slightly lengthened barrier to keep migrants off their rolls. The law did very little, in the end, to prevent the problems that had precipitated Paisley's fiscal collapse, and it forced them to reorganise the management bureaucracy that they had only recently established.

Nevertheless, the town had no time to resist further. With only weeks between the law's passage and the date it took effect, Paisley's existing poor law structure was adapted to fit the letter of the new law. On 12 August the hospital board added the title Inspector of the Poor – the title mandated by law – to James Shaw Brown's reappointment as Hospital Governor, a change from his previous title of Supervisor of the Poor. His salary remained unchanged, at £100.[40] No one then realised that Brown had thus been tasked to serve two masters: the hospital board and the town council

38 Hansards, 'Commons Sitting of Monday July 21, 1845', *19th Century House of Commons Sessional Papers*, Third Series, vol. 82.

39 HCP Town Council, vol. 1–28, 29 July 1845.

40 HCP Hospital, vol. 6–4, 12 Aug. 1845.

that was by law supposed to organise the new system of poor relief. To compound confusion, the Law mandated that the Board of Supervision would first meet at the same time as the new parochial boards were forming, so there was initially no higher level of oversight or guidance. In addition, the powers given to the Board of Supervision were primarily for inquiry and examination, unlike the English Poor Law Commissioners who were specifically empowered to issue 'Rules, Orders, and Regulations for the Management of the Poor' and had an energetic cadre of assistant commissioners prepared to pressure parishes as they implemented the law.[41] Paisley was one of more than 800 parishes that were thus empowered to interpret the requirements of the new law on their own.

The town council met on 20 August to the news that the bill had become law with none of their proposed revisions included. After some discussion (that was excluded from the minutes) Provost David Murray moved the formation of a committee, convened by himself, to put in place the required bureaucracy: a parochial board, a system to elect members to it, and 'generally the whole provisions of the Bill, as affecting the Town'.[42] Again, they were given no guidance in this practice beyond the text of the Act itself.

On 9 September, the subcommittee reported their findings regarding the new law back to the council. The Law demanded that the new parochial boards meet on the third Tuesday in September, the 16th, just one week away. At that meeting the board was to cause to be made up a roll of the parish's poor, appoint an Inspector of the Poor, and determine the mode of raising the funds to support the rolls. If all this could not be accomplished in a single meeting, they were permitted to put off the decision about raising funds for no longer than a fortnight.[43] The committee noted that the decision of greatest urgency for Paisley was the method of assessing poor rates, as the options available created a great difference in what individual rates would be.

41 *Poor Law Act (England)*, Sec. 15; A. Brundage, *The Making of the New Poor Law: The Politics of Inquiry, Enactment, and Implementation, 1832–9* (New Brunswick, NJ: Rutgers University Press, 1978), 87–92.

42 HCP Town Council, vol. 1–28, 20 Aug. 1845.

43 HCP Town Council, vol. 1–28 9 Sept. 1845; *Poor Law (Scotland)* Sec. 32.

The mode of assessment was a technical element of the Law that had tremendous importance for a parish like Paisley. Decisions regarding assessment method and amount absorbed hundreds of hours of committee meetings and were hotly contested issues for board elections. The Law outlined three possible methods for assessing poor rates: (1) based on property values, evenly divided between owners and tenants; (2) raising half the necessary amount from property owners and the other from all the parish inhabitants based on their 'means and substance'; or (3) as a flat percentage on income, whether from lands or other sources.[44] The question of method was not only based in fairness, but also in who was most able and likely to pay their share and how high a rate they could bear.

The committee recommended the first, 'rental', method, in which half the tax for each property would be paid by the landlord and half by the occupier. This would have the desirable effect of taxing landowners who did not themselves reside in the parish – a severe gap in Paisley's funding stream under the old system. Being based in the rental value, though, this method might affect rents in the burgh and require rate payments beyond what a tenant would pay if they were taxed purely on their income. The committee justified their recommendation with an analysis concluding, 'that the amount leviable from several persons … would be augmented, and that in some instances persons at present paying the highest sums of assessment would be much reduced, but from the introduction of the non-resident landlords, who have hitherto been exempted, assessment would in the great majority of the rate payers be lessened'. The committee recognised that such a dramatic change would cause significant outcry from some of the wealthiest members of the community. As their minutes noted, 'It is the opinion of the Committee that the pure rental system should be adopted, but as this is a subject of great importance to the Community, the Committee suggest that any final determination of the point should be postponed as long as practicable to afford the parties interested an opportunity of fully considering the whole subject.'[45]

44 *Poor Law (Scotland)*, Sec. 34.

45 HCP Town Council, vol. 1–28, 9 Sept. 1845.

Accordingly, on the appointed date the council (repeating an act already performed by the hospital board) officially named James Shaw Brown to be the Poor Law Inspector and approved the salary he was offered by the hospital. The salary would be confirmed or adjusted by the not-yet-composed parochial board, after the full responsibilities of the position were known.[46] Brown was officially ordered to make up the required roll of 'poor persons claiming, and by Law entitled to relief, from the Town parishes, and of the amount of Relief given or to be given to each of such persons'.[47] As proposed, the decision about how to raise the necessary funds was put off until a meeting ten days later. At that meeting, they did determine to assess based on a percentage of the annual value of lands and heritages within the burgh, split equally between owners and tenants, not on non-property income. With that decision, the barest outline of the New Poor Law was in place.

While they were working out the details of administration and resources, the timetable imposed by the Act meant that Paisley also had to quickly restructure how it directly managed the poor. Here, the parish was in much better shape than some others in Scotland. The roll of poor demanded by the Act was simply a continuation of the system Paisley had begun in 1839. It seemed such a natural transition, in fact, that the managers of the hospital were perplexed to discover they had no official role in the new process. Only on 18 September (two days after the town council put plans in motion to begin administering the New Poor Law) did the penny drop. After some debate they ordered Brown (as Supervisor and their clerk) to write a direct communication to the new Board of Supervision (bypassing the town council), 'containing an account of the Constitution of the Hospital Board and asking advice as to whether the said Board is now legally constituted, the New Poor Law having now passed and whether in existing circumstances the future proceedings of said Board are to be considered as legal'.[48]

46 HCP Town Council, vol. 1–28, 16 Sept. 1845.

47 HCP Town Council, vol. 1–28, 16 Sept. 1845.

48 HCP Hospital, vol. 6–4, 18 Sept. 1845.

In the same meeting, Inspector Brown revealed just how awkward the transition was. While he was employed by the hospital board in his role as Supervisor of the Poor, Governor of the Hospital, and clerk to the board, his new position as Inspector of the Poor answered directly to the town council until the new parochial board was in place. The council ordered him to create the poors' roll mandated by the Act, the entire substance of which already existed in the hospital's records. Brown thus had to request as a personal favor from the hospital board to be allowed to make extracts from his own records to create the 'new' returns. Accordingly, a motion was made to grant him the permission. Then, as the hospital directors considered what had happened, the question of proper jurisdiction arose. Mr Melvin, one of the managers who had earlier maintained there was no need to ask for the Board of Supervision's guidance, proposed specifying it was by the authority of the hospital board that the rolls were made up, not due to the town council's order.[49] Melvin's amendment carried, making a statement that it was the hospital board's responsibility – not the town council's – to see that the Board of Supervision's instructions were fulfilled.

For a few weeks, Brown worked at his double positions, both overseeing the hospital and preparing the required documents for the new system. It must have been an overwhelming amount of work, because at the next hospital board meeting, on 14 October, the directors acknowledged the necessity of hiring one or two men to act as Inspector's Clerk and [rate] Collector. The board decided to ask the town council for the authorisation to fill the positions.[50] A deputation of seven hospital directors was duly dispatched to the town council meeting the following evening.

There were three council members appointed to the Hospital Board of Directors, including Councilor John Campbell, the board's convener, but there was nevertheless some miscommunication and the delegation received an unpleasant surprise. While couching their response in respectful terms, the council asserted,

> that the whole duty of carrying the Poor Law Amendment Act into effect, until a new Board is appointed devolves on the Town Council: and that the Council will

49 HCP Hospital, vol. 6–4, 18 Sept. 1845.

50 HCP Hospital, vol. 6–4, 14 Oct. 1845.

> be ready to give the Inspector of the Poor all necessary assistance, in working out the provisions of the Act or carrying into effect the instructions of the Board of Supervision; and further that Mr Brown the Inspector be requested to communicate solely with the Town Council, all correspondence with the Board of Supervision.[51]

It took two days, until 17 October, for Brown to officially receive this news in his role as Governor of the Hospital.[52] On the 23rd, a special Thursday meeting of the hospital board was called to consider the council's reply. It must have been a long and angry discussion, barely hinted in the official minutes Brown took in his continuing role as the board's clerk. He wrote, 'This reply of the Town Council and the whole subject therewith connected having been maturely considered by the meeting and each of the members having expressed his opinion, it was moved by Mr John Paton that the Members of the Board do now agree to Resign the office they hold as Directors and Overseers into the hands of the Town Council. Which motion was … unanimously carried.'[53] After making plans to publicise their action and voting their esteem to the Governor (Brown) and matron, the Board was declared dissolved.[54]

While this was no doubt a satisfying action for the slighted directors, the next day brought new insult. Informed of the hospital board's dissolution, the town council responded that the directors of the hospital were legally unable to dissolve the board under their own authority. The council hoped that they would reconsider, but if the directors' intent was to no longer serve in that capacity they would have to submit individual resignations and could not eliminate the body itself.[55]

Brown brought this response to another special meeting of the hospital directors on 28 October. 'Which communication having been considered at some length', the board resolved that they could not 'consent to alter [their decision] or to resume office until' the town council's resolution of the 17th was withdrawn or modified 'as to allow to the members

51 HCP Town Council, vol. 1–28, 15 Oct. 1845.
52 HCP Hospital, vol. 6–4, 23 Oct. 1845.
53 HCP Hospital, vol. 6–4, 23 Oct. 1845.
54 HCP Hospital, vol. 6–4, 23 Oct. 1845.
55 HCP Town Council, vol. 1–28, 24 Oct. 1845.

of the Hospital Board free access to the Inspector's Correspondence with the Board of Supervisors, the same being absolutely necessary to the legal administration of the Hospital Funds and the proper treatment of applicants for parochial relief'.[56] Mr Brown was instructed to communicate this ultimatum back to the Council.

Having asserted their overall authority, the town council was prepared to concede a point and claimed there had been a misunderstanding. '[I]t was not the intention of the Council to withhold from them any part of correspondence with the Board of Supervisors having reference to the administration of the Poor's funds and that the Inspector be instructed to submit all such correspondence to the overseers and Directors of the Hospital for their guidance in all matters legally subjected to their control.'[57]

This concession, such as it was, came with a sour taste and not a little rancor. When the board received the communication in mid-November, their meeting minutes noted,

> Whereas it appears that at the meeting of Town Council held on the 7th current, certain statements were made injurious to Mr John Campbell [recall that he was a Councillor as well as Convener of the hospital board] it was moved … and unanimously carried that the Directors and Overseers deem it expedient and necessary hereby to place on record their cordial approbation of the conduct of Mr Campbell since his appointment as Chairman of the Hospital Board and to express their conviction that he has faithfully discharged the duties of his office and fairly represented the interests of the Directors.

Then, as if to prove a point, 'The Inspector laid before the meeting and read certain parts of his correspondence with the Board of Supervisors.'[58]

None of this struggle over precedence resolved Mr Brown's issue of too much work to accomplish in his many roles regarding the town's poor. The hospital board – members of which met Mr Brown daily in the course of his work – found a solution that did not involve the town council. Rather than hiring an Assistant Inspector, as they had suggested in October, on 2 December the board voted to hire an 'Assistant to the Governor'.[59] Keeping

56 HCP Hospital, vol. 6–4, 28 Oct. 1845.
57 HCP Hospital, vol. 6–4, 8 Nov. 1845.
58 HCP Hospital, vol. 6–4, 8 Nov. 1845.
59 HCP Hospital, vol. 6–4, 2 Dec. 1845.

the job description within the bounds of the hospital, rather than the poor law, skirted the issue of authority. Brown was no doubt relieved; there was an immediate shift in the hand that kept the board's minute book, evidence of a reapportionment of duties.[60]

The spat over which town body was in charge of implementing the New Poor Law was only the tip of the iceberg regarding confusion over the operation of the law. Paisley Burgh had worked hard for nearly a decade to bring order, efficiency and reasonable compassion to their management of the poor, and Parliament in passing the new act intended to leave in place homegrown structures that were working. Even the powers of the Board of Supervision were meant to be supportive rather than dictatorial. They required regular reports and had the ability to conduct inquiries, but they had no power of enforcement or to dictate procedures beyond the minimum detailed in the law. The result in Paisley (and this must have been true across Scotland) was uncertainty over what the Law actually required.

In spite of the town council's assertion that they were responsible for the implementation of the Act and the theater of resignations, the hospital board ultimately carried on – as they had for years – as if they were the Town's authority in the matter of poor relief. In their second December meeting, Brown must have confessed to confusion in his role as Inspector in wedding the old and new systems. The minutes noted, 'Some doubts having arisen as to the practical application of certain clauses of the Poor Law Amendment Act, the Inspector was instructed to communicate with the Board of Supervision in order to obtain the necessary explanations and if possible to obtain a personal interview.'[61] They made no mention of including the town council in the business.

Over the course of the next three decades Brown would repeatedly make such communications, both with the Board of Supervision and his fellow Inspectors. While the new law provided space for parishes to carry on with many policies or practices that had worked in the past, it also provided a framework into which all the policies of all the parishes must integrate. Unlike the English Poor Law, in which a strong central body

60 HCP Hospital, vol. 6–4, 17 Dec. 1845.
61 HCP Hospital, vol. 6–4, 17 Dec. 1845.

implemented a relatively uniform policy across the nation, the Scottish Poor Law attempted to lay an organising structure over the top of existing local systems. The remainder of James Shaw Brown's long career was spent negotiating the differences between systems as he and other local practitioners determined together what the New Poor Law actually required.

Meanwhile, the town council turned its attention to the funding and management of the poor law rather than specific care for the poor. In December they finally determined and submitted to the Board of Supervision for approval the amount and means of assessment proposed for the year August 1845 – August 1846, their desired structure for the new parochial board, qualifications for board members (now to be called Managers), and recommendation that James Shaw Brown be appointed an interim collector of the rates in addition to his other duties.[62] The hospital took on the new name of Paisley Poorhouse. These arrangements were approved on 5 February, and the election of Managers set for just a few days later. The inaugural meeting of the Paisley Parochial Board took place on 5 March 1846, and the New Poor Law had arrived in Paisley at last.[63]

62 HCP Town Council, vol. 1–28, 30 Dec. 1845.
63 HCP Town Council, vol. 1–28, 10 Feb. 1845.

CHAPTER 3

The Case of the Girl Who Lived on Her Clothes: How the People of Paisley Met the Poor Law

Inspector Brown and the Girl Who Lived on Her Clothes

A young woman called Jean Watson asked for help on the last Tuesday in July 1854. The statement Inspector Brown recorded in the Poor Law Office is the only record of her life that is now recoverable, though it is impossible to say if that was by accident or design. Watson declared she was unmarried, 25 years old, and she held a 1-month-old child in her arms. Since she was forisfamiliated at age 14, she had worked as a domestic or farm servant with eight different households. The longest stretch was three years with a family in Gorbals, followed by two and a half years with a Mrs Brown in Barony. Most recently – until May 1854 – she had worked for James Kerr in Neilston, a neighboring parish to Paisley. She declared that the father of her boy was John Anderson, a farm servant in Kilbarchan, giving no particular evidence of how they were acquainted. Although she had parents living in her native Ayrshire, when her term with Kerr ended in May she came to Paisley and lodged in the cheap rooms at 6 Hospital Lane (across the street from the poor house), where her son was born. With no hope of finding a job in the late stages of her pregnancy or while nursing an infant, she turned to the economy of makeshift and dissolved the capital she had accumulated over a decade of service. In the words of the poor law statement, she had 'been living on her clothes' since coming to Paisley.[1]

1 HCP Statements, vol. 11–8, Statement 7077.

When Watson came asking for relief, Inspector Brown was 43 years old. He was nearly seven years married to the former hospital matron Elizabeth Baird and was the father of two little boys, David and John. The Browns had moved in 1852 from their apartments in the poor house to the family building at 3 Back Sneddon, where James Shaw's mother and sisters still lived. He was the only one of his siblings to marry, and the boys must have been doted on as the only children in the extended family. James Shaw's experience as a teacher and with establishing the boarding out system, not to mention his lifetime as an older brother, suggests he was a compassionate man who looked with sympathy at this threadbare woman and her child. One can imagine Watson wearing the few clothes she had remaining to her, dandling a fussy infant Thomas, while Brown asked intimate questions with the same unflappable air with which he once oversaw a crowded classroom or answered questions to a Parliamentary inquiry. His greatest talent, though, was in pursuing accuracy. The carefully collected statistics and the letter and practice of the poor law system provided a lens to mitigate sympathy, control the interaction between the pauper and the managers, and to spread the parish's assessment as broadly and fairly as possible.

The intake system for paupers had been well established over the nine years since the New Poor Law was inaugurated, as Brown matured in his role as Inspector. On every lawful day (Sundays excepted) he visited the Parochial Office in the Poor House building at 8 New Sneddon in the morning and evening to receive communications from the parochial directors and to 'attend to applications for relief'.[2] A person in need of relief might see him there or wait for him to call after an incomplete schedule was delivered by a doctor, overseer, or clerk. It was a rare day when no new applicant appeared, and much of Brown's professional day must have been dominated by the Statements of Cases. While some information may have been completed by clerks, Inspector Brown was responsible for the accuracy of the information and presenting it to anyone who asked.

Two different hands completed Watson's statement, suggesting that the inspector or his assistant visited her at her lodging after receiving the

2 HCP Hospital, vol. 6–3, 15 July 1839.

schedule in the office. Watson answered queries regarding her personal history from birth to the present day, including where she had lived, employment, her family, literacy and religion, as well as what she knew about the father of her child. The Inspector likely gave her a small amount of aid at that interview if he deemed it urgent, but entering her onto the roll as a pauper had to be approved by the Administration of Relief Committee, one of four major committees that managed the parochial board's business. The Relief Committee was meeting infrequently that summer, but their first meeting since the start of the fiscal year on 15 May was just a few days after Watson's application. Her case was not even addressed by the committee, which was not unusual. Inspector Brown had proved his good sense in the first few years of the New Poor Law, and Relief Committee meetings must have carried on for hours when each case was individually examined in the early days.[3] The infrequency of committee meetings in 1854 suggests that Brown was empowered to provide immediate relief without direct oversight. Many cases were left to the Inspector's discretion and approved *en masse* or ignored entirely in the committee minutes.

The Managers of the Poor

Inspector Brown's relative independence in granting or withholding relief for applicants rested on a general confidence that the poor law in Paisley was administered locally, by men who were known to and respected by the rate-paying community. Paisley's Parochial Board, as mandated by the Poor Law and the Board of Supervision, included twenty-three men, with representation of the ratepayers, the town council, and the General Kirk Session.[4] The board elected their own Chairman, who typically served

3 HCP Parochial Board, vol. 7–19, 27 March 1846.

4 The Act did not directly acknowledge the schism in the Kirk following the Disruption, but provided that in any parish with more than one kirk session, the sessions had to cooperate in the selection of their representatives to the board. *Poor Law (Scotland)*, Sec. 17.

two consecutive years. There was some turnover on the board from year to year, always returning enough old members to maintain institutional memory. Men who served on the board were, generally speaking, in manufacture and trade, with a few from other professions such as medicine or accountancy.

The men who stood for the parochial board each year were fulfilling an obligation to their community broadly called 'civil society'.[5] This idea, coined during the Scottish Enlightenment after the Union of Parliaments removed national government from Edinburgh, recognised that Scotland generally lacked an institutionalised political or bureaucratic class. Instead, there was an obligation for men of a certain social standing to participate in the governance of their community in addition to their commercial occupations. The Kirk, voluntary organisations and local needs gave rise to a multitude of boards, committees and societies that oversaw most of the day-to-day needs of communities without having any clear central oversight. Like all Scottish communities, Paisley's government for most of the nineteenth century was primarily at the Burgh and County level. There were rarely acts that were imposed on a national level, because such acts had to be passed at the Westminster Parliament where Scottish issues rarely rose to the top of the agenda. Justice was administered by local Magistrates and Sheriffs' courts. Disputed cases could be appealed to the Court of Session, and very occasionally a case would be further appealed to the House of Lords for final disposition.

The members of the parochial board were well-known members of the community. Taking the listing in *Fowler's Commercial Directory* in 1853–4 as an example, the truly 'Great Men' of the town, the wealthiest magnates such as the Coats family, did not serve on this particular civic government body, though their names do appear in other offices and societies. Rather, men who stood for election to the parochial board were in the next level

5 G. Hassan, 'The Rise and Fall of Civil Society in Scotland, *Scottish Review* 12 Aug. 2020; G. Morton, 'Civil Society, Municipal Government and the State: Enshrinement, Empowerment and Legitimacy. Scotland, 1800–1929', *Urban History* 25:3 Special Issue: Civil Society in Britain (Dec. 1998): 348–67; and C. Smith, *Adam Ferguson and the Idea of Civil Society: Moral Science in the Scottish Enlightenment* (Edinburgh: Edinburgh University Press, 2020).

of the population, such as the Board Chair, thread manufacturer Robert Farquharson; the builder and contractor Hugh Hamilton; William Steven, who manufactured or sold rope, sacks, and sheeting; William Burns, an accountant and feuar; and Andrew Nairn, accountant and house factor.[6] Service on the parochial board was generally only one of several civil society roles these men undertook. According to *Fowler's*, only five had membership on the board as their sole leadership position on a board or voluntary society.[7] The parochial board and similar bodies were likely a kind of rotating obligation rather than a calling or passion project for most of the men who served. Surviving directories from 1845, 1853–4 and 1862–3 show significant differences over time. Just one board member from 1845 was serving in 1853, and only three from 1853 were also on the board in 1862.

Men who served on the parochial board frequently took other governmental or quasi-governing roles in the burgh. As the hospital and town council had worked closely together in the years before the New Poor Law was passed, there continued to be significant overlap between the parochial board and the town council in the 1850s. While the town council had the obligation to appoint four of their members to the board, an additional four members of the council won positions on the board through election by the ratepayers in 1853. Three board members were also Justices of the Peace, two were on the Police Commission, and six were trustees overseeing the town's financial affairs following the bankruptcy and rescue of 1843. Nine served in school leadership and six were on the governing committee for firemen. Banks, the Gas & Light Company, the Infirmary and Dispensary, the Athenaeum, the Cemetery Company and a litany of other institutions and charities established for the support and enlightenment of Paisley's inhabitants all had parochial board members in their leadership. For these men, participating in the governance of and care for the community of Paisley, including the poor, was at least a pastime and conceivably a calling.

6 Listings in *Fowler's Commercial Directory and General Advertiser, for 1853–4* (Paisley: G. Fowler, 1853). 'Feu' is an old form of lease; as a feuar Burns received payments from tenants for land on which he held the feu.

7 *Fowler's Commercial Directory*; *Paisley Herald and Renfrewshire Advertiser*, 25 Feb. 1854, 2.

Remarkably, it is more difficult to trace and reconstruct the families of these public worthies than it is for the applicants for relief. Without the demographic goldmine of a Statement and with common use of relatively few given names in nineteenth-century Scotland, it is difficult to be certain of record-matching through directories, censuses, and vital records. Minute books preserve hints of personality but never any clue of the members' concerns outside the board room, including how their engagement with the poor law fit into their family or business obligations. In lieu of extensive investigation of the dozens of men elected to the board from 1845 onward, a son's memoir of one particularly active member must suffice. While twice-Provost David Murray was an extreme case, his life illustrates the extensive public engagement available and required by the civil society, as men answered the needs of their communities.

Born in Paisley in 1807, David Murray trained for medicine as a young man but ultimately joined his father's business of house painting and selling related supplies.[8] His son suggested that he was influenced by the radical unrest in Paisley in 1819–20, linking it to his support for Parliamentary and then burgh reform in the early 1830s.[9] His first role in public service was as a Manager of the Poor in 1832, and he became active in town government as soon as the municipal councils were reformed.[10] He served on the town council throughout the crisis of the 1840s and was a member of the delegation sent to London to plead for assistance from the Government. In 1844 he was elected Provost (Chief Magistrate), a position he held until 1850. He became an elder in a secessionist congregation, the radical Free Church congregation at St George Street headed by Reverend Dr Robert Burns.

Married in 1830 to a member of the Clark family, Murray, like several other members of the board, lived in the town centre. His family building sat on Gilmour Street, near the train station (opened in 1840), two doors away from the Government School of Design (of which he was the founding President), and a stone's throw from the county buildings and prison. The building held six commercial apartments, including Murray's

8 J. C. Murray, *Memoir of David Murray, Late Provost of Paisley, with Sketches of Local history in His Time* (Paisley: Alexander Gardner, 1881), 4, 31.

9 Murray, *Memoir of David Murray*, 47, 53.

10 Murray, *Memoir of David Murray*, 65, 57.

own establishment, two unrelated business offices, and a spirit dealer's cellar. Murray's family – his wife, seven children, and a live-in domestic servant – occupied a 6-room flat valued at an £18 annual rent.[11] In 1854, in addition to his service as an elected member of the parochial board and whatever duties he had to the School of Design, Murray was a Justice of the Peace, served as a Trustee for Cart Navigation, was the Chairman of the National Security Bank, a manager of the Infirmary, a Director of the Paisley Coffee Room, Governor of the Paisley Cemetery Company, the Convener of the Corporation of Merchants and President of the Society for the Reformation of Manners.

In the 1850s Murray's firm employed over a dozen men and boys, but his son implied that most of his father's energy went to public service:

> It is unnecessary now, and to him it would have been distasteful at any time, to dwell upon the extent to which his private interests were sacrificed in his public labours. ... Whether, if he had had the opportunity, his fine business energies could ever have been thrown into a private enterprise with the enthusiasm which he displayed in the management of public affairs, it is useless to inquire.[12]

Quite aside from other obligations, Murray's service on the parochial board took up considerable time. It required at least one evening meeting per month, when the board reviewed and generally ratified committee actions. Board members served on one or more of the committees, which would generally entail at least one more meeting per month per committee, and potentially much more when there was a particular concern to address. Throughout his career Murray served regularly on the Poorhouse Committee, and at times on the Administration of Relief Committee and the Assessment Committee. Each board member also took a regular turn to complete a weekly inspection of the poor house. Some of Murray's other obligations may have required minimal time, but presuming that he was also engaged in running his business it seems that many of his evenings were devoted to his public service and not his family life.

11 Murray, David: Valuation Rolls VR006600001-/34 Paisley Burgh 1855; Census 573/51/18 1851; Census 573/32/5 1861 *ScotlandsPeople*.

12 Murray, *Memoir of David Murray*, 64–5.

Provost Murray's extensive involvement is probably not typical of middle-class participation in civil society. No other member of the parochial board appears across so many areas of town life for such a long period of time. Nevertheless, key features of his life are representative of many men who oversaw the poor law. In spite of his marriage into a branch of one of Paisley's leading families, he was solidly middle class, engaged in the daily economic and political life of the burgh. Where it is possible to connect an occupation to the parochial board members, they were overwhelmingly merchants and tradesmen, and more than half had addresses in the respectable tenement and terraces of Paisley rather than detached, named houses on the outskirts. Their work for the poor law was fit into the hours after their professional obligations and perhaps before their family ones. The levels of urgency were not comparable, but there is a resonance between the scarce, carefully budgeted time Murray and his colleagues allocated to their poor law work and the scanty patchwork of resources and need that brought Jean Watson and other paupers to the poor law office.

Participation in government and oversight was a voluntary social obligation for the parochial board. For another cadre of men and women, managing the civic work of the burgh was a profession. The numbers employed in this area grew as the New Poor Law became more established. At first, in the name of convenience and efficiency, James Shaw Brown served as both House Governor and Poor Law Inspector, but a sharp suggestion from the Board of Supervision in 1852 persuaded the parochial board to split the positions and hire a new Governor and Matron, prompting Inspector and Mrs Brown's move to Back Sneddon.[13] In addition to the Inspector and an Assistant Inspector, the parochial board employed: the new Governor and Matron of the Poorhouse; a 'keeper and his wife' who oversaw the paupers of unsound mind; domestics, cooks, and maintenance men for the institution; an assessor and a number of collectors of rates; not to mention doctors and clergymen who were contracted to provide services as needed. Dozens of families 'in the country' were compensated for fostering pauper children. Thus, the poor law was not a phenomenon isolated in a small segment of Paisley's community. Every person assessed

13 HCP Parochial Board, vol. 7–19, 27 Jan. 1852.

Illustration 1. Notes on the Case of Alexander Getheral

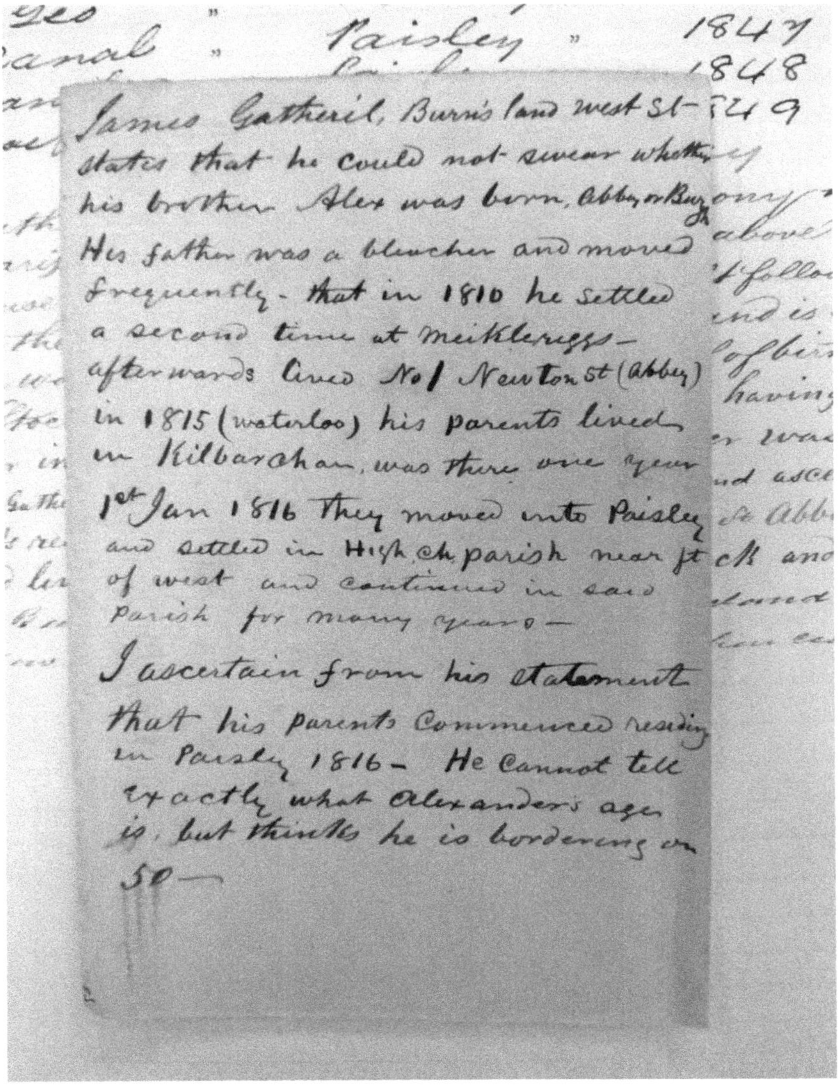

James Gatherel, Burn's land west St-
states that he could not swear whether
his brother Alex was born, Abbey or Burgh
His father was a bleacher and moved
frequently - that in 1810 he settled
a second time at Meiklerigs -
afterwards lived No 1 Newton St (Abbey)
in 1815 (waterloo) his parents lived
in Kilbarchan, was there one year
1st Jan 1816 they moved into Paisley
and settled in High Ch parish near ft
of west and continued in said
Parish for many years -
I ascertain from his statement
that his parents commenced residing
in Paisley 1816 - He cannot tell
exactly what Alexander's age
is, but thinks he is bordering on
50 -

HCP Statements vol. 11–56, Statement 5025. Courtesy of National Records of Scotland/Paisley Heritage Centre

for poor rates (which included both owners and tenants of properties) was entitled to cast ballots for members of the board and had their own opinions about the generosity or parsimony of relief. Residents at every social level touched and were touched by the poor law at multiple points in their lives, regardless of whether they ever applied for relief themselves.

Applicants for Relief

Of course, no one was more directly affected by the poor law than the applicants and paupers themselves. For Jean Watson and others like her, contact with the poor law was personified by the polite, diffident Inspector Brown and his probing questions. Inspector Brown's process began with the applicant. He took her responses as they were presented, pausing to ask for details of dates and locations. A hint of how he worked to jog memory survives in a scrap of notes tucked into the volume of Statements from 1851 regarding Alexander Getheral, who re-applied for relief in 1862. One side, a torn-off corner of preprinted stationery, carried the penciled question, 'Alex 30 then now 49. When father made application he had lived 26 years in Paisley. Query when did he come to Pais?' On the reverse he (or the assistant he dispatched) wrote a summary of his interview with the applicant's brother.

> James Gatheril, Burn's Land west St states that he could not swear whether his brother Alex was born, Abbey or Burgh. His father was a bleacher and moved frequently. That in 1810 he settled a second time at Meikleriggs – afterwards lived No 1 Newton St (Abbey) in 1815 (Waterloo) his parents lived in Kilbarchan, was there one year 1st Jan 1816 they moved into Paisley and settled in High ch parish near ft of west and continued in said parish for many years -
>
> I ascertain from his statement that his parents commenced residing in Paisley 1816. He cannot tell exactly what Alexander's age is, but thinks he is bordering on 50 -[14]

14 HCP Statements, vol. 11–6, Statement 5025.

The parenthetical note, '(Waterloo)', suggests the Inspector used the landmark event to coax out and date faded memories.

From notes like this one, it appears the first step was to take the applicant at their word – only after those first answers were recorded would Brown and his staff check facts and revise or amend the statement if necessary. In some cases, there was nothing more to do than pass the applicant a shilling or two and write to another parish seeking reimbursement. When the initial statement suggested the applicant might have a settlement in Paisley, Brown sought out witnesses to confirm the crucial parts of the life history. Ministers were asked to check their registers, and birth and migration stories were verified by recourse to relatives or neighbors placed to corroborate the applicant's story. For example, when David Richmond and Margaret Moodie, claiming to be married and with one or two children, applied for relief in June 1851, there was no data entered at all, only a penciled note, 'send for evidence of marriage'.[15] A few days later, a request came from one of the Glasgow parishes to pay support for Thomas Boyd, an unmarried weaver and a 'drunken wretch' who was nevertheless born in Paisley, which information was provided 'by his sister … who has a good recollection of his birth'.[16]

Not all fact could be verified, however, and some or all of Jean Watson's statement may have been falsified, starting with her name. Her son was born six months before civil registration of births was instituted in Scotland, and none of the other details from her statement can be definitively linked to other records. It is impossible to tell at this distance if she gave a false name or just slipped through record keepers' fingers. Such falsehoods were not uncommon, especially (though not exclusively) from unmarried mothers. A few years before Jean Watson applied for relief, Inspector Brown took a statement from Flora O'Neil (alias Jean Martin) who admitted giving a false name for 'fear that we might write home to her own parish regarding her'.[17] James Lowrie and Ann Robertson's statement carried the notation, 'The whole of this statement of residence appears to be incorrect. He and

15 HCP Statements, vol. 11–6, Statement 4693.
16 HCP Statements, vol. 11–6, Statement 4697.
17 HCP Statements, vol. 11–6, Statement 4604.

his wife cannot or will not give a proper account but from all that can be gathered regarding them it appears they have a settlement no where excepting it be in Paisley.'[18] Regardless of Watson's veracity, in July 1854 there was a young woman and an infant, and they were so unsurprising to the poor law authority that they needed only perfunctory treatment. Jean Watson's details were carefully recorded but there are no notes from further inquiry or any further action.

Among a Mass of Paupers

Jean Watson was one applicant for relief among many in need. From 1845 to 1876, more than 16,000 individual Statements of Cases were recorded, while the town's population never passed 50,000 souls. The town averaged over 430 new applicants for relief each year and in 1851, the closest study year to Watson's application, Inspector Brown recorded 519. There were large fluctuations in the number of applicants from year to year, skyrocketing in years when the economy floundered and declining when times were flush. There was a more gradual shift across the decades as interpretations of the Law altered who was likely to be granted relief. The year 1851 was a reasonably representative year for the decade, including a double-dipped trade slump but not an overwhelming collapse such as was seen in the 1840s.

While there are discernible patterns (women with children and without partners were especially vulnerable, for example), each applicant came to the poor law carrying a unique set of circumstances and particular individual need. The statements were recorded by the managers of relief, but they reflected and sometimes directly recorded the applicants' own words and reveal their expectations of what was due to them from the law or from their personal relationships. In addition to the simple facts of the case that were so carefully examined and verified, the manner and voice of the applicant carried meaning beyond the facts of their situation.

18 HCP Statements, vol. 11–6, Statement 4705.

It was a point of pride for Inspector Brown to make a correct, just determination of an applicant's eligibility for relief from Paisley, and his colleagues remembered him rarely making an error. The provisions of the poor law meant that any errors could quickly become a public embarrassment (at least within bureaucratic circles). Not only could parishes argue with one another over which had responsibility for a pauper, but applicants themselves could protest the inspector's or parochial board's determination. The right to relief was secured by Section 73 of the Law, 'if relief shall be refused to any poor person who shall have made application for relief, it shall and may be lawful for such poor person to apply to the sheriff of the county … and the said sheriff shall forthwith, if he be of opinion that such poor Person is … legally entitled to relief, make an order upon the Inspector of the Poor … directing him to afford relief to such poor person' while the case was considered further.[19] Many managers of the poor in Scotland chose to give very small amounts of relief to questionable cases, rather than refusing outright, because that tiny aliment meant avoiding the sheriff's potential intervention. Poor law inspectors from time to time bemoaned the tendency for sheriffs to approve applications that in the inspectors' opinions had no merit.[20] In considering Jean Watsons case, then, Inspector Brown had to be sure he was making a judgment based on the woman's economic situation, not her moral condition.

There was certainly a flood of assumptions, performance and judgments that went into any application for relief, but overt judgments regarding the character of applicants based on their appearance or manner are remarkably rare in the Paisley record. Just three of 519 applicants for relief in 1851 were described with the loaded term 'respectable' in their statements, a judgment passed by the Inspector or his assistant based on now-lost details of their perceived refinement. Margaret (Dechman) Walker, a 63-year-old widowed pirn winder who had two grown daughters and a stepson in Paisley, was noted to be 'a very respectable well doing person'.

19 *Poor Law (Scotland)*, Sec. 73.

20 For example, 'R.' wrote to the *Poor Law Magazine* in 1862, 'If [the parochial board] refuse even well-known and undoubted cases of unworthy applicants, the Sheriff has the power of interfering in a most injudicious way.' 'Correspondence', *The Poor Law Magazine for Scotland* 4 (April 1862): 401.

She was, nevertheless, turned down for relief as being able-bodied and with family that could support her.[21] A few months later, Margaret McKenzie, a 40-year-old unmarried warehouse worker (sewer) applied due to 'delicate health and want of work' and the Inspector added the note, 'respectable appearance'.[22] The final 'respectable' applicant was John Laird, a 50-year-old native of Paisley, widowed less than a year, who was living in Glasgow when he applied for relief because lumbago left him unable to carry on his trade. The inspector noted that Laird, 'had a respectable hairdressing shop & trade in Paisley for many years – has ruined himself by intemperance'.[23]

While these notations of respectability stand out, leaving one to assume that the remaining applicants were not notably respectable, the statements generally are equally free of critical judgments. The strongest words were reserved for individuals who seemed unsteady, like Isabella Thomson, 29 years old and unmarried, who, 'was in a warehouse but ill doing and has had no regular employment for 9 years … Resided with parents … till she had a bastard child 9 years ago but ever since she has led an irregular life and has been a common prostitute – no certain place of abode and after in prison.'[24] Another 'ill doer' was Kenneth McKenzie, for whom Edinburgh asked Paisley to pay relief and the Inspector recorded, 'An ill-doing blackguard fellow. … This man has cohabited for sometime back with a woman named Ann Stevenson. … they were not married but she has 2 children by him. … They have been travelling the country and have become chargeable to many parishes within the last twelve months.'[25] The clear moral judgment passed on Thomas Boyd, the 'drunken wretch', came from his sister, who further supplied he was, 'Never married but cohabited with a woman named ___ [no name was provided] for some time and has some children by her ….'[26] Unlike these examples, most cases gave simple statements of

21 HCP Statements, vol. 11–6, Statement 4539; Relief Committee, vol. 7–27 14 March 1851.

22 HCP Statements, vol. 11–6, Statement 4646.

23 HCP Statements, vol. 11–6, Statement 4768.

24 HCP Statements, vol. 11–6, Statement 4956.

25 HCP Statements, vol. 11–6, Statement 4608.

26 HCP Statements, vol. 11–6, Statement 4697.

fact, such as Jean Watson's disability, 'on account of having this child',[27] and left the judgments on the eligibility for relief up to the readers.

Moral objectivity was not an attitude an applicant could expect from a poor law inspector, though. If Jean Watson was telling lies about her situation, she was doing so to craft an image that would gain sympathy and relief while protecting her actual identity. The Statements of Cases and other research in Scotland show that children were born out of wedlock into all sorts of circumstances and their mothers were not necessarily outcast or shamed. Nevertheless, a woman who could name and pursue the putative father of her child, perhaps with a story of a promise of marriage, was generally a greater object of sympathy than one who, like Isabella Thompson, was suspected of engaging in sex work.[28]

Paisley's Applicants by Numbers

Applying for aid from the parish may have been a momentous, shameful decision worthy of falsehood for Watson and other applicants, but for Inspector Brown and his colleagues each statement was one glittering drop in the torrent of need; perhaps the volume of applicants was so high that taking extra time to engage in moral investigations was simply untenable. There were large fluctuations in the number of applicants from year to year, and many applicants required aid multiple times in their lives. Application numbers gradually declined across the decades as court decisions narrowed the range of who was considered eligible for relief.

For the purposes of this book, Statements of Cases from the census years 1851, 1861, and 1871 were transcribed and counted in terms of sex, family status, and the events that preceded their initial applications for

27 HCP Statements, vol. 11–8, Statement 7077.

28 The question of premarital sex and birth out of wedlock in Scotland is a great deal more complicated than Victorian stereotypes would suggest, and well beyond the scope of this study. See A. Blaikie, *Illegitimacy, Sex, and Society: Northeast Scotland, 1750–1900* (Oxford: Clarendon Press, 1993).

relief. Some cases were then record-matched to census enumerations, valuation rolls, and vital records to flesh out a fuller picture of the applicants' lives. Each individual statement provides a snapshot of the moment in a person's life when they first requested public aid. If the individual was accepted to Paisley's roll of paupers, additional snapshots were added over time. Far from being the charity-addicted, life-long paupers that continued to haunt commentators' nightmares,[29] applicants came from a social stratum of workers that walked a border between poor and pauper, moving in and out of dependence as circumstances changed. Like Jean Watson in the weeks before and after her child was born (and like many struggling people today), they generally lived in the cheapest housing they could find, ate meagre and monotonous meals, engaged in a wide variety of miscellaneous occupations, and utilised pawnbrokers to draw cash from their personal possessions before or while deciding to request poor relief. For many recipients of relief, reliance on the poor law was temporary or sporadic, exactly as outdoor relief was designed to be. At the moment of application, applicants were not dramatically different from their neighbors; individual life circumstances, one turn of fate at a crucial moment, rather than key characteristics, determined who would need relief.[30]

Most of the statements Inspector Brown recorded included a qualitative description of the applicants' 'disablement', a plain-language description of what brought the applicant to the poor law office. For Jean Watson the entry was, 'on account of having this child'.[31] The entry could

29 For example, 'Once a pauper, the person is not unwilling to continue one, and makes no particular effort to escape from the condition.' George Taylor, 'On the Moral Effects of the Poor Law', *Poor Law Magazine for Scotland* 4 (June 1862): 484.

30 W.M. Gordon, 'The Demographics of Scottish Poverty: Paisley's Applicants for Relief, 1861 and 1871', *Journal of Scottish Historical Studies* 30:1 (2010): 25–42; W.M. Gordon, 'Seeking Relief on Love Street: Gender, Mobility and Pauperism in Mid-nineteenth Century Scotland', in *Gender and Mobility in Scotland and Abroad*, ed. S. Dye, E. Ewan and A. Glaze (Guelph: University of Guelph, 2018), 103–18; and A. Blaikie, 'Nuclear Hardship or Variant Dependency?: Households and the Scottish Poor Law', *Continuity and Change* 17:2 (2002): 272–3.

31 Statement 7077.

be brief, as for James Gibson 'Labouring under palsy', or extensive, as for Ann McCordock who reported,

> Daughter was engaged as a domestic servant to Mr Fauld's Coal Mercht or clerk to a colliery Renfrew on 23rd December last and entered on her duties on Monday 30th Dec. Was in her service only 5 days when she became unwell, remained two days sick in her masters house and was then sent by him per rail to Paisley where she arrived on Tuesday night the 8th Inst.[32]

Many descriptions of disablements carry the weight of traumatic events brought about by the strain of poverty or sheer bloody-mindedness, such as Margaret Galbraith who reported of her husband John McManus, 'he gave wife a very severe beating on 19th inst and has since absconded'.[33] Another Margaret, married to William Graham, applied when '[h]e put in jail on Friday last for assault upon John Slater. Throwing him downstairs by which he is some hurt.'[34] When trade failed in June, statement after statement simply said, 'Out of work' or 'Idle'.

Summarised and aggregated, the precipitating events that drove Paisley's residents to apply for relief fall broadly into major categories of those disabled by individual health conditions, those who fell prey to vulnerability of their particular life stage, and those impoverished by an economic crisis. While each applicant was experiencing their own unique ordeal, the kinds of distress they would encounter were remarkably predictable.

32 HCP Statements of Cases, vol. 11–6, Statement 4525, Statement 4528.
33 HCP Statements of Cases, vol. 11–6, Statement 4625.
34 HCP Statements of Cases, vol. 11–6, Statement 4629.

Table 1: Precipitating Events as a Percentage of Applicants, 1851, 1861, 1871

Sample Year	1851 (n = 519)	1861 (n = 591)	1871 (n = 347)
Health Conditions	*32.57*	*41.12*	*59.08*
Chronic Illness	10.02	21.83	19.02
Discrete Illness	14.26	8.80	25.65
Injury	5.01	6.09	5.48
Mental illness (including Intemperance)	3.28	4.40	8.93
Life Stage	*26.98*	*32.31*	*31.99*
Infancy	1.35	0.85	3.75
Pregnancy/Childbirth	3.47	5.58	3.75
Husband absent	10.79	12.35	8.36
Young Children	5.20	6.26	5.76
Old Age	4.05	5.92	6.34
Burial Costs/Death	2.12	1.35	4.03
Economic Crisis	*34.11*	*16.92*	*0.29*
Travel/Footsore	0.58	3.55	0.29
Unemployed (not disabled)	33.53	13.37	0
Other Causes	*6.55*	*9.64*	*8.64*
Other	3.85	1.86	2.30
Not Listed/Blank	2.70	7.78	6.34

Family Condition

Based on his inquiry and observation of the applicant, Inspector Brown would determine if the person was 'disabled and destitute' as the poor law required for relief. By the terms of the Act Brown had discretion to grant immediate and continuing aid as needed, while the Relief Committee approved his actions at their meetings that might be held weekly, monthly, or not for several months at a time.[35] Disability was generally easier to determine than 'destitution', because family members had a legal obligation to support their relations, as illustrated by the case of the 'respectable' Margaret Walker who was denied relief because her daughters were deemed able to support her.[36] Thus, learning an applicant's family condition was key to appropriate disposition of a case and dominated the questions on the Statement. People at every stage of life appear in the statements, from infancy to extreme old age, from their first days forisfamiliated from their parents to middle-aged widowhood with many children to elderly couples. Although the tables that follow are simply three snapshots in a complex 20-year history, the differences evident from decade to decade can be linked more closely to changes in how the poor law was interpreted and implemented than to changes in applicants' behavior or need. The most important of these changes, the provision of relief to unemployed able-bodied workers, is the subject of the next chapter.

This caveat aside, the sample of cases amply demonstrates that applicants for relief in Paisley came from a wide range of circumstances. In each sample year, widows and orphans accounted for at most one-third of the applications, which meant a majority of those asking for relief did not fit the model of the 'deserving poor' assumed by the language of the poor law. Instead, they were people like Jean Watson, who needed support in spite of the poor law's prejudice against the unfettered and able-bodied.

35 *Poor Law (Scotland) Act*, Sec. 70; HCP Committee Minute Books, vol. 7–27 & 7–28.

36 Statement 4539; *Poor Law (Scotland) Act*, Sec. 71.

Table 2: Sex and Marital Status of Applicants for Relief 1851, 1861, 1871[37]

Sex/Status	1851	1861	1871
All Applicants	*n = 519*	*n = 591*	*n = 347*
Unmarried	22.1	30.8	30.3
Married	53.0	44.2	36.3
Widowed	18.3	20.6	27.0
Men	*n = 271*	*n = 235*	*n = 152*
Unmarried	11.4	22.6	13.3
Married	74.5	54.9	18.2
Widowed	8.5	16.2	8.1
Women	*n = 246*	*n = 356*	*n = 195*
Unmarried	34.1	36.2	30.3
Married	30.1	37.0	32.3
Widowed	29.3	23.6	33.8

Although knowing the sex and legal marital status of applicants is tidy, even a casual perusal of the Statements shows a messier truth. Marriage could be irregular and was always difficult to dissolve. Injury and infectious disease could disrupt a family with horrific rapidity. The simple three-pronged identification of marital status (Unmarried, Married, Widowed) was inadequate to describe the real complexity of relationships. Chapter 5 explores in more detail how a complex family structure could tangle the provision of poor relief. Before delving deeply into the legal consequences, the following table illustrates the distribution of applicants for relief based on their apparent relationship to a co-resident family at the time of their application (see note for a definition of terms).

37 The numbers and percentages in this table do not equal 100 percent because individuals without discernible marital status were not included.

Table 3: Family Condition of Applicants for Relief in Paisley, 1851, 1861, 1871

Condition	1851	1861	1871
	$n = 519$	$n = 591$	$n = 347$
Child	1.5	1.5	4.3
Single Person	22.8	32.0	30.0
Married Couple	41.2	20.6	15.6
Married Applying Alone	4.0	11.8	4.6
Separated/Abandoned Spouse	9.4	10.7	12.4
Widowed Person	19.0	22.0	28.0
Not Known	1.9	1.4	5.2

Note: The condition terms used to label the table are shorthand for complex situations. Applicants were identified and grouped according to the following considerations. '*Child*:' most applicants in this category were under 16, orphaned or deserted by their relatives. Sick or injured young people gained access to relief through their parents, who were then the applicants of record. '*Single Person*:' A person who had never been legally married and was economically responsible for themselves and any minor children with them. '*Married Couple*:' Names of two people, identified as married, appear on the Statement and were apparently co-resident at the time of application. '*Married Applying Alone*:' Names of one or two people, identified as married, appear on the Statement. Evidence from the statement shows they were not currently co-resident (due to incarceration, emigration, illness, or other causes) but the relationship was ongoing. '*Separated/Abandoned Spouse*:' At least one person's name, identified as married, appeared on the Statement. Evidence from the statement shows they were living apart from and were primarily economically independent from their legal spouse. Circumstances ranged from a mutually agreed separation to sudden abandonment. Most married women whose husbands had gone 'in search of work' were placed in this category because of the uncertain nature of the husband's ultimate return or current economic contribution to the household. '*Widowed Person*:' Individual named on the statement is identified as widowed, usually with the name of their deceased spouse (of either sex). May be living in a wide variety of family situations, from complete isolation to with a large number of small children, with adult children or in a new marriage-like relationship. '*Not Known*:' primarily incomplete Statements, frequently of deceased individuals.

Over the course of the decades, the proportion of married male applicants declined, which was linked to the eventual exclusion of the able-bodied unemployed from even casual, in-kind relief from the poors fund. Again setting the issue of unemployment aside for the next chapter, individuals, especially women, outside a stable relationship were far more likely than married people to appear in the Statements of Cases. It is difficult at this remove to know if the families headed by a married couple were genuinely less poor, if unmarried individuals were more likely to apply because they knew they were more likely to fit the poor law's expectations for relief, or if married men in 1871 were simply turned away before any schedule was completed, a bias in the administration of relief rather than the distribution of need. Conceivably – though it's rather unlikely – the Statements actually provide an accurate cross-section of poverty in Paisley rather than a selection biased by law, prejudice or self-doubt. For the modern historian, statistics drawn from the Statements provide a wavery image of poverty in Paisley, never a true reflection.

Each statement did more-or-less accurately record the lives and experiences of individuals, and that is what Inspector Brown was charged to examine. While family condition could be crucial to determining whether or not a person was eligible for relief, their physical location and history of residence was key to deciding which parish was responsible for paying that relief.

Location and Migration

After nearly two decades working with Paisley's poor and almost ten years' experience under the New Poor Law, Brown likely had an idea of what to expect as soon as he learned Jean Watson was staying at Hospital Lane. Although applicants for relief could come from virtually anywhere in the town, they clustered thickly in the First and Second Wards, and in 'the Sneddon' behind the Gilmour Street train station, including Hospital Lane, Old Sneddon Street, parts of Love Street and Back Sneddon Street. On the other side of the tracks, they filled tenements on Moss Street and School Wynd, or scattered along High Street. The tenements where workers lived, by the time they applied for relief, were the cheapest housing available in Paisley. Flats at 6 Hospital Lane took an annual rent of only £1.19/-, just about the lowest that could be found in the burgh.[38]

It was common (although not universal) for applicants to report many residences over the years before they applied for relief, showing significant physical mobility.[39] Jean Watson, reportedly aged 25 when Brown took her statement, said that she left her family home at age 14, a typical age for girls to begin independent work as a domestic or farm servant. She lived in eight different locations over the next ten years. Servants' contracts were typically for six months, and at first Jean stayed with families over several contracts, claiming to have been with the McLauchlans in Gorbals (Glasgow) for three years. More recently, Watson or her employers had been less satisfied; after coming to Renfrewshire around 1852 she spent just a single term with each of four employers in four different parishes before she left service entirely in advanced pregnancy. It was common for single women – who depended on their employers for housing – to move locations frequently. Even for people who were not servants, shifting housing was a common strategy to respond to changes in employment or family status. Individuals migrated over all sorts of distances, sometimes across the street and sometimes across the nation or overseas. Many moved in and out of Paisley in search of work, and others escaping or pursuing family members.[40] Elisabeth Rough, for example, migrated to the Paisley area from Stirling for work as a domestic servant, and in 1851 reported that her fiancé James McCormick left the burgh to escape their forthcoming marriage, leaving her with an infant to support.[41] A dressmaker, 28-year-old Catherine McKinnon, was born

38 Valuation Rolls VR006600001-/179, Paisley Burgh, *ScotlandsPeople*. – Valuation Rolls.

39 Most moves came in May, coinciding with the regular end of the year-long house leases. Regular residential mobility was common across much of Scottish urban society, not limited to the poor. I.G.C. Hutchison, *Industry, Reform and Empire Scotland, 1790–1880* (Edinburgh: Edinburgh University Press, 2020), 106.

40 Gordon, 'Seeking Relief on Love Street'.

41 HCP Statements, vol. 11–6, Statement 4547.

in Leith and migrated as a child with her family to Greenock. When she was about 19 she followed her trade to Paisley, where she lived in at least five different locations in Abbey Parish before being struck with rheumatic fever in 1851.[42]

Migrants to Paisley also included immigrants – particularly from Ireland – and their applications for relief were accepted along with all the others.[43] One hundred applicants in 1851 were natives of Ireland, most from the counties that make up modern Northern Ireland. While Irish immigrants made 19.2 percent of the applicants, a census sample showed 14.3 percent of the general population was Irish-born. The over-representation of people from Ireland in applications grew in subsequent decades, which seemed to be a symptom of an aging population reliant on unskilled labour rather than an ongoing influx of support-seeking immigrants.[44] Even in 1851, a quarter of the Irish applicants had lived in the town long enough to qualify for relief in the same terms as their native-born neighbours.

Paisley natives also emigrated to America and Australia, sometimes with support from a charitable or friendly society.[45] In the 1819 radical crisis and onward it had been positively encouraged as a means of escaping a volatile economy.[46] Sometimes this was a response to poverty or a lack of employment, in others it was an escape, as the case reported by Mary Entriken,

42 HCP Statements, vol. 11–6, Statement 4548.

43 Which is not to say there wasn't significant prejudice against the immigrants, displayed especially in testimony about potential revisions to settlement law.

44 W.M. Gordon, 'Demographics of Scottish Poverty: Paisley's Applicants for Relief, 1861 and 1871', *Journal of Scottish Historical Studies* 30:1 (2010): 25–45.

45 'America' was often reference to the continent rather than a nation; it's not always clear if a person meant the United States or Canada.

46 HCP Town Council, vol. 1–28, 14 April 1840; Assisted emigration has been more studied regarding England, Ireland, and the Scottish Highlands than urban schemes for the relief by emigration of skilled workers, but Lucille Campey noted the significance of coordinated emigrations to the Canadian Maritimes from Paisley and Glasgow throughout the 1820s. L. Campey, *An Unstoppable Force: The Scottish Exodus to Canada* (Toronto: Natural Heritage Books, 2008), 49–51.

> The father of her [2-month-old] child, Samuel McReady, pastry baker ... has paid his proportion of aliment viz 3/- per 2 weeks from the birth till now. She understands that he is going off immediately to America to leave her with the burden of the child, and she applies to have him compelled to take the child with him or to make some arrangements for its future support.[47]

Whether across the ocean or across the street, physical mobility was a constant possibility for the workers of Paisley and a frequent headache for Inspector Brown and his colleagues. Each of Scotland's parishes was responsible for their own poor, and all this movement complicated the effort to determine to which parish each applicant rightfully belonged.

Settlement

In collecting information about family relationships and residential history, Inspector Brown's ultimate purpose was to determine a deserving applicant's settlement. It was a fundamental premise of the poor law that individuals were linked to communities, and communities had obligations to support their members in poverty. A pauper's parish of settlement was legally obligated to pay their aliment, whether that was a direct payment for outdoor relief, reimbursement to another parish to which the pauper had migrated, or accommodation in a poor house. It was every inspector's job to identify the paupers that 'belonged' to their own parish and those for whom others were responsible. Determining settlement could be immensely complex and was frequently argued in court, as is explored more fully in Chapter 5. Yet the law itself seemed simple. The Act of 1845 only defined settlement by residence: a migrant must live in a new parish for five years, without requesting relief, in order to gain the right to be relieved by that parish.[48] All other (and more common) means of gaining a settlement were not defined by the New Poor Law but rested on the older Law of Settlement, which was itself a patchwork of laws

47 HCP Statements, vol. 11–6, Statement 4584.
48 *Poor Law (Scotland) Act*, Sec. 76.

and traditions.[49] A Scot had an automatic settlement in the parish where they were born. This birth settlement was irrevocable – if no other settlement could be identified the birth parish was responsible. A migrant who gained a residential settlement must continue to live in the new parish for at least one year in five to retain it; failing to meet this requirement they reverted to their birth settlement.

The New Poor Law barely addressed the most common way to gain a new settlement, which was through marriage and maturity.[50] Wives and dependent children automatically took the same settlement as their husband/father – a policy so obvious to the crafters of the law it barely needed mention except by occasional reference to a pauper and his wife and children.[51] For women the settlement they gained through marriage could be life-long, even lasting into widowhood. Children followed their father's or unmarried mother's settlement until they became self-supporting, when their own birth parish became responsible – until the young adult married or gained a new residential settlement in their own right. The fine points of interpretation sparked thousands of letters between parishes and hundreds of cases in the courts, but in broad strokes these rules were widely understood and easily applied. In the case of Jean Watson, it was immediately evident that she did not have any settlement in Paisley. Since she went to service at age 14, the longest time she had lived in any parish was three years in Barony.[52] She had lived in Paisley for only a few months, so Inspector Brown could be confident that Jean was not Paisley's responsibility. The infant Thomas Anderson would have a birth settlement in Paisley when

49 'The Law of Settlement', *Poor Law Magazine for Scotland*, vol. III (Nov. 1860), 122.

50 *Poor Law (Scotland)*, Sec. 80.

51 *Poor Law (Scotland)*, Sec. 77.

52 Domestic and farm servants faced a particular hurdle in establishing settlement because of the way their residences changed with their employment, and because they did not live independently. A servant who maintained frequent contact with her family in a nearby parish might be held to still live in that parish, not where she was employed. The concerns and arguments are summarised in *Welsh* v *Lowden*, *Cases Decided in the Court of Session, Court of Justiciary, and House of Lords from August 25, 1894 to July 29, 1895*, Fourth Series, vol. XXII, Winter Session (Edinburgh, 1985).

he reached adulthood, but as long as he was in his mother's care it was her parish of settlement that must pay for his relief.

Not all cases were determined so easily. Although the terms in the Law seemed clear – birth, marriage, and residence all seemed to be readily understood – individual circumstances constantly called these conditions into question. Was an irregular marriage declared before witnesses a marriage in terms of settlement? Could a man deployed with the army be said to actually live in the parish where his wife and children were? Did a child born when their mother was overtaken by labour on the road have a birth settlement where their mother was staying or where they were literally born? These complexities emerged from the life stories of perfectly honest and well-meaning applicants for relief. Adding the fallibility of human memory and desires to obfuscate for advantage meant that each claim for relief needed to be carefully examined. In this examination, Inspector Brown excelled. His experience and clear understanding of the law, combined with his evident compassion for the poor led to trust from the parochial board and his fellow inspectors around Scotland that he would conscientiously and appropriately balance the resources of the parish with the needs of its poor.

Patterns of Pauperism

Inspector Brown's charge was to determine if any given individual was eligible for relief from Paisley Burgh. Aside from annual tallies of the numbers granted indoor and outdoor relief, it's unlikely he indulged in any broader analysis of the experiences that led to poverty and pauperism. From a modern perspective, freed of the urgency to relieve individual want, patterns are evident. For Inspector Brown, each applicant sat in a web of their own context, the unlucky centre of swirling circumstances. Unique individual situations were overlaid on residential histories, relationships, and occupations to determine if a person would seek poor relief. Reviewing a year's worth of Statements together reveals that factors of life stage and economic conditions intersected in predictable patterns; encountering illness, injury, unemployment or pregnancy at a crucial moment could push an individual or family to apply for relief when at another time they might have weathered the difficulty without becoming paupers.

Five of the fourteen questions posed by the Statement were aimed at finding relationships with potential income earners, but they also served to explain why family or community supports did not exist or had failed. Marital status was immediately the first determinant of who should be supporting the potential pauper, and one of the easiest patterns to identify. Unmarried applicants, like Jean Watson, were most likely to be female, single women outnumbering single men in the 1851 Statements by almost three to one. 'Unmarried' should not be equated with 'young'. The 115 unmarried applicants in 1851 ranged in age from 14 to 65, with twenty-six aged forty or older. Perhaps fewer than expected of the unmarried women were applying because of the effect of childbearing on their ability to support themselves; only 22 percent of the unmarried women were disabled by pregnancy or recent childbirth or were unable to work due to having young children. The remaining majority of unmarried applicants (both men and women) were disabled by a chronic or discreet episode of illness, by injury, or were unemployed without being disabled. For a single person without co-resident family members (or with children too young to contribute), being unable to work due to a 'shock of paralysis', being 'in disease venereal', having taken 'a fall down stairs', or being 'unwell from intemperance' was enough to push unmarried people of any sex or age to request relief.[53]

While the unmarried applicants for relief were most likely to be women, the opposite was true for those in marriages. Of 276 applications with a married person as the primary applicant (couples were covered by a single statement), 202 were in male-headed households. Although the law of *feme covert* did not explicitly exist in Scotland, men were legally obligated to support their own children and wives and were generally recognised as the economic and social head of the family.[54] If a couple was

53 HCP Statements, vol. 11–6, Statements 4531; 4831; 4854; 4639.

54 *Poor Law (Scotland)* Sec. 80; L. Leneman, '"A Natural Foundation in Equity": Marriage and Divorce in Eighteenth and Nineteenth-Century Scotland', *Scottish Economic & Social History* 20:2 (2000): 199–215.

co-resident, the husband was entered as the primary applicant for relief unless he was entirely incapacitated or incarcerated. The family's troubles were interpreted as his disability.

Unemployment was the most common reason in 1851 for a married man to apply for relief. Leaving aside unemployment for consideration in the next chapter, married people next-most commonly applied for poor relief when they or someone in their family required medical care or burial. Couples who could ordinarily just barely cover normal expenses were unable to meet sudden medical needs. For example, James Meiklin, a weaver, had moved from his birthplace in Paisley to Barony (Glasgow), where he lived with his wife and four children aged 10 and younger. His application for relief came to Paisley on 4 July 1851 due to 'fever the whole family'.[55] Another weaver, John Jamieson, applied on 7 October 1851 because of 'having had a child to bury and wife confined on childbed delivered of twins'.[56] To meet these and similar needs the parochial board employed four doctors to care for the town's poor for a set annual fee, and access to this care began with an application for relief.[57] They also maintained contracts to acquire coffins in various sizes and to pay for a minimal burial.

After receiving this kind of support, a family might live for years or a lifetime without requesting aid again, as Jamieson's family apparently did. For others, a successful request for medical relief was the first step in incorporating poor relief into their family economies. One year after paying for the Meiklin family's treatment, Inspector Brown entered the note, 'Mrs [Meiklin] has again become chargeable to Barony. … Husband in America with children Margaret and Hugh. The children at home with her are Wm James & Mary. Husband sailed 13 weeks ago to America to Montreal and is now in Toronto.'[58] Contemporary commentators wrote both of the shame inherent in applying for relief and of the potential for inveterate pauperism, but for most families the decision to re-apply for relief came from a balance of need and potential eligibility. Pride was an

55 HCP Statements, vol. 11–6, Statement 4776.
56 HCP Statements, vol. 11–6, Statement 4858.
57 HCP Parochial Board, vol. 7–19, 1 May 1846.
58 HCP Statements, vol. 11–6, Statement 4858.

immeasurable factor that an applicant had already overcome before contacting Inspector Brown.

The first application for relief might come at any stage of a couple's family life. In 1851 the youngest married couple to apply was 22-year-old John Reid and his wife Mary Sinclair. Reid had migrated from Ireland and Sinclair was a foundling raised by the parish of Paisley. Reid reported his trade was 'labourer' and the Inspector recorded simply that he or Mary was 'unwell'. Sinclair was probably pregnant, but there is no explanation of which partner was ill and the term unwell was not exclusively euphemistic. When the couple first asked for relief, sometime in the summer, Inspector Brown gave them a little money and sent them away. When they tried him again in early October he completed the formal statement. Their recent struggles were revealed through a series of moves since Reid's immigration in 1849, 'Paisley 6 mos; Glasgow 2 mos; Storie Street Paisley 1 mo; Sneddon Street Paisley 1 mo., Love Street Paisley 5 mo; 11 Shuttle Paisley 7 wks'. The conclusion of the process was foregone, though, which Brown must have suspected when he started. Reid, and by extension Sinclair, was not entitled to relief from Paisley because he had not lived long enough in the parish.[59] Casual generosity aside, the only official aid Paisley could offer the couple was passage to Ireland. After this refusal the couple turned to other strategies for survival and did not reappear in Paisley's record.

At the other end of the life cycle, the oldest couple to make an initial application for relief in 1851 was 80-year-old Patrick McGrath and Helen M'Queen, aged 67, who lived at 69 Love Street. Both McGrath and M'Queen were born in County Tyrone, Ireland, but they had married in Paisley around 1810 and had lived in the town ever since. Over these years M'Queen had borne fourteen children, only one of whom was still living in 1851. McGrath, a weaver, had been unable to work since the previous August. The Inspector wrote he was 'not bedfast, but seemingly disabled for any employment'. M'Queen, who previously had wound pirns for McGrath's work, began to do 'washing and cleaning for anyone who employed her'. Like Reid and Sinclair, this couple had received a small amount of casual relief once before their formal statement was completed, when they 'got a

59 HCP Statements, vol. 11–3, Statement 4853.

few shillings 3 years ago'.[60] Unlike Reid, though, their long residence and labour in Paisley made them eligible for relief there.

Neither this elderly couple nor the very young couple had children in the home to care for or to add to the household income, but most applicant couples did. Of the 214 couples who applied for relief in 1851, 168 had at least one child living at home and 39 had one or more children under 5 years old. Children and childbearing were a nearly inevitable part of family life in Paisley, regardless of income level. Almost 12 percent of applicants for relief in 1851 were applying directly because of pregnancy, childcare, sick or dead children, or were children themselves. From a modern perspective children began earning at a shockingly young age, but before they reached that age they were considered 'disabled' by definition and could merit relief if their parents were unable to provide sufficient support.

While most applicants with children were (or had been) married, Paisley Parish made little distinction over whether a child was born within or out of wedlock. Unmarried mothers were regularly received onto the town's poor rolls and given the same relief as a widow while their children were small. Unmarried fathers, however, were not given the same consideration to help them parent their children. Putative fathers of children were named and pursued for support, with rare success. Widowers were never expected to take on direct care of their children in place of waged work. If there was no grandmother, aunt, neighbour or housekeeper available, the children would most likely be swept into the custodial poor law system and boarded out along with the town's orphans and other waifs.

As was true for single applicants, medical or funeral needs were the most common reasons after unemployment that couples applied for relief in 1851. It is hard, indeed, to determine the exact lines between a sudden, discreet illness or injury, a chronic illness like William Stewart's 'asthmatic complaint',[61] or debility brought about by old age. Health-related issues were clearly included in the poor law's insistence that recipients of relief be both destitute and disabled. Even when a family's primary problem was a lack of income, the inspector might search for a reason to justify relief. When

60 HCP Statements, vol. 11–6, Statement 4591.

61 HCP Statements, vol. 11–6, Statement 4887.

John Picken and Rebecca McNaught applied for relief because Picken (a weaver) had no work, the Inspector noted in the space for disablement, 'want of work. Health good. Child James delicate'.[62] That delicate child could become a rationale to give some relief to the struggling family.

Some married couples received a small aliment to support a helpless dependent, even if both parents were deemed able to work. When Alexander Porterfield and his wife Fanny Murray first applied for relief in March 1851, they were refused as able-bodied. Porterfield was an Irish-born labourer and jobbing gardener, and Murray worked as a white-seam sewer.[63] They had an 18-year-old daughter, Nancy, and an 11-year-old son. The family initially applied for relief because the boy had a hernia and needed a medical belt for treatment. The Inspector noted that Porterfield, who was 62 years old, 'was somewhat worn out by age; applies chiefly for the boy … and the girl is deficient in mind and disabled in limbs'. After the initial rejection by the Relief Committee because the parents were able-bodied an additional notation was made, 'The girl Nancy is a very great object indeed – neither able to speak, walk nor use her hands in any way. Her body has the appearance of being that of a child aged 2 or 3 years.' In the following October the family was granted 4/- per month to aid specifically in supporting the children, although both parents were still earning.[64]

Children's economic role in a family changed over time. Early in a marriage, children were an economic liability, as they were for James Noble, aged 45 or 46, and his spouse Mary Stewart, aged 31. They had seven children at home, aged 12 years to 3 months, when they applied on 19 September, five from prior marriages and two together. Noble had a 1/- per day pension from 20 years' service as a Rifleman and further provided for the family as a weaver, with Stewart winding and her oldest son assisting. The second son was training as a tobacco spinner, and the five younger children were not earning at all. This stable life was upended when Nobles's eyes became inflamed and 'by erroneous treatment … had the sight of both eyes entirely

62 HCP Statements, vol. 11–6, Statement 4627.

63 White seam was a Scots term for plain sewing, as opposed to decorative or fancy needlework. HCP Statements, vol. 11–6, Statement 4606.

64 HCP Statements, vol. 11–6, Statement 4606; Relief Committee, Committee Minutes, vol. 7–27, 15 April 1851; 3 Oct. 1851.

destroyed for life'.[65] While the pension continued, this accident cut the heart out of their family economy and may have forced the Noble children into wage earning earlier than their parents had anticipated.

In contrast, later in life children in the home could add significantly to the family's income, as in John Ritchie and Janet Hepburn's case. The couple had five children at home, aged 23 to 6. The oldest girl, 23-year-old Margaret, added her 6/- weekly to her father's 10/-. Ritchie turned to the parish for relief not because of the family's economic need, but because another daughter, Jean, aged 17, had recently given birth to a baby boy. Ritchie hoped to use the power of the poor law to pursue the baby's father for support.[66] A large family could also compound misfortune; an illness or downturn in trade that brought a couple to apply for relief might strike down all or nearly all members of the family simultaneously. Samuel Craig and Elisa Mitchell must have been beside themselves when they came looking for help from the parish in November; their three children, 7-year-old Elisa, 4 ½-year-old John, and 2-year-old Hugh, were all in fever.[67] Children did die so easily.

The applications for co-resident couples largely bear out the assumption that under 'normal' circumstances of health and employment families with two or more adults in the home would not need additional support to survive. Lack of evidence is not proof of achievement, but families that through fortune or favor maintained good health and steady employment do not appear in the poor law record. Simply being married, though, did not guarantee such stability. Sixty-eight applicants in 1851 reported they were legally married but not currently living with their spouse. In some cases, separating appeared to be a mutually agreed upon strategy. Helen Cairne, with two small children in tow, sought help from the parish in late November 1851 due to her husband's absence. The inspector reported, 'He went to America with wife's consent on 1st May last. She has had a letter but no money.'[68] When the economy slumped

65 HCP Statements, vol. 11–6, Statement 4840; 1851 Noble, James (Census 573/52/8); 1861 Noble, James (Census 573/31/10). *ScotlandsPeople.*

66 HCP Statements, vol. 11–6, Statement 4953.

67 HCP Statements, vol. 11–6, Statement 4897.

68 HCP Statements, vol. 11–6, Statement 4983.

men sometimes traveled in search of work, which may well have been a jointly-agreed-upon strategy. In addition to the hope for income, the resulting female-headed households were more likely to be approved for casual or formal relief.

Whims, accidents, and illness could also cause separations of various duration. Some applications in 1851 came from spouses who were separated with no apparent plan to reunite, such as James Donaldson and Janet Thomson. When Thomson, a clipper and winder who was ill with jaundice, applied for relief, she reported that she and Donaldson had married in Paisley in 1832 but 'he was too fond of company, fiddling, singing &ct, [and] deserted her in 1833 and she has not seen him since'.[69] In other cases, separations were imposed upon couples, as when one impulsive event apparently separated fruit and fish hawkers Agnes McLean and Catherine McDonald from their husbands in December. Both women applied (separately) for relief because their husbands were in prison for assault and they were left to care for small children. Presumably McLean and McDonald knew when their husbands would be released, but many separations were less certain, such as Margaret McCanon who reported on 17 June that her husband James Watson 'left home on 13 curt had been drinking previously'.[70]

The needs of and responses to these separated spouses could be quite different. Janet Thomson, separated from her husband for two decades, was for all intents and purposes a single person, applying for medical relief. Further investigation revealed her husband was long dead, and she was subsequently supported by the parish as a widow. McLean and McDonald's situations continued chaotic; over the next decade both applied repeatedly for support when their husbands were imprisoned or simply absent. Presumably they were rewarded with small payments or medical aid each time – or at least some of the times – they applied, using the poor law as one resource to hold together fragile personal economies. McCanon, on the other hand, seemed to hope the poor law authorities could force her husband back to providing support for her and their four

69 HCP Statements, vol. 11–6, Statement 4985.

70 HCP Statements, vol. 11–6, Statement 4730.

children. In the event, though, this did not happen. By 1852 McCanon was receiving relief from her husband's parish of settlement and he was nowhere to be found.

Faced with a woman claiming the absence of a husband Inspector Brown made note, when he could, of where, when, and by whom the applicant was married, but marriage itself was sometimes a questionable status. Scotland's tradition of irregular marriage, which could require only a statement of intent before witnesses or the 'habit and repute' of living as man and wife led to cases like Elisa Cochran's. When her partner Peter Stewart left her and their three children she admitted they were 'never regularly married but acknowledged themselves man and wife before witnesses 7 years ago and have lived together ever since'.[71] Such irregular marriages, informal separations, deployments, migrations, and old-fashioned adultery all complicated the most important question of who was responsible for the support of the poor person if they were in fact destitute and disabled. A great deal of this complexity was eliminated by death, as it had been for Janet Thomson. Widowhood provided proof, usually, of a sanctioned, respectable relationship (regardless of what the reality had been) and supported the assumption of need. There was no hesitancy to helping a widow as there could be when examining the case of a deserting or deserted spouse.

Three times as many widowed women as men applied for parochial relief in 1851. In many ways the widows were similar to other applicants – illness and unemployment commonly pushed them into the need for relief. Widowed applicants might apply as young as their twenties or at the end of a long life. What defined them most clearly was their deceased partner. Widows (mostly but not exclusively female) clearly knew they were entitled to poor relief to help replace the support they had had from a spouse. While unmarried women with children most often were pursuing the father of their children for support, widows expected the parish to give direct support in place of the missing parent. In 1851 thirteen able-bodied widowed mothers applied to Paisley specifically asking for relief for their children rather than themselves. Flora McDougal, for example,

71 HCP Statements, vol. 11–6, Statement 4626.

applied in February. Her late husband, Archibald McIntosh, was a night watchman and 'drowned in Cart [Water] ... on one of the foggy nights in December last'. McIntosh's employer had paid for the burial and given the widow some support, but by February McDougal planned to 'labour out of doors' to support her three daughters, and she was given 6/6 per month from the parish to supplement her wages.[72] The assumed responsibility of a man for his children could continue well beyond his death. When Henry Marr died of cholera in 1849, he left a wife, Mary Boothman, and seven children, the oldest of whom was 13 or 14 years old. Boothman remarried, but her new husband proved to be 'an unsteady young man' who could not support the large family. Boothman turned to Paisley parish asking support for the children based on their father's settlement, but not for herself or her unsteady husband.[73]

The Aliment

The inspector's inquiry into family relationships established as far as possible the applicants' support network and needs, and he granted an aliment roughly aligned to that need. Funds were often declared to be for a particular family member, but in practice it was impossible for the poor law managers to dissect a household budget and ensure any relief funds they paid went only to the approved recipient. When monetary relief was granted the funds most likely went to rent, food, and fuel, none of which were easily divisible to those members of the family officially on the poor roll. The money granted was enough to make a difference within the broader economy of makeshift, but never enough to truly support the pauper. Until 1855, the aliment was allotted in a per-month amount and paid out monthly, which likely meant many paupers had some hungry days as they reached the end of the month. After that date, the allocation

72 HCP Statements, vol. 11–6, Statement 4569.
73 HCP Statements, vol. 11–6, Statement 4877.

changed to a weekly amount that was paid once a fortnight.[74] In 1851, aliments awarded to paupers ranged from 2/6 to 15/- per month, with 4/- or 6/- the most common amount.[75]

Conversion to new money and modern pricing make equivalent values nearly meaningless; one inflation calculator places the 2023 value of an 1851 shilling at £8.93, which makes the highest monthly aliment nearly £134 in modern funds.[76] This raw conversion cannot accommodate the change in the relative value of commodities; the rent on the flat where Jean Watson stayed (if it had been paid monthly) was just shy of £30 in modern money, out of reach for her but a ridiculously low-cost today. Using the same conversion, Provost Murray's 6-room home would rent for £267/month.[77] It is easier to understand the value by exploring what goods or services could be purchased with a given sum. Retail prices for the period are difficult to find; one surviving newspaper series from Paisley recorded prices at the Glasgow Bazaar in 1854, which gives a reasonable approximation for what paupers might be able to purchase with their relief.

Watson was not entered as a pauper for Paisley, so she received only a few pennies or a shilling – if that – when she applied. Two other unmarried mothers, each 24 years old, were found to have settlements in Paisley and received relief from the parish in 1851. Margaret Steel had a newborn daughter when she applied for relief in March, and Helen Boyle had two children, Charles and Margaret Sweenie, aged 5 and 1, respectively. Steele was put on the roll at 10/- per month. Boyle, who lived with her mother and sometimes worked in Blackhall Mill, was granted just 4/- per month.[78]

74 HCP Relief Committee, Committee Minutes, vol. 7–28, 11 May 1855.

75 In this year, the relief granted or refusal was traceable for only forty-seven applicants. More were accepted as paupers, but the amount granted is not known.

76 CPI Inflation Calculator, in2013dollars.com/UK-inflation (accessed 12 April 2023).

77 My 4-room holiday rental in Paisley in 2022 (generously supported by a grant from the Society of Antiquaries of Scotland) went for £1689/month including service fees.

78 Both of these women were formally added to the poor roll by the Relief Committee in January 1852. They had most likely been receiving the same amount informally since their application, at the discretion of the inspector. One shilling (1/-) was worth twelve pennies (12d.).

Assuming that Boyle's rent was paid by her mother, the relief would have gone for food from one of the town's many grocers or hawkers. The prices in those shops were likely somewhat higher than those at the Glasgow Bazaar, where provisions were sold in bulk. In July 1854, 'inferior' cheese sold at the Bazaar for 48/- per hundredweight, which works out to about 5d. per pound. Turnips cost 3d. per bunch, new carrots 2d. for a dozen and cresses 1d. per pint. This modest basket – with no grocer's markup – plus perhaps a small lump of butter at 10d. the pound, would have exhausted Boyle's aliment for a week.[79] Other staples would be out of reach at 9d. per dozen eggs or 1/4 for the cheapest pair of chickens for the pot. As for fruit, gooseberries might be an occasional treat at 2d. per pint, but currants at 8d. or strawberries at 10d. per pint were probably inaccessible. Margaret Steel, with less (if any) family support, would have needed to allocate about 3/6 from her monthly relief payment for her rent, and something for coals that cost around 9/6 per ton.[80] If the aliment was her only income, she would be left with barely more than a shilling per week to feed herself and her baby. Depending on the family's situation, some of the groceries – especially the cress and soft fruits – might be turned around for sale in even smaller quantities from baskets in the streets.

The largest aliment recorded in 1851, 15/- per month, went to a weaver, Archibald McLaren who, though he was only 51 years old, was reported to be 'far gone in decline'. He was born in rural Abbey Parish but had lived in Paisley since 1825, working as a weaver and warper. His two children still at home were legally considered too young to work at 11 and 8 years old, although the census a few months earlier had shown them to be a draw boy and an errand girl – crossed out. There was no income-generating activity recorded for his wife, though she likely was a winder while McLaren could work. The large aliment, meagre though it was in real terms, recognised the economic disaster of losing a family's main income source. Importantly, there was no evident effort made to seek out alternative support for McLaren's widow and children, although her parents were living and there was also an adult married daughter. In this case the

79 'Glasgow Bazaar July 19', *Paisley Journal & Renfrewshire Gazette*, 22 July 1854: 7.

80 HCP Poorhouse Committee, Committee Minutes, vol. 7–27, 9 Oct. 1855.

family fell neatly into the 'deserving' category assumed by the poor law and the community support provided was correspondingly unquestioning and generous.[81]

Poor Relief in a Makeshift Economy

Applying for poor relief could be a one-time event, or it could be the beginning of an ongoing relationship with the parish. The young woman calling herself Jean Watson vanished from the record after her encounter in Paisley. She may have – in a best-case scenario – married the father of her child and gained a life of respectable stability. It seems more likely that she returned to Largs (if that is truly where she came from) with her boy and continued working in what service positions she could find, got married or did not, and spent her life scraping and struggling and occasionally turning to the poor law for a little help. Other paths could lead her to mendicancy, illness, incarceration, intemperance, or dozens of other personal tragedies that befell workers and paupers in Paisley. While independence from or reliance on poor relief seems to have been largely a product of chance and personal choices, here also there are patterns to be seen in the Statements of Cases. The situations that caused an individual or a family to apply for poor relief – such as chronic disease or sudden death – were often unpredictable, striking apparently randomly at vulnerable people teetering on the edge of pauperism. That teetering population, however, did have identifiable characteristics that made them vulnerable, the most significant one of which was occupation.[82]

81 HCP Statements, vol. 11–6, Statement 4804; 1851 McLaran, Archibald (Census 573/17/6) *Scotland'sPeople.*

82 The role of poor relief in an economy of makeshift has been better studied in England and regarding the Old Poor Law, but that research suggests the patterns shown in Paisley were likely long-standing and common across the United Kingdom. See, for example, S. Williams, 'Earnings, Poor Relief and the Economy of Makeshifts: Bedfordshire in the Early Years of the New Poor Law', *Rural History* 16:1 (2005): 21–52; J. Harley, 'Material Lives of the Poor and Their

The town's economic crises were especially cruel to the handloom weavers and related occupations. In the early years of the century when figured shawls were first produced in Paisley, harness weaving was a highly skilled and well-paid trade, proudly passed down through families along with a literary and radical political tradition.[83] Even before the collapse in the 1840s, though, weavers were losing economic ground. The trade was still highly skilled and a source of pride and activism, but the demand for Paisley shawls in general and harness-loom-woven shawls in particular declined through most of the century. Virtually as soon as figured shawls became the height of fashion, alternate methods of production such as embroidery and block printing began to let women get the Paisley look without the sky-high price.[84] In 1851, weaving and related trades were the most common occupational group among applicants for relief; in fact, they appeared in the group of applicants at nearly double their presence in the general population.

Table 4: Percentage of Individuals in Handloom Weaving-Related Occupations

Census Year	Applicants for Relief	General Adult Population (employed)
1851	50.96	26.62
1861	20.47	18.21
1871	13.48	11.48

Note: Based on HCP Statements and a 10 percent sample of adults in census enumeration books for Paisley Burgh.

Strategic Use of the Workhouse During the Final Decades of the English Old Poor Law', *Continuity and Change* 30:1 (2015): 71–103; J. Healey, ' "By the Charitie of Good People": Poverty and Neighbourly Support in Seventeenth Century Lancashire', *Family & Community History* 19:2 (2016): 83–94; and of course S. King and A. Tomkins, *The Poor in England 1700–1850: An Economy of Makeshifts* (Manchester: Manchester University Press, 2003).

83 M. Blair, *The Paisley Shawl and the Men Who Produced It: A Record of an Interesting Epoch in the History of the Town* (Paisley: Alexander Gardner, 1904), 42–4; 61–5.

84 P. Clabburn, *Shawls: In Imitation of the Indian* (Haverfordwest: Shire Publications, 1981), 18–19.

Many weavers who first applied for relief in 1851 subsequently turned to the parish again and again as part of their regular survival strategy. For example, Daniel Leitch and his wife Helen (or Elin) Hill, were in their early twenties and had a 7-month-old infant in May 1851, when they applied for relief after Daniel had been without work for ten weeks. Leitch was a weaver, Hill wound his pirns, and they had a flat on Maxwelton Street. They likely did not own a loom, and so relied on manufacturers to provide Leitch with a 'web' (the materials and an order for a length of fabric) and rent a loom in another's shed. After the emergency in 1851 receded the family returned to the Poor Law Office with regularity, often coinciding with the town's fortunes. The Inspector's notes on their statement recorded,

> 12 Dec 1854 applies being idle 6 weeks. … 16 Nov 1857 ap[plies] … wife & 3 [children] … idle 3 weeks. … 9 Dec 1859 again applies able-bodied and working but has a child dead and is without means to bury it. … 19 Feby 1861 again ap being ill health off work and idle 3 mos. … wife and 4 children. … 10 Sep 1861 Wife ap husband in prison since Friday had been drinking and theft of plaid … has 3 young ch oldest with grandmother. 25 Nov 1861 ag ap … same condition. … 11 Nov 1875 ag ap disabled by abscess in back last 2 weeks wife & 5 children.[85]

Some of the Leitch family's misfortunes were tied to their individual circumstances, but most of their episodes of pauperism were tied to weaving's economic vulnerability. Among the 148 weavers who first applied for relief due to a lack of work in 1851, 42 applied again during a later period of widespread unemployment in 1854, 1857 or 1861. A majority of the remainder re-applied for relief for another reason – deaths, separations, illnesses and other misadventures dogged this population even when they were able to stay in work, and their incomes could not always absorb the extra cost. In the terrible year of 1861, Leitch and Hill must have been desperate to keep feeding their children; his drunkenness and theft could have been an act of desperate impulse. After that, the family was able to stay off the poor roll for fifteen years until Leitch's abscessed back pushed him to request medical relief. In part the family's struggles eased as their children began to contribute wages, and they also benefitted from the town's diversifying economy. In 1871 the family was

85 HCP Statements, vol. 11–6, Statement 4641.

living in a one-room flat on Queen Street. Daniel was still a weaver, but the three oldest of the children were working in other fields: as a slater, a brick worker, and a factory girl.[86]

Weavers were at risk of periodic or chronic poverty, and many joined weaving with other work such as carting, hawking, or casual labour. Yet a significant number of men remained in the trade in spite of the economic risk they faced. Handloom weaving gave workers a remarkable level of self-determination in an industrialising age. Although weavers might be reliant on manufacturers for webs and rent their looms, they continued to determine their own work hours. The work was done in a comparatively small, communal-but-not-crowded room, quiet when compared to a factory floor in spite of the thump and clatter of the looms. Weaving was less physically taxing than the building trades or carting. In spite of the risk of poverty it was a trade-off significant numbers of men were willing to make as long as webs and looms were available.[87] Weaving was so intertwined with both Paisley's identity and her poverty that at least as early as the 1830s and through the 1870s the poor house and asylum included a weaving shed so that men who were able to could continue their craft even when they could not sustain themselves.[88]

When he had completed his investigation into Jean Watson, handed her a few coins and one hopes wished her well, Inspector Brown's final task was to write to the Largs Inspector of the Poor seeking reimbursement for the handout.[89] The odds are good that he was successful in getting it. In years to come Brown's colleagues would remember that he was virtually never mistaken in his interpretation of the poor law.[90] Yet while he was a stickler for accuracy, Inspector Brown must have had a deep sympathy for these families and individuals who came to his office door, whether it was once

86 Leitch, Daniel (Census 573/118/6) 1871, *Scotland'sPeople*.

87 Shaw, *Paisley Shawl*, 46–8. I am grateful to Dan Coughlan of the Paisley Museum and volunteers at Sma' Shot Cottages in Paisley for their qualitative descriptions of weavers' lives and benefits of the occupation.

88 HCP Hospital, vol. 6–3, 7 June 1839.

89 The letterbooks that would have recorded such a letter have not survived.

90 'Death of Mr James S. Brown Inspector of Poor for Burgh of Paisley', *Paisley Herald and Renfrewshire Advertiser*, 18 April 1876: 4.

or time after time. His own family's success would not insulate him from the need that permeated the Sneddon; he could have seen Jean Watson's lodgings from his own front door. The restrictions of the poor law on who could receive relief, filtered through the framework of the Statement form, provided a means to balance the ravening demands of poverty against the very real economic limitations in the town.

However, one key feature of the poor law conflicted badly with Paisley's situation and Brown's conscience. The Scottish Poor Law (unlike the English) denied the right to relief to any able-bodied person. When Paisley's economy faltered so that weavers and labourers and even factory operatives were put out of work, the plain reading of the Law prevented Inspector Brown from adding them to the roll as either casual or ordinary poor. Throughout the 1850s and 1860s, as the economy repeatedly cratered, the poor law authorities in Paisley struggled to support men and families who were only disabled by their hunger.

CHAPTER 4

The Case of the Starving Men: Relieving the Able-bodied Unemployed: 1847–66

A Half-Century of Employment Crises

By mid-century, Paisley already had decades of experience with poverty related to market cycles, with the crisis of 1841/2 only the worst of many bad seasons. Since at least 1819 there had been periodic times of mass unemployment and hunger in the town. Before the New Poor Law was enacted, private money and charities were organised to keep the workers in Paisley fed. This was not wholly an altruistic act. The radical teens had shown that hungry men could turn to violence, and every plea for funds to support the unemployed able-bodied poor was tinged with the potential for violence if the workers were not placated. Community relations were complex however, as Tony Dickson and Tony Clarke argued, stating that there was a special sympathy between the manufacturers in Paisley and their operatives.[1] 'A large proportion of the manufacturers in Paisley were themselves from fairly humble origins, having begun life as weavers or packmen. One result of this was that a potential existed in Paisley for common action by weavers and manufacturers, based on their similar social origins and the lack of any great "social distance" between the two groups.'[2] Manufacturers frequently held seats on the parochial board, and they may have felt even more acutely than other town leaders

1 T. Dickson and T. Clarke, 'Social Concern and Social Control in Nineteenth-Century Scotland: Paisley 1841–3', *The Scottish Historical Review* 65:179 part 1 (April 1986): 48–60.

2 Dickson and Clarke, 55.

a responsibility to do something in response to the impersonal forces throwing men out of work.

Paisley before the New Poor Law had responded to widespread unemployment with charity that came from beyond the meagre means of the regular system of relief. It came primarily from subscriptions (i.e., voluntary donations) which were sometimes given to the poor as cash payments or 'store tickets' to local merchants. Since this system supported local trade and permitted recipients to spend the relief as they saw fit, it was used in combination with in-kind relief until the great distress of 1841. In 1832, when a downturn in trade coincided with an outbreak of cholera in the town, a series of soup kitchens were opened to feed hundreds throughout the Spring.[3] The plethora of relief agencies in the town means that today it is not clear when and in what proportions the funds came from kirk-door collections, assessed poor funds, or charitable donations. When trade collapsed again in 1837, a public subscription permitted the establishment of soup kitchens throughout the town, delivering as many as 1800 quarts of soup daily. The able-bodied men in this case were given work in exchange for their food although the work offered – breaking rocks – could badly damage hands needed for the delicate work of weaving when trade revived in September.[4] At first, the major distress in the early 1840s was addressed the same way, until surplus funds in the town were entirely exhausted and relief was begged from around the kingdom. The initial distributor of English aid at that time, Assistant Poor Law Commissioner Edward Twistleton, condemned the cash system because recipients were (he claimed) likely to spend the money on alcohol or to redeem clothes from pawn. After 1843, relief for unemployed men in Paisley was provided primarily through soup kitchens and sometimes with direct provision of uncooked staple foods.[5] The economic downturn in 1847 was the first to test the provisions of the New Poor Law that made poor relief an entirely centralised and civic affair.

3 J.W.C. *The Town of Paisley: Historical Sketch* (Paisley: Daily Express, 1878), XV.
4 J.W.C. *Historical Sketch*, XVII.
5 'Select committee on Distress', 15–17.

The Crisis of 1847–8

Blighted potatoes were rotting for the second consecutive season in Highland Scottish as well as Irish plots in the winter of 1847. The whole nation experienced economic stress related to the famine while simultaneously sending massive donations for relief of the victims.[6] Unemployment was again widespread in Paisley. A voluntary Committee for Relief of Destitute Operatives had been formed (as had been the practice to address such emergencies before 1845) and was feeding up to 7,000 individuals a day, but could not raise enough to meet the need. Almost as soon as the crisis was evident the parochial board had disagreed over whether and how unemployed operatives should be given relief from assessed poor rates, even as they were voting an increase in payments to the regular poor in recognition of high prices.[7] In January 1848 the Sheriff of Renfrew, the Provost, and the Magistrates of Paisley wrote formally about the crisis to the parochial boards of both the Burgh and Abbey Parishes. The Burgh Board Chairman and former Provost, thread manufacturer Robert Farquharson, duly called a meeting of the Paisley Parochial Board to consider the matter, but since the current provost himself and two baillies were on the board, there was doubtless little genuine surprise expressed at the letter's contents.[8]

The letter recounted the lack of employment available in Paisley for most of 1847, and that the voluntary committee formed for the purpose of aiding the unemployed operatives was out of funds, could not raise more, and in fact the magistrates and members of the Relief Committee had given their personal pledges for a bank loan. The magistrates insisted, in short, that the parochial boards could and must use their funds to support the able-bodied unemployed. They argued that the Poor Law Act's 68th section, stipulating that assessments levied for the poor 'shall … be applicable to the

6 T. Devine, *The Great Highland Famine: Hunger, Emigration and the Scottish Highlands in the Nineteenth Century* (Edinburgh: John Donald, 1988), 115–16.

7 HCP Parochial Board, vol. 7–19, 12 Feb. 1847.

8 HCP Parochial Board, vol. 7–19, 3 Jan. 1848.

relief of occasional as well as permanent poor'[9] covered the men thrown out of work in the crisis. They concluded with their concern that hunger would drive the operatives to theft or violence, 'Should the unemployed be thrown on their own resources, the Magistrates are charged with the preservation of the peace of the community, must vindicate the law, by punishing any outrage against the lives or property of the inhabitants.'[10]

A subcommittee of the Paisley Parochial Board was charged to consider the magistrates' demand, and on 11 January 1848 they submitted their report. The report refuted the idea that unemployment could be grounds for recognition as 'occasional poor', acknowledging that all major authorities on the poor law of Scotland 'have always considered it as a recognised principle to refuse relief from the ordinary poors fund for the support of persons applying on the mere ground of temporary suspension of employment'.[11] In addition, they argued that even if supporting the operatives from the Burgh assessment were legal, the board simply could not afford it because of the stress the economic emergency was placing on support for the ordinary poor. The regular assessment of £6,000 (drawn from 4 shillings per pound of annual rental) was proving inadequate and the board anticipated an extra assessment of £1500–2000, without doing anything for the unemployed, able-bodied poor. Any further collection, the board maintained, 'even although it were legal must be utterly impracticable'.[12]

Even though they refused to authorise new aid for unemployed operatives, the parochial board insisted they were in fact doing everything they could. They had, they claimed, 'invariably put the most liberal construction on the terms of the statute and extended relief to every case which could be fairly included within the classes of either permanent or occasional poor and ... parties have been and are at the present moment in receipt of parochial relief in Paisley whose claims if made in other parishes, would not be readily sustained'.[13]

9 *Poor Law (Scotland)* Sec. 68.
10 HCP Parochial Board, vol. 7–19, 3 Jan. 1848.
11 HCP Parochial Board, vol. 7–19, 11 Jan. 1848.
12 HCP Parochial Board, vol. 7–19, 11 Jan. 1848.
13 HCP Parochial Board, vol. 7–19, 11 Jan. 1848.

Parsing the Poor Law

Unemployment was a cyclical problem in Scotland in the nineteenth century, yet the provision against able-bodied relief in the New Poor Law meant that the most common precursor to poverty was not automatically recognised to qualify for relief. Rosalind Mitchison made a compelling argument that the inclusion of the disablement rule in the 1845 Act was a product of Whigs' Malthusian preferences rather than settled national sentiment or experience.[14] Studies of unemployment and welfare provision in Scotland have commonly examined the mature phase of the New Poor Law, following Ian Levitt to analyze the last half-century of the poor law from 1890 to WWII and to examine unemployment insurance as a phenomenon arising from the vacuum left by poor relief.[15] Yet this firm stance against relieving the able-bodied unemployed only solidified over more than a decade of debate, as Levitt himself noted.[16] In spite of the active argument over the rule, scholars have generally accepted the exclusion of the able-bodied unemployed from relief as a universal truth instead of a contested practice after the Poor Law (Scotland) Act was passed.[17] Examining the implementation period of the law illuminates

14 R. Mitchison, 'The Creation of the Disablement Rule in the Scottish Poor Law', in *The Search for Wealth and Stability: Essays in Economic and Social History presented to M.W. Flinn*, ed. T.C. Smout (London: MacMillan, 1979), 199–217.

15 I. Levitt, *Poverty and Welfare in Scotland: 1890–1948* (Edinburgh: Edinburgh University Press, 1988); R. Johnston '"Charity that Heals": The Scottish Labour Colony Association and Attitudes to the Able-bodied Unemployed in Glasgow, 1890–1914', *The Scottish Historical Review* LXXVII:1 no. 203 (1998): 77–95.

16 Levitt, *Poverty and Welfare*, 11.

17 B. Harris, 'Parsimony and Pauperism: Poor Relief in England, Scotland and Wales in the Nineteenth and Early Twentieth Centuries', *Journal of Scottish Historical Studies* 39:1 (2019): 66; H.J. MacDonald, 'Boarding-Out and the Scottish Poor Law, 1845–1914', *The Scottish Historical Review* LXXV:2 no. 200 (1996): 197. A notable exception to this rule comes from other scholars working in Paisley, who have noted the same chaffing against the disablement rule that I examine in this chapter. L. Peters, 'Paisley and the Cotton Famine of 1862–3', *Scottish Economic & Social History* 21:2 (2001): 126.

the legal argument and negotiation that led to the able-bodied exclusion. Poor law managers and the town government in Paisley fought hard for their belief that there was a social obligation to support men and families through cyclical unemployment, in defiance of the clear meaning of the Poor Law's text. In Glasgow, as well, the managers of the poor saw poverty caused by widespread unemployment as no different from poverty caused by illness or abandonment, and the national *Poor Law Magazine for Scotland* gave prominent place to their views. Even the first President of the Board of Supervision, Sir John McNeill, assured parochial boards that under the correct circumstances unemployed men could receive support from the poor law.[18] Rather than accepting Article 68 as understood on the surface, managers struggled to find a legal license to give parochial support to able-bodied workers when there was no work to be had.

Paisley Parochial Board's initial response to the crisis of 1847/8 was typical of Inspector Brown's legalistic approach to relief. While being very careful not to violate the law, they parsed the Law's language to fit their community needs. Raw feelings over the passage of the law had clearly not passed in the three intervening years; the subcommittee examining the Sheriff and Magistrates' request could not resist a dig at the law, 'If indeed the statutes for relief of the poor had been more wisely framed … support for the unemployed might be possible.'[19] The board was careful to go no further, though. Rather than acceding to the Magistrates' request, the board determined to write to the Government regarding the state of Paisley's economy and requesting revision to the poor law.

Their argument in favor of supporting the unemployed with funds assessed from the community dated most recently to an 1804 decision, *Pollock* v *Darling* in the parish of Dunse, Berwickshire. In that instance, successive crop failures and a well-established system of poor rate assessment was expanded to support the so-called 'industrious poor', whose wages could not keep up with the price of food.[20] Although *Pollock* v *Darling* was decided

18 'Relief to Able-Bodied but Unemployed Poor', *The Poor Law Magazine for Scotland* 5 (May 1863): 423–8.

19 HCP Parochial Board, vol. 7–19, 11 Jan. 1848.

20 *Adams* v *M'William* and *Thomson and M'Tear* v *Lindsay*, *Cases Decided in The Court of Session, Teind Court, and Court of Exchequer, from July 24, 1848 to July 20,*

in favor of using poor rates for the hungry unemployed, the majority in the decision was a narrow one, and debate over the practice continued in the decades following.[21] Justices after the New Poor Law was passed considered that the new Act drew a line under that precedent.

Of course in January 1848 Paisley was not alone in their suffering, nor in their attempt to resolve the problem of poverty due to widespread unemployment. In nearby Gorbals, William Lindsay, an able-bodied, unemployed man with four children, refused to accept the decision when his application for relief was denied. As was his right, Lindsay applied to the Sheriff of Lanarkshire for consideration of his claim.[22] To the poor law officials' great surprise, in early January 1848 the sheriff determined that while Lindsay was not entitled to support, his *children* were, and that the Gorbals parish must give Lindsay an allowance to sustain them.[23] Gorbals, in turn (in the person of the Inspector John Balderston), took the unusual step of appealing the sheriff's decision to the Court of Session and wrote to other parishes for financial support to pursue the appeal. Paisley's board refused to aid that cause, and they specifically refused because they disagreed with Gorbals's position. As they noted, 'it has been and still continues to be the practice of the Parochial Board of [Paisley Burgh Parish] to extend relief to persons in the destitute and helpless condition of William Lindsay the Pursuer.'[24] Indeed, as illustrated in Chapter 1, well before the Poor Law (Scotland) Act was passed, it was the Burgh's policy to 'interpret the poor law as liberally as possible, and ...extend relief to such persons as from age and distress are proper objects of parochial assistance'.[25] Not only did they disagree with Gorbals's position, the Paisley board immediately capitalised

1849. Reported by George Young, et al., vol. XL (Edinburgh: T. & T Clark, Law Booksellers: MDCCCXLIX), 786–7.

21 Mitchison, 'Disablement Rule in the Scottish Poor Law', 203–6.

22 One of the changes in the New Poor Law for Scotland was the right to relief that was given to parish residents. Not only did they have the right to apply, they had a right to appeal to the local sheriff if they were turned away by their parochial board. If the sheriff determined that the applicant was justified, the Board would have to give relief.

23 HCP Parochial Board, vol. 7–19, 25 Jan. 1848.

24 HCP Parochial Board, vol. 7–19, 25 Jan. 1848.

25 HCP Hospital, vol. 6–4, 29 Nov. 1839.

on the legal moment to grant poor rate funds to the Relief of Destitute Operatives' Committee. A motion by Mr James Millar instructed the Administration of Relief Committee to grant up to £500 of relief toward supporting Paisley families who were receiving assistance from the soup kitchens.[26]

The Court of Session, however, did not share the same intimate understanding of need in Scotland's industrial communities and ruled against the Sheriff of Lanarkshire in 1849. When the *Lindsay* case went before the Court of Session in February 1849 it was joined to a similar case, *Adams* v *M'William*, to be considered and argued before the whole court of thirteen justices. Where William Lindsay in Gorbals was trying to get support for his children, not himself, William M'William had applied for relief from the Parish of Glasgow to save himself from starvation after being unable to find work anywhere in Glasgow, Paisley, Kilmarnock, or Greenock. Turned down by the Glasgow Inspector, M'William turned to the Sheriff's Court and after some dispute was found entitled to relief so long as he was destitute and unable to find work.[27] The Court's argument over these two cases was extensive. They turned to Scottish legal precedent to interpret the meaning of the 1845 Act, reinforcing the idea that able-bodied unemployed people had never been considered among the ordinary poor (*Pollock* v *Darling* carefully excepted) and that Section 68 of the Poor Law Amendment Act did genuinely exclude men like Lindsay and M'William from demanding parochial support. The conclusion of the Lindsay and M'William cases held that 'an unemployed, able-bodied man has no legal right to parochial relief, although unable to find employment, and destitute of the means of subsistence', and further, 'has no legal right to demand parochial relief for his children in pupillarity'.[28]

The decision did nothing, though, to actually feed the hungry children or their unemployed parents. Unemployment continued to stalk Scotland's urban regions, and the men who worked daily with the poor understood

26 The soup kitchens in 1848 were arranged by the voluntary Relief Committee. In later crises, as will be seen, the parochial board established and paid for a soup kitchen within the walls of the poor house.

27 *Adams* v *M'William* and *Thomson* v *Lindsay*.

28 *Adams* v *M'William* and *Thomson* v *Lindsay*, 719.

the desperation they saw. Many inspectors, parochial boards, and even the Board of Supervision grasped at a linguistic loophole, declaring, 'This clause [Section 68] leaves an optional power in the hands of any parochial board to relieve this class of applicants during a season of distress.'[29] This interpretation led the Paisley parochial board to support soup kitchens throughout the 1850s and into the Cotton Famine years. The argument was subtle: while the able-bodied unemployed had no *right* to demand relief from the poors' funds raised by assessment, the parochial board could *choose to spend* their funds on outdoor relief for the able-bodied unemployed, especially if that relief was given in kind.

Feeding the Hungry

The grant awarded in 1848 established it as normal practice that Paisley's Parochial Board would fund soup kitchens in periods of high unemployment. The board was encouraged by the magistrates to impose additional assessments for the purpose of supporting the unemployed, rather than relying on the uneven generosity of public subscriptions.[30] Slack times continued in the early 1850s and some members of the board chaffed at the provision of support to able-bodied workers but the Relief Committee agreed unanimously to instruct Inspector Brown 'to receive and examine such applications as may be lodged with him by poor persons suffering from want of employment and upon finding the distress to be urgent and the applicants though able bodied to have a legal settlement in Paisley to extend to them Parochial Relief by placing them on the Roll of Casual Poor till the first meeting of the Board'.[31] As a result of this policy, a full one-third of first-time applicants for relief in 1851 were marked as able-bodied but unemployed.

29 'Relief to Able-Bodied but Unemployed Poor', *Poor Law Magazine for Scotland* 5 (May 1863): 123.
30 HCP Parochial Board, vol. 7–19, 31 Oct. 1851.
31 HCP Relief Committee, vol. 7–27, 16 May 1851.

It was no small thing that these men were entered into the formal record. An application for relief negated progress toward earning a residential settlement, even if the application was denied. For men born in Scotland the lack of a residential settlement only meant that a possibly-more-parsimonious birth parish was responsible for their support. For those from Ireland, however (at least 21 of whom are in the group of those pauperised by unemployment only), gaining and maintaining a settlement in Paisley protected them from physical removal. Inspector Brown and his colleagues understood the significance of formal application, even if the unemployed men themselves did not. As was shown in the previous chapter, a first visit to the Poor Law Office could result in casual aid with no schedule completed, at least temporarily preserving their progress toward a settlement.

By May 1852, the board was supporting 102 families through soup kitchens at a weekly cost of £13 (2/6 per family), the majority of which went to families with an able-bodied head of household. By their June meeting the Relief Committee had decided they must begin to ask for labour in exchange for the relief. They were edging closer to the English system of testing the poor to prove their worthiness before giving support, fearful that unencumbered relief would promote sloth. The Relief Committee expected that imposing a labour test would preserve 'a spirit of industry amongst the population'.[32] Trade revived before a scheme for the labour test was put into practice, but the recovery was shaky and another dip soon followed.

The unemployment crisis in 1854 was short and shallow enough that it bore no particular mention in the town's contemporary histories, but the weavers' applications for relief show it was dramatic. Paisley Parochial Board at first did not see the slump as an issue of concern. In late November (always a hungry time in the town) the Relief Committee refused aid to nine applicants, all of whom had received relief in the past. As the meeting minute recorded, 'cause of application want of work, ground of refusal being able bodied and in good health'.[33] Yet only a few days later,

> Inspector [Brown] reported that a deputation appointed by a … Weavers Committee had this day placed in his hands a list of 40 persons, weavers to trade, being heads of

32 HCP Relief Committee, vol. 7–27, 11 June 1852.

33 HCP Relief Committee, vol. 7–27, 28 Nov. 1854.

> families residing in different districts of the town, who are represented as being out of employment for several weeks, and as being in such circumstance of destitution as to render immediate relief absolutely necessary. The Inspector reported that since the receipt of the list he had visited a number of these parties in their own houses, and found that to all appearances the destitution complained of was real. On consideration whereof the Committee resolved that the Inspector be authorised to grant interim relief in the most urgent cases and that a special meeting of the whole Board shall be called on an early day next week to consider and direct what ought to be done with reference to this class of applicants.[34]

The board decided to use poor funds to support the able-bodied unemployed, while imposing a work test. In this crisis the parochial board showed more sensitivity to the men's chosen crafts than they had in the crises of the 1830s and early 1840s. Rather than sending the men to break stones or pick oakum, they allocated the money to open a soup kitchen and purchase cheap shirting webs, which would be doled out to the weavers. Payment was set at 2d. per ell. and a tidy profit was expected.[35] In 1838, hospital looms had produced more than £120 in cash as well as meeting the needs of the house with the same simple fabrics.[36]

The board had not accounted for two decades of development in industrial textile production. When the crisis eased, the total cost of producing the finished cloth was calculated to be 4 ¾ d. per ell.[37] Yet when the board offered the fabric for sale at that price, no buyers could be found, and the market value of the cloth was judged to be no more than 2 ½ d. per yard.[38] The handloom weavers' skills were wasted on the plain shirting webs the board was willing to supply, and the fabric produced was of no better quality than machine-made. While some of the cloth was finally sold in the name of charity at 3 ¾ d. per yard, most of it was used in the poor house itself.[39]

34 HCP Relief Committee, vol. 7–27, 1 Dec. 1854.

35 An ell was the length of warp filled by 5,000 shots of weft, measuring approximately one yard but varying by fabric. Plain fabrics like those commissioned by the parochial board might be woven at a rate of 4–8 ells in a workday. House of Commons, *Hand-Loom Weavers' Reports*, 27 March 1839, 33, 36–7.

36 HCP Hospital, vol. 6–3, 7 June 1839.

37 HCP Relief Committee, vol. 7–27, 19 Jan. 1855.

38 HCP Relief Committee, vol. 7–28, 19 April 1858.

39 HCP Relief Committee, vol. 7–28, 15 April 1858.

The food and employment support continued into early February 1855. At that time 125 families were on the soup list. In all 178 webs were distributed to 134 weavers. The downturn was easing; fifty-two men on the weavers' list had already returned to better-paying work, including twelve who enlisted in the militia. Although the fabric produced during this crisis was not valuable, it established an important principle for the board: they would not give cash to able-bodied unemployed men, but make-work and food could be provided from the public coffers.

The 1854–5 crisis eased with the Spring weather, but again the respite was short. An international economic crisis emerged in 1857 and hit Paisley harder than any downturn since the New Poor Law was passed. Linked by historians to trade disruptions of the Crimean War, related grain production in the western United States, and bank panics on both sides of the Atlantic, the 1857 crisis is most often interpreted as a prelude to the enormous disruption of the American Civil War and the Cotton Famine it sparked in Britain.[40] Unemployment among the weavers and factory operatives surged. On 3 November 1857, a public meeting sent a deputation to Provost Robert Brown and the magistrates to report more than 1,000 residents were out of work and 'that so destitute were they in their circumstances, many of them had been compelled to part with various articles of clothing and household furnishings to preserve life'.[41] They asked the town leaders to institute a public subscription for the relief, such as had been used in the past.

40 W.O. Henderson, 'The Cotton Famine in Scotland and the Relief of Distress, 1862–4', *The Scottish Historical Review* 30:110 part 2 (1951): 164. J.R.T. Hughes, 'The Commercial Crisis of 1857', *Oxford Economic Papers* new series 8:2 (1956): 194, 222; J. Huston, *The Panic of 1857 and the Coming of the Civil War* (Baton Rouge: Louisiana State University Press, 1987); C. Calomiris and L. Schweikart, 'The Panic of 1857: Origins, Transmission, and Containment', *The Journal of Economic History* 51:4 (1991): 807–34; D. Ross, 'Savings Bank Depositors in a Crisis: Glasgow 1847 and 1857', *Financial History Review* 20:2 (2013): 183–208; C. O'Grada and E. White, 'The Panics of 1854 and 1857: A View from the Emigrant Industrial Savings Bank', *Journal of Economic History* 63:1 (2003): 213–40.

41 'The State of Trade – Meeting of the Unemployed', *Paisley Herald and Renfrewshire Advertiser*, 7 Nov. 1857: 4; HCP Parochial Board, vol. 7–19, 12 Nov. 1857.

The magistrates refused. Instead of turning to private donations, they drew on precedent and wrote to Inspector Brown and his counterpart in Abbey parish, recommending in the strongest possible terms that the parochial boards or relief committees of the two parishes 'authoris[e] relief to [the unemployed] under the discretionary powers vested in them by the Statute', asking that they work together to ensure efficient and fair support across the burgh.[42] Since the provost and two of the magistrates were also serving on the parochial board, this communication must have been to some extent performative, intended to reassure the public rather than directly affect policy.[43] The effect of the letter was to bring into the public parochial board meeting a discussion of the legality of such support. A few days later the *Paisley Herald* reported the conclusion of the joint meeting, 'They were to the effect that while the boards did not recognise any legal responsibility for the support of able bodied poor, yet under the present circumstances it was advisable, in the meantime to extend relief to them.'[44] While acknowledging the rampant need, the aid offered was carefully restricted to ensure no fraud was practiced. A nine-point resolution kept them within the legal boundaries of the law, reiterating the exclusion of able-bodied workers from relief and emphasising the emergency nature of these relief actions. They authorised make-work projects and soup kitchens in both Paisley and Abbey, with prohibitions against anyone being fed who was on strike, who refused employment, or to young single men at all.

It was enough to keep the peace that relief was being offered at all. In the first three weeks of November more than fifty heads of families, most of them weavers and winders, had applied for relief because they were out of work. The soup kitchen opened on the poor house grounds as soon as it was authorised. It was just as quickly discovered to be insufficient to the need, so that additional boilers had to be added.[45] By the first week of December, more than 1,500 men, women and children were getting daily rations of bread, soup and oatmeal. Men (in particular) receiving relief

42 HCP Parochial Board, vol. 7–19, 12 Nov. 1857.

43 There is no digitised directory available for 1855–61, so further analysis of crossover between the two bodies is not currently possible.

44 *PHRA*, 14 Nov. 1857, p. 4.

45 HCP Poorhouse Committee, vol. 7–28, 20 Nov. 1857.

had to work for the food, and the parochial boards issued handbills asking farmers to provide ground for digging.[46] Weavers, even in desperate circumstances, may have been reluctant to accept the aid offered under such conditions; on 9 December the Relief Committee authorised giving out webs of 'low-priced Galas … reserved for weavers who up to this date have not applied for relief except special cases'.[47]

Throughout the winter demand for relief remained high. There must have been very little opportunity for earning extra pennies here and there, because it is clear the soup kitchen rations were all some families had to eat. At the end of December, the size of rations was increased to eight (up from six) ounces of bread and six (raised from four) ounces of oatmeal. The soup ration remained at 1 ½ pints per day. Everyone over 4 years of age qualified for this full ration, which had previously been given only to those ten and older. There was no room in the recipients' budgets for any non-essentials: in February, a portion of soap was added to the regular ration.[48]

The situation at last began to improve in March 1858, after the Burgh had spent in excess of £1,760 on supporting the able-bodied poor. The soup kitchen was closed at the end of the month, leaving thirty-one people still unemployed and destitute. Those men and their families were offered the poor house.[49] The more than 10,000 yards of fabric unemployed weavers had produced over the year were again kept for use within the poor house, estimated to be a three-year supply.[50]

Paisley had not well recovered from the 1857 crash when the Cotton Famine arrived.[51] The parochial board again assumed responsibility for the men made unemployed by the collapse in trade, handloom weavers chief among them. On 1 November 1861, two separate applicants, 'being destitute able-bodied weavers out of employment', were accepted for relief. James Shaw Brown was directed, 'to give them work within the [Poor] House and

46 HCP Joint Abbey/Paisley Relief Committee, vol. 7–28, 23 Nov. 1857.
47 HCP Joint Abbey/Paisley Relief Committee, vol. 7–28, 9 Dec. 1857.
48 HCP Joint Abbey/Paisley Relief Committee, vol. 7–28, 21 Dec. 1857.
49 HCP Relief Committee, vol. 7–28, 30 March 1858.
50 HCP Relief Committee, vol. 7–28, 15 April 1858.
51 Henderson, 'The Cotton Famine in Scotland', 156.

assist their families with food'.[52] It is not clear if the men were physically housed in the poor house of if they traveled there to work. The food was provided by the reopened soup kitchen and by mid-November seventy-eight families, totaling more than 300 individuals, were being fed in spite of the Relief Committee's misgivings about the legality of the practice. As their minutes recorded, 'Having considered the present state of the law on this subject with special reference to their powers of applying the poor funds for the support of this class of the poor, [the Committee] delay making any determinate arrangements till a meeting of the whole board be called. And meantime authorise the Inspector to grant relief in cooked food as was done in 1857–58 to the most necessitious cases.'[53]

The meals provided by the soup kitchens were not, themselves, likely to discourage recipients from seeking something better. The kitchen provided literal soup, made of boiled beef houghs (hocks), barley, peas, and other vegetables and served with wheat bread (the ration back down to 6 ounces) and oatmeal (4 ounces). These three hundred people were fed at a cost of under 10d. per person, totaling £12 per week paid from the assessed poor rates.[54] Perhaps because of the difficulty obtaining inexpensive cotton, there was no attempt to secure webs for the weavers: the parish prepared to set work for the operatives at picking oakum and breaking rocks, saving the board the embarrassment of trying to sell cloth at a loss.[55]

Yet while the managers of the poor were trying to keep their costs low, they did not lose sight of their humanitarian obligation. In December 1861 the Poorhouse Committee minutes reported, 'Examined, this day's supply of Beef and Houghs for the poor house, found it defective. The beef being partly hough and bull beef, and the houghs not entire.'[56] A few months later, the committee noted the bread they were purchasing was short weight and demanded a new batch at full weight. Whether this insistence on quality was for the health of the paupers or to ensure parish money was well spent, the effect was to set a standard of care for those receiving relief.

52 HCP Parochial Board, vol. 7–19, 1 Nov. 1861.
53 HCP Relief Committee, vol. 7–28, 15 Nov. 1861.
54 HCP Relief Committee, vol. 7–28, 22 Nov. 1861.
55 HCP Relief Committee, vol. 7–28, 28 Nov. 1861.
56 HCP Poorhouse Committee, vol. 7–28, 16 Dec. 1861.

Paisley found their rolls swelled in 1861 by their disproportionate generosity. In November, Inspector Brown reported to the board that there were a number of applicants for relief who fell into the category of able-bodied unemployed who had settlements in neighboring Abbey Parish. After correspondence with the Abbey Parish board, the Paisley board voted to refuse relief to Abbey-settled able-bodied applicants (presumably in retribution for a similar stance from Abbey). Their strategy was not successful. When Brown wrote as instructed to the Abbey inspector, the Abbey board continued to refuse any payment for the men or their families. They went so far as to claim that in this instance – when relief itself was being granted in a legal twilight, 'relief granted to persons of the class [i.e. able bodied unemployed] should come not from the parish of their legal settlement, but from that of their interim residence'.[57] The Paisley board was defeated by Abbey's greater parsimony. Recognising that the voluntary nature of able-bodied relief gave them no legal claim against Abbey, the board determined, 'in order to prevent suffering which might otherwise arise', to grant relief to the men, if only in the form of stone breaking and soup.[58]

The work entailed in accepting and managing these applications for relief was telling on Inspector Brown, though he was loath to complain. In 1855 the Board of Supervision, frustrated with the erratic quality of book-keeping in parishes across the nation, issued regulations for the schedules and other records the inspectors kept.[59] For years Inspector Brown dutifully completed the required forms, but also continued to use the schedules designed in 1839, maintaining the sequence of data he was collecting. When the annual number of new applicants neared 600 in December 1861 the parochial board learned,

> For a long time an Historical Register of Poor has been kept in folio form, which gives all the particulars required by the regulation form of Register which Mr Brown has carefully also kept up. As the substance of these books is the same, it would be a

57 HCP Relief Committee, vol. 7–27, 4 Dec. 1861.

58 HCP Parochial Board, vol. 7–19, 4 Dec. 1861.

59 *Tenth Annual Report of the Board of Supervision for the Relief of the Poor in Scotland* (Edinburgh: Murray and Gibb, 1855), Appendix A.

> considerable relief to the Inspector if he was permitted to substitute the folio form, which he prefers, for the regulation form.

With the acquiescence of the Board of Supervision they subsequently resolved,

> That in the opinion of this Board the Historical Register of Poor Folio form, which has been kept by the Inspector from 1839 down to the present date is more convenient and better adapted for this parish than the Regulation form of Register and recommend that the Inspector be in future relieved of the duty of keeping the latter form as unnecessary.[60]

This decision about record keeping illustrates the continuing contest over centralised versus local control of the New Poor Law. James Shaw Brown showed that he was entirely willing to take some direction from Edinburgh, even at the expense of his own time and labor, but he was not willing to give up his own process in exchange. Similarly and with more import, the contretemps between Paisley and Abbey over able-bodied relief in the depths of a slack winter illustrates the tension produced by the law's decentralised nature. More than fifteen years after the law was introduced, such niggling points of interpretation still rose to the surface and worked their way ponderously through the courts, rather than having power even nominally housed in the central Board of Supervision to determine a universal reading of the Law. How the law was going to be interpreted in any parish depended on the sympathies of the men who governed and administered the law in the place. In Paisley, whether because of a fear of unrest or simple humanity, men and women whose only disability was a lack of employment during hard times were consistently granted (meagre) support as a matter of policy, while that mercy was denied in another part of the same town.

Among the 591 new applications for relief in Paisley in 1861, 45 specifically mentioned a lack of work in explaining their need for relief.[61] Those are the applicants applying for the first time – the numbers reliant on the

60 HCP Parochial Board, vol. 7–19, 11 Dec. 1861.

61 HCP Statements, vol. 11–12 and 11–13, 1 Jan. – 31 Dec. 1861. At least a dozen of the people first relieved when unemployed in 1851 also re-applied during 1861.

soup kitchen show that most of the people in need were re-applying (as described in the previous chapter) or were relieved entirely outside the official poor law system of documentation. More than half of these new applicants (24) were married couples residing and applying together. Seven were married women whose husbands were out of the home – six gone in search of work and one imprisoned for poaching. The remaining applicants in this group were never married (9) or widowed (3), both men and women and ranging in age from 18 to 48.

Unemployment came in waves as the crisis deepened throughout 1861. The first pulse of able-bodied unemployed applicants appeared in June, when seven of the forty-six applicants in that month (15 percent) were unemployed for periods ranging from 1 to 11 weeks. These applicants had worked in a variety of areas – mill workers, a block printer, a miner and two weavers. When amplified distress descended on Paisley in November, it hit the weaving community much harder. In that month twenty-nine new applicants (of 79) were noted to be unemployed without further disability; twenty-one of them were weavers. The following month, twenty-seven more new applications were made by individuals or families with no disability beyond destitution due to unemployment. In December, there were fifty-seven applicants – the unemployed accounted for 47 percent of them. It is clear that the slump had spread throughout the town's economy; only 9 of the December group were weavers. They were joined by labourers, various mill workers, and hawkers.

Worker Response to Unemployment Crises

Workers in Paisley were well used to the ebb and flow of trade in the town. Relatively few were wholly unprepared for slack times or eager to turn to the parish as soon as their regular wages stopped. Yet critics of poor relief often proclaimed the problem of poverty among the able-bodied was a problem of self-control or improvidence. 'Scotus', writing about the Scottish Poor Laws in 1870, maintained that the guarantee of parochial relief to the able-bodied unemployed would sap them of their resilience and will to work. 'Scotus' declared that voluntary relief efforts were the best tactic to address an unemployment crisis, while parochial relief was best suited to the grinding daily care of the disabled and impotent poor. Further, 'Scotus' harked back to the old 'Speenhamland' system in England to argue the English experience of guaranteed relief to able-bodied men led to 'a breaking down, not only of the independence of the poor, who soon began to show indifference to getting employment and to obtaining sufficient wages, but of the morality of manufacturers, who succumbed to the temptation, and rewarded labour with unremunerative wages'.[62]

The Statements of Cases, however, suggest that a majority of workers had some savings or other resources to use before turning to the parish. Only two of the forty-five applicants for whom a length of unemployment was specified in 1861 applied more or less immediately after losing work. Agnes Kerr, a millworker without living parents and with a 4 ½-year-old son, and the couple James Gibb and Christian Hutcheson, a weaving family with three children under 5 years old, both applied when they had been unemployed for a week or less.[63] Nine more in this group applied after being out of work two or three weeks. The large majority turned to poor relief only after a month or more of unemployment. At the extreme end, John Wilson and his wife Elis[abeth] Gillies saved enough from his 12 s. salary as a trainer at Coats Mill that they did not apply for parish aid until he had been out of work a full nine months.[64]

Of course personal savings was not the only – or even the main – way that workers in Paisley survived unemployment. It was inevitable that families faced unemployment with the same strategies the poor used to survive throughout the period. When Wilson and Gillies, along with their 2-year-old daughter, applied for relief in September, they reported they were living with Gillies' parents in a 2-room flat on St. Mirren Street. Six months earlier, when the census was taken, they had had their own single-end flat on Storie Street.[65] Already laid off at Coats when the census came, Wilson's

62 'Scotus', *The Scottish Poor Laws: Examination of Their Policy, History, and Practical Action* (Edinburgh: Edmonston and Douglas, 1870), 187.

63 HCP Statements, vol. 11–12, Statement 11037; vol. 11–13, Statement 11304.

64 HCP Statements, vol. 11–12, Statement 11164.

65 1861 Wilson, John (Census 573/17/14), *ScotlandsPeople*.

occupation was recorded as a plain weaver. Although handloom weavers were losing economic ground it was an occupation a trained hand could turn to when the big firms were closing down. The Wilson family likely sold or pawned every household or personal item they could when they changed houses to join Elisabeth's parents and multiple younger siblings. There must have been dietary changes and long nights and days wracking their brains for a way to earn or save a few more pennies.

Other men (especially) left the struggling Paisley economy to look for opportunities elsewhere. Thirteen of the sixty-seven married women in 1861 who applied for relief without their husbands specified that the men had left them to search for work. A further nine women in 1861 drifted or came to Paisley in search of an absent husband, such as Agnes Muir who, with her three children, applied for relief in July. She claimed her plasterer husband 'left her in Storie Street on 25 May last and she remained there till 29 June when hearing he was in Greenock she went down there from a chance'.[66] Returning unsuccessfully to Paisley, she asked for help after sleeping rough for a night at the brick kiln on Caledonia Street. All the effort to save money or find alternate work nevertheless in the end led some families to Inspector Brown's office and the lines at the soup kitchen for their bowls of soup and few ounces of bread.

Able-Bodied Relief in the Courts, 1859–1866

While unemployment and hunger stalked workers in the early 1860s, Paisley was not alone in concluding that voluntary, rate-supported soup kitchens were a viable response to unemployment. The Chairman of the Board of Supervision assured parishes that it was a legally sound strategy, but this interpretation of the law was not universally accepted. The question of able-bodied relief also intersected with the question of settlement because even applying for relief (never mind being added to the roll) negated any progress a migrant had made toward gaining a new settlement

66 HCP Statements, vol. 11–12, Statement 11086.

through five years' residence in a parish.[67] The legal process to settle this question was working its way through the courts in the same years that Paisley's soup kitchens were feeding thousands.

The case began in a squabble between Barony and Carmunnock (both areas of Glasgow) and Mearns (in eastern Renfrewshire) in 1859. A block printer, Joseph Collingwood, was born in Barony, moved to Carmunnock in 1846, and stayed there until 1853 – long enough to gain a residential settlement in the new place. However, during the unemployment crisis of November 1848 the Carmunnock Parochial Board had (similar to Paisley) directed payments to able-bodied unemployed applicants. In Collingwood's case this aid totaled 6 shillings. Then, since the printer had not yet earned his settlement in Carmunnock, the inspector there, George Hunter, billed C.S. Meek, the Barony inspector, for reimbursement. Remarkably, Barony paid the bill, agreeing that Collingwood had been relieved appropriately. This exchange demonstrates that in the western industrial region of Scotland, it was accepted in the late 1840s that parochial boards had this ability to relieve the able-bodied unemployed.[68]

Collingwood, along with his wife and family, migrated to Mearns in 1853. About eighteen months later, in the hungry month of November 1854, he deserted them by enlisting and was not heard from again. Mearns Inspector Alexander Petrie relieved the now-destitute Mrs Collingwood and children, then applied for reimbursement from Carmunnock. Inspector Hunter refused, claiming that the 6 s. paid in 1848 had interrupted the Collingwoods' acquisition of a settlement there. This case – like so many others – went before Sheriff-substitute Bell, worked up to the Court of Session and in 1859 was decided against Carmunnock because the 1848 relief was improperly given and thus could not be counted against the acquisition of a settlement.[69] This decision negated the practice of relief for the unemployed as it had been practiced for more than a decade.

67 *Poor Law (Scotland) Act*, Sec. 76.

68 *Meek* v *Hunter* and *Petrie*, 4 March 1859, *The Scottish Jurist: Being Reports of Cases Decide in the Supreme Courts of Scotland, and in the House of Lords on Appeal from Scotland*, by J. Lorimer, et al., vol. XXXI (Edinburgh: Thomas Constable and Co., MDCCCLIX), 334–5.

69 *Meek* v *Hunter* and *Petrie*, 334–48.

The *Meek* v *Hunter and Petrie* decision threw parochial boards into a flurry. As the *Poor Law Magazine*'s editor reported, 'The result of that decision has been to cause a divided practice, and throw confusion and doubt in the dealings of the Boards with persons who may be within the definition laid down by courts of law as able bodied.'[70] From this confusion, Inspectors of the Poor from across Scotland discussed strategies for a concrete resolution. *The Poor Law Magazine* recounted,

> Parochial Boards represent their constituents, who entrust their interests to their management, and there must always be a large discretion in such matters. … It happens every day in parochial management, that to give a small temporary relief to a poor man would be the means of keeping him from becoming a permanent burden on the funds. Such a discretionary power, therefore, is advantageous to the ratepayers, and no Inspector of Poor has any interest to give such temporaries unnecessarily. It by no means follows that although such a discretion should be in the Board that the occasional able-bodied person should have a legal claim to demand relief, or that the rights of the Board to give are only to be measured by the right of the applicant to demand. We cannot follow this view of it at all, but it is time that the point was set at rest.
>
> The Lord Advocate was applied to some months ago to legislate on the subject of the able bodied poor. He expressed his doubts how far the decision of the Second Division [Court of Session] in *Petrie* v *Meek* was truly the law of Scotland.[71]

Bolstered by this opinion from the Lord Advocate seemingly in support of their position, the inspectors nevertheless feared what the English-dominated Parliament would do with the question if it was brought forward for clarification by amendment of the Law. Sir John McNeill, Chairman of the Board of Supervision, stated that the entire board shared his fear, 'that if such a question were to be raised in Parliament, we might run the risk of having thrown on us the English rule of able-bodied poor being declared legally entitled to relief'.[72] The Scottish inspectors imagined with horror the costs that such an alteration of the law would impose on their ratepayers.

70 'Able Bodied Poor', *The Poor Law Magazine for Scotland*, vol. 6 (Sept. 1863), 2.
71 'Able Bodied Poor', Sept. 1863, 2–3.
72 'Able Bodied Poor, Sept. 1863, 3.

Someone – recorded as 'high authority' – suggested that if the case were raised in court, the justices could confirm 'that the parochial boards have the discretionary power which heretofore (before the *Meek* case) they have been claiming and exercising'.[73] In this instance, no adjustment to the legislation would be necessary, the parochial boards would simply be confirmed in their preferred interpretation of the law. For reasons now lost to history, the Parochial Board of Dundee was selected to bring the case, presenting the unusual situation of a member of the Dundee Parochial Board, Robert Isdale, bringing suit against Henry Jack, Dundee's Inspector of the Poor.

The obvious importance of *Isdale* v *Jack*, which carried with it 'imminent danger to the whole Scotch system',[74] led to it being heard and argued by the entire 13-justice Court of Session. The justices, unlike the *Lindsay* case in which they argued precedent and intent prior to 1845, based their arguments primarily in the text of the New Poor Law itself. In addition to the troublesome 68th section regarding able-bodied relief, they drew on Section 33, about the purpose of poors' funds, Sections 70 and 71 regarding settlement, and the 76th section concerning the effect of receiving parochial relief on achieving a settlement. The most significant lines of argument turned on the 33rd section that authorised assessment for the purpose of 'the relief of the poor persons entitled to relief from the parish' and on the able-bodied exclusion, 'nothing herein contained shall be held to confer a right to demand relief on able-bodied persons out of employment'.[75] If they did not have a right to relief, the justices pondered, could they be considered 'entitled?' Some justices found the text-based argument conclusive; others pointed to past practice since well before 1845 that responded to economic collapse with aid. They made a tortured linguistic argument that if the able-bodied unemployed were not accepted as a regular part of the occasional poor mentioned in Section 33, there would be no need to explicitly exclude them in Section 68.

73 'Able Bodied Poor', Sept. 1863, 3.

74 'Able Bodied Poor', Sept. 1863, 4.

75 *Poor Law (Scotland) Act*, Sec. 33, Sec. 68.

In the end, six justices wrote or concurred with opinions that parochial boards could use their discretion to give relief to able-bodied applicants when they were convinced no work was available. Seven justices found the opposite. By the time *Isdale* v *Jack* was through the Court of Session the urgency of the Cotton Famine was receding, but no inspector in Scotland could hope it would be the last such emergency. Still convinced of their own legal interpretation and the necessity of protecting their uniquely Scottish system (thus wary of asking Parliament for legislative relief), 'an influential meeting of delegates from a number of the larger parishes in Scotland' determined that the case should be appealed to the House of Lords.[76] They asked parochial boards across Scotland to contribute funds to the cause. There is no record of whether or not Paisley contributed to this action, but they were undoubtedly aware of it and following intently.

Isdale v *Jack* came to the House of Lords in February 1866 and was not the resounding vindication for which the parochial boards had hoped. The subtlety of the Scottish arguments entirely escaped the Lord Chancellor. Flanked by Lords Chelmsford and Kingsdown, he declared, 'I am unable to distinguish or to see any difference in principle between being entitled to relief and being entitled to demand relief'.[77] Harking back to the decision in the *Lindsay*, etc. case, he moved that the appeal be dismissed, and his fellow Lords concurred. They maintained the Court of Session's decision, and relief for the able-bodied unemployed in Scotland was ended. In 1871 only one applicant for relief in Paisley was listed as able-bodied and unemployed, a 36-year-old washerwoman who was chargeable to Greenock.[78] No one would contest the little aid Inspector Brown passed to this widowed mother, but for every other unemployed person in Paisley he either recorded a plausible disability or turned them away.

76 'Able Bodied Poor Action – Appeal to House of Lords', *The Poor Law Magazine for Scotland* 7 (Feb. 1865): 210.

77 *Jack v Isdale*, 12 Feb. 1866, *Cases Decided in The Court of Session, Teind Court, &c. and House of Lords*, reported by Middleton Rettie, et al., Third Series, vol. IV (Edinburgh: T & T Clark, Law Booksellers, MDCCCLXVI), 3.

78 HCP Statements, vol. 11–17, Statement 16140.

Inspector Brown Explains His Position

At the end of the 1860s, the Member of Parliament for the Ayr Burghs, Mr Edward Craufurd, spearheaded a new inquiry into the workings of the Scottish poor law. Craufurd focused his call for the subcommittee on alleged corrupt inefficiencies in the law of 1845 and its administration.[79] The committee's inquiry was wide-ranging, including examining witnesses on parochial support given to the able-bodied unemployed. Inspector Brown, called to London to testify, recounted Paisley's response to the successive employment crises. In 1826, 1842 and 1847, he said, they 'were met by voluntary contributions, and the relief was administered by committees of local gentlemen'.[80] When jobs collapsed in 1851, many of the men who had contributed in the past refused to give again, on the grounds that they were paying poor rates for the purpose of supporting the poor, the destitute unemployed included. Brown described the consternation of the town parochial board authorities, pressured by both magistrates and the starving workers. They had dithered until the President of the Board of Supervision, Sir John McNeill, visited the town and assured the Paisley and Abbey Parochial Boards 'that the distress ought to be met by the poor rate;' the legal opinion of 'eminent counsel … was entirely in favour of it'. On the strength of that opinion, Paisley aided the able-bodied poor with poor rates in periods of distress in 1851, 1855, 1858, 1862 and 1864. Although Paisley had not seen another crisis since 1864 Brown admitted that in light of the *Isdale* v *Jack* decision, 'I am quite sure that the community of Paisley, in the event of any distress occurring, would be in the greatest possible difficulty to know what to do.'[81]

79 Hansards, 'House of Commons Sitting of Tuesday, 2nd March, 1869', Third Series, vol. 194, 19th Century House of Commons Hansard sessional Papers.

80 House of Commons, 'Report from the Select Committee on Operation of the Poor Law (Scotland): Together with the Proceedings of the Committee, Minutes of Evidence, Appendix, and Index', 6 July 1869, 297.

81 'Operation of the Poor Law', 297.

When a commissioner, Mr Armistead, expressed some skepticism that relief on such a scale could really be targeted to those who deserved aid, Inspector Brown replied acerbically, 'The ground of relief given was not so much ascertaining that the applicant was deserving as that he was starving.' Recovering himself Brown went on, 'I should say … that I think the relief was judiciously administered, that is to say, that it was given to those who stood in absolute need of it, and who had no other way of living or getting through the period of distress.'[82] Even after *Isdale* was decided, Brown admitted, Paisley would very occasionally provide make-work and payment to able-bodied individuals when 'it was found that they really were in want, that they had no visible means of living'.[83]

Brown's questioners pounced on that admission, asking if the Inspector thought such discretion to support the able-bodied unemployed should rest centrally, with the Board of Supervision. Brown replied strongly in favor of parochial control, 'I would not be disposed to limit the power of parochial boards in any way further than they are limited now, either in that or in any other department. … They are perfectly competent to judge whether relief should be given or no, and they will not give it too readily, for they have to pay the money.'[84]

In spite of Brown (and others') advocacy, a provision for able-bodied relief was not included in the committee's final report, although it admitted the suggestion came 'from many quarters'. Instead, they recommended the creation of an English-style poor house test, particularly in connection with unmarried mothers, and to make Scottish poor houses more punitive than supportive.[85] Significant elements of the proposed revision to the poor law were opposed by the Scottish poor law establishment, and upon the bill's second reading even some members of the committee had turned against it. The bill was recommitted, then reintroduced in 1873, and failed to gain traction. The death of that bill was the last opportunity in Brown's career to regularise and authorise relief for able-bodied unemployed people. Had

82 'Operation of the Poor Law', 298.

83 'Operation of the Poor Law', 298.

84 'Operation of the Poor Law', 298.

85 House of Commons, 'Report from the Select Committee on Poor Law (Scotland): With the Proceedings of the Committee', 3 July 1871, xi.

it passed, it would have gained that ability at the expense of local control and the workers' freedom (as relief would have been mandated through a workhouse test). Although the united voice of so many Scottish parishes was not enough to gain the interpretation of the law they wanted to see, it was at least enough to prevent the imposition of an even stricter and more centralised rule.

The decision against using poors' funds to support the able-bodied unemployed held in Scotland until the end of the nineteenth century, although the problem did not disappear. While maintaining the letter of the law, local governing bodies continued seek ways to mitigate the suffering that came with economic downturns, ultimately constructing tools outside the poor law.[86] Poor law managers and the town government had fought hard for their belief that there was a social obligation for the government to support men and families through cyclical unemployment, in defiance of the clear meaning of the poor law's text. Once the legal case was settled, however, they complied.

The question of what to do with able-bodied, unemployed workers in times of economic crisis was a broadly acknowledged problem that received significant interest from commentators as well as poor law managers for most of two decades. Over many of the same years, but without the same public interest, Inspector James Shaw Brown was working through a far more complex question – complex because it was virtually unaddressed in the New Poor Law. The question was to what extent a woman, once married, had control over her own legal settlement. The problem was personified in the case of Elisabeth Cousland.

86 R. Johnson, '"Charity that Heals": The Scottish Labour Colony Association and Attitudes to the Able-bodied Unemployed in Glasgow, 1890–1914', *The Scottish Historical Review* LXXVII:1 no. 203 (April 1998): 77–95; Levitt, *Poverty & Welfare*, 107–8.

CHAPTER 5

The Case of the Widow's Settlement: The New Poor Law and Women's Agency: 1850–61

A Complicated Family

Elizabeth Cousland presented herself to Inspector Brown on Monday, 9 September 1850. The day before, Cousland's husband, Peter McMurrich, had become critically ill with the consumption that must have been developing for months or years.[1] With seven children to support, including a 3-month-old daughter, Cousland was desperate to gain some aid. Brown met her immediate need, assuring medical care for McMurrich and food for the children, and set about determining who was responsible for her support. It took more than a decade for him to find the answer. The Cousland case wound through not only the intricacies of the poor law but also the shifting social landscape in Victorian Scotland, turning on a changing recognition of women's individual rights and abilities as independent actors within Scottish society.

Inspector Brown included Cousland's name and details on the statement he completed, but he gave primary place on the application to her

1 HCP Statements, vol. 11–6, Statement 4402. While Peter's last name was recorded as McMurrich in the poor law record and the *Poor Law Magazine* article based on the case, it was reported as McMurray in census and statutory records. Elizabeth Cousland is referred to by her maiden name throughout this chapter in part for clarity, but also because married women were routinely identified by their birth names on poor law documents throughout the century. Portions of this chapter were originally published as 'The Obligation to Support the Widow: Settlement, the New Poor Law and the Scottish Local State', *Journal of Scottish Historical Studies* 35:1 (2015): 45–69.

ailing partner. He noted that both Cousland and McMurrich had earlier marriages and were wed to each other by a Justice of the Peace in Glasgow in August 1844. It was perhaps a first clue there was something off about the relationship when Cousland could not recall the name of the officiant, though she did name two witnesses. The seven children included McMurrich's son with his first wife, three children Cousland had had with her first husband, James Hutton, and three daughters McMurrich and Cousland had together, including the infant, Jean. McMurrich was 42 years old and, when he was well, worked as a calico printer and gamekeeper. Cousland was ten years younger than her husband. The two oldest children, James Hutton (13) and John McMurrich (10) each were recorded as earning 2/6 per week as tearers (printers' assistants), but if they had been working assisting their father/step-father their income stopped when he fell ill. Cousland was considered unable to work due to caring for little Jean.[2] Block printing was a skilled trade, but like many reliant on textile work the family fluctuated in and out of pauperism with the times and circumstances. They had received relief in Abbey Parish during the 1847/8 downturn, and before that Cousland and her children were relieved for ten months between her first husband's death and her remarriage. With this history, Inspector Brown was comfortable placing the family on Paisley's casual roll when McMurrich died two days after their application. Since other parishes had already accepted responsibility for the family it should have been a simple process to obtain recognition and reimbursement from one of them for the family's current care.[3]

The case turned out to be more complicated than it first appeared. The one thing that was certain was that, aside from their current residence in the town, the family had no claim on Paisley. Since McMurrich was a native of Cardross, Dunbartonshire, and in fact had only lived in the Paisley Burgh Parish for a year and a half before his death, he did not have a settlement in the parish. While he was entitled to poor relief generally, he did not have the right to receive funds raised by the poor rates in Paisley for either

2 Statement 4402.

3 Report of the Cousland case in 'Arbitration Cases', *The Poor Law Magazine for Scotland* 3 (Dec. 1860): 183–7.

himself or his family. During the crisis of 1848 he had received relief on behalf of the children, paid by Abbey Parish and reimbursed by Cardross. Since paying relief constituted an admission of settlement, Brown wrote first to the Poor Law Inspector in Cardross requesting reimbursement for the aid given to McMurrich's children. The Hutton children, though, did not gain a settlement through their parents' marriage. Their support, Inspector Brown determined, should come through their late father. He accordingly also requested reimbursement from the parish where Cousland had lived with her first husband and where two of the children had been born: Bonhill, Dunbartonshire.[4]

On 19 September, Cardross's inspector responded to the request and Cousland's claim for relief began to come apart. While Cardross was willing to repay McMurrich's expenses and a small allowance for his son John, the Cardross inspector reported that McMurrich's first wife was alive, was last known to be in Glasgow, and had purportedly gone off with a soldier.[5] However they may have lived and been regarded by their neighbours, Cousland and McMurrich could not be legally married, the three youngest children in the family were bastards, and Cousland herself was of suspect morals. Cardross would absolutely not admit responsibility for Cousland or her children.

Inspector Brown was caught out. Under the Act, the parish that first acknowledged a pauper needed relief was responsible for sustaining that pauper until the parish to which they rightfully belonged could be billed for the expense.[6] Brown was absolutely certain that Cousland and her brood did not have a settlement in Paisley, but the question of where in fact responsibility for them lay would be argued over the entire course of the 1850s. Throughout that decade Brown and his fellow inspectors grappled not only with the facts of the Cousland/Hutton/McMurrich case but also with the shifting landscape of the poor law in Scotland and how it considered the legal status of married women. Over the decade through which Cousland's case was debated, the accepted interpretation of the poor

4 'Arbitration Cases', 183.
5 'Arbitration Cases', 183.
6 *Poor Law (Scotland) Act*, Sec. 70.

law changed repeatedly, each new decision altering where responsibility for her and her family might lie.

Recent scholarship regarding the poor and their access to relief has sought out the voices of the poverty-stricken, most often in the form of petitions for relief, and these show women (widows in particular) taking an active role in obtaining support for themselves.[7] Yet the language of the law assumed a male head of household and expected a uniform settlement for a nuclear family. When actual applicants contradicted these expectations, as previous chapters have shown, the law was not so clear-cut. Women advocating for their own relief faced poor law inspectors in each parish who interpreted the law as they went along, compensating for the morass of practical detail omitted from the 1845 Act, including how to determine a widow's proper settlement.[8] The legal angles pursued to resolve the details were contingent on the imagination, experience and expectations of the managers, and thus on their assumptions about the society in which they lived. James Shaw Brown's personal experience meant he was unlikely to underestimate women's abilities in his administration of the law.

When Paisley blacksmith David Brown, James Shaw's father, passed away in 1837, there was no fear that his widow would be forced onto the poor law. His will provided her liferent in the houses and other profits from his small ventures in moneylending, but only if she did not remarry.

7 In addition to Blaikie's extensive work in rural Scotland, see, for example, L. Baker, 'Survival Strategies of Widows in Dijon during the French Revolution', *Women's Studies* 31 (2002): 53–65; P. Sharpe, 'Survival Strategies and Stories: Poor Widows and Widowers in Early Industrial England', in *Widowhood in Medieval and Early Modern Europe*, ed. S. Cavallo and L. Warner (Harlow: Routledge, 1999), 220–39; M. Levine-Clark, 'Engendering Relief: Women, Ablebodiedness, and the New Poor law in Early Victorian England', *Journal of Women's History* 11:4 (2000): 107–30; and N. Muller, 'Deceit, Deservingness, and Destitution: Able-bodied Widows and the New Poor Law', *Journal of Victorian Culture* 26:1 (2021): 89–102.

8 In spite of England's more centralised system of poor relief, scholars have noted the same irregularity of practice as the century progressed, particularly in reference to people like able-bodied widows who fell between clearly-defined categories. See, for example, Muller, 'Deceit, Deservingness, and Destitution', 93–4; P. Jones and S. King, eds, *Obligation, Entitlement and dispute under the English Poor Laws* (Newcastle upon Tyne: Cambridge Scholars Publishing, 2015), 12–13.

He further provided that following his widow's death the remaining property would be split evenly between his six surviving children: James Shaw, John, and four daughters – Euphemia, Margaret Weir, Ann, and Janet. In making this bequest he ensured that the women would have independent control of the money even if they married, declaring that 'they shall have full power and authority by themselves alone to uplift and discharge their respective shares of my said estate and the rents and profits and duties thereof without the consent of any such husband or husbands, any law to the contrary notwithstanding'.[9] The Misses Brown, who ranged in age from 17 to 29 when their father died, took to their needles and their sums. In 1841 their mother appeared in the census as "Independent," while Euphemia and Janet were "Sewers." A decade later, Widow Brown had passed away and Euphemia, Margaret, and Ann were sewing at home. The four sisters apparently lived in one household throughout their lives, although one or another happened to be away at census time. Throughout these years sewing and "Income from House Property" maintained a substantial enough family economy that they were able to keep a live-in servant.[10]

Census and property records cannot fully reveal the dynamic in the Brown family or detail who was managing the money. The house on Back Sneddon belonged to James Shaw, and his sisters were recorded as his tenants, but there is no knowing how (or if) money actually changed hands. Inspector Brown's own salary, which topped out at £200, was not enough to maintain two respectable households without the extra income from their inherited property. Financially independent and active women were not such an anomaly in mid-nineteenth century Scotland as was once thought, however. David Meredith and Deborah Oxley found that in general, working-class women in Paisley received a greater share of household resources than similar women in the London satellite Wandsworth in the latter half of the nineteenth century, suggesting a more important

9 1837 Brown, David (Wills and testaments Reference SC58/42/10, Paisley Sheriff Court) *ScotlandsPeople*.

10 1841 Brown, James (Census 573/35/27); 1851 Brown, Euphemia (Census 573/55/16); 1861 Brown, James S (Census 573/36/11) *ScotlandsPeople*. A number of 'Miss Browns' appear as dressmakers in town directories; some of these are verifiably not members of this family, but some may have been.

economic role for the Scotswomen relative to their husbands and sons.[11] Eleanor Gordon and Gwyneth Nair, examining middle-class women in nineteenth-century Glasgow, found these propertied Scottish women took surprisingly public roles in society. They were frequently accorded a substantial degree of power in businesses and other financial matters, sometimes while their husbands or fathers were still living.[12] As historians pry ever more deeply into the details of family life and finances in the nineteenth century, it becomes more and more evident that a great many women exercised significant economic autonomy.[13] Inspector Brown, whose wife Elizabeth had gone out to work for her living while her own father was alive and then continued to earn an income after her marriage, quite likely expected Elizabeth Cousland to act independently on behalf of her family.

Focusing on the legal arguments in cases relevant to Cousland's reveals the developing discourse regarding women and the nature of marriage in Victorian Britain, encompassing debates that led to acts regarding divorce (in England) and married women's property as well as considerations of settlement. Similar to the regulations regarding relief for the able-bodied unemployed, the language and assumptions of the poor law concerning married women did not necessarily reflect what Scots considered common sense.[14] In 1850, a woman was assumed to take on her husband's legal persona – including his poor law settlement – at marriage and to retain it throughout the rest of her life, even when widowed.[15] By the time Cousland's

11 D. Meredith and D. Oxley, 'Blood and Bone: Body Mass, Gender and Health Inequality in 19th Century British Families', University of Oxford *Discussion Papers in Economic and Social History* no. 118 (September 2013).

12 E. Gordon and G. Nair, *Public Lives: Women, Family and Society in Victorian Britain* (New Haven: Yale University Press, 2003), 161–6.

13 J. Maltby, '"The Wife's Administration of the Earnings"? Working-class Women and Savings in the Mid-Nineteenth Century', *Continuity and Change* 26:2 (2011).

14 L. Leneman, '"A Natural Foundation in Equity": Marriage and Divorce in Eighteenth and Nineteenth-Century Scotland', *Scottish Economic & Social History* 20:2 (2000): 199. See also B. Griffin, 'Class, Gender, and Liberalism in Parliament, 1868–82: The Case of the Married Women's Property Acts', *The Historical Journal* 46:1 (2003).

15 Most scholarship regarding coverture has addressed issues of property or citizenship (and exclusively addressing English law), but it is evident that settlement fell under the same set of (vague) legal rules. See M.P. Baldwin, 'Subject to Empire: Married

case was concluded in 1860, however, a woman's personal settlement was considered merely suspended throughout the duration of her marriage, to be restored to her upon widowhood. This changed interpretation of settlement developed from a series of poor-law-related arguments regarding women's legal competence, ability to head families, and generally to affect their own situations.

Any arguments regarding poor relief were also weighted with knowledge of cost and the desire to shift paupers off the parishes' rolls when possible, no matter what the rationale given. Nevertheless the change from an assumption of perpetual dependence to one of interrupted independence is significant, and congruent with developing historical interpretations of women's position in nineteenth-century Scotland. The existence of these debates around the proper settlement of widows argues that ideas about gender and marriage were far from uniformly settled in favor of women's disability. In the guise of arguments regarding settlement, bureaucrats and judges were articulating their beliefs relevant to their own wives, sisters, and daughters. Elizabeth Cousland's poor law case responded to dual pressures from Westminster and conflicting local interpretations to develop a national practice that reflected Scottish values.

Determining Settlement

The primary issue in Cousland's case was the question of settlements, which was assumed by the New Poor Law to be readily determined.[16] Only one section of the ninety-two-section law defined a rule regarding settlement, setting the five-year rule for gaining a residential settlement.

Women and the British Nationality and Status of Aliens Act', *Journal of British Studies* 40:4 (Oct. 2001): 522–56; A. Erikson, 'Coverture and Capitalism', *History Workshop Journal* 59:1 (Spring 2005): 1–16; L. Tabili, 'Outsiders in the Land of Their Birth: Exogamy, Citizenship, and Identity in War and Peace', *Journal of British Studies* 44:4 (Oct. 2005): 796–815.

16 *Poor Law (Scotland)*, Sec. 70.

Every other rule about settlement was not articulated but assumed, and rested on the Law of Settlement. This English law predated the New Poor Law by centuries and sat uneasily on Scottish tradition. It was supposed to define exactly to which parish an individual belonged, but was simultaneously quite straightforward and maddeningly vague.[17] It recognised two primary types of settlement: birth and residential. Every Scot was born with a settlement in the parish of his birth, which the new law made irrevocable by omitting any suggestion it could be lost.[18] If he should happen to move out of his birth parish after reaching adulthood and live in a single parish for five years without requesting relief, the birth settlement would be suspended in favor of a residential (sometimes also called industrial) settlement in the new place.[19] To maintain his acquired settlement he had to live in the new parish for at least one year in five without begging or applying for relief.[20] As shown in the previous chapter, relief for unemployment during an economic crisis, such as what McMurrich received in 1848, complicated settlement. Unemployment relief was not legitimate, the courts determined, so in some cases receiving such relief was held not to have affected the acquisition of a residential settlement. In other cases, getting such relief was a deciding factor against a settlement. If a person was absent from a parish in which he had a residential settlement for four years and one day (and so could not meet the 1 year–in–5 requirement), the residential settlement was lost and his birthplace was again liable for his relief. Every individual, on any given day, had just one parish of settlement – the trick was to properly determine which parish that was.

The forgoing description uses the male pronoun advisedly. Although the Act of 1845 specified, 'every word importing the Masculine Gender shall

17 'The Law of Settlement', *Poor Law Magazine* 3 (Nov. 1860): 120–1; *Greig* v *Carse and Waite* [usually and hereafter referenced as *Prestonpans* v *Dunse*] in 'Supreme Court Decisions', *Poor Law Magazine for Scotland* 2 (May 1860): 469.

18 *Poor Law (Scotland)*, Sec. 77.

19 'Law of Settlement', 121; House of Commons, 'Report from the Select Committee on Poor Removal; together with the Proceedings of the Committee, Minutes of Evidence, and Appendix', July 1879, 961.

20 *Poor Law (Scotland)*, Sec. 76.

extend to a Female as well as a Male', and women were at least half of the applicants for relief, in practice paupers were assumed to be adult males.[21] The principle of settlement rested on the possibility of removal, the physical relocation of paupers to the parishes responsible for maintaining them.[22] The Act required that in the case of a removal to Ireland or England, the 'poor person, his wife, and such of his children as may not have gained a settlement in Scotland' would be sent away.[23] The law encouraged parishes to exchange funds in lieu of removal, and arranging to pay and receive such bills were a large part of Inspector Brown's responsibilities. The spectre of removal nevertheless haunted legal debates regarding settlement, bringing with it the potential for forcibly separated spouses and abandoned children. Thus, married women and children derived a settlement assigned to them from the person responsible for them, superseding any settlement based on that dependent's own personal history. Such 'derivative' settlements were supposed to ensure that removal would not split up families.

Alas for the Law, applicants' lives did not reliably fit into the model imagined by those who wrote it, and the New Poor Law's passage was followed by years of variable policies as the theory of the law was worked out in practice. As illustrated in Chapter 3, women, in particular, applied for relief when they were living outside the model male-headed family, and caused consternation for poor law officials. Historians examining the English poor law have explored the conflicting gender dimensions of the English law as women were variously (and sometimes simultaneously) defined as able-bodied workers, inherently disabled workers, and dependent domestic creatures with no proper economic role at all.[24] In Scotland, where

21 *Poor Law (Scotland)*, Sec. 2.

22 *Poor Law (Scotland)*, Sec. 72.

23 *Poor Law (Scotland)*, Sec. 77.

24 P. Thane, 'Women and the Poor Law in Victorian and Edwardian England', *History Workshop* 6 (1978): 30–51; A. Clark, 'The New Poor Law and the Breadwinner Wage: Contrasting Assumptions', *Journal of Social History* 34:2 (2000): 261–81; M. Levine-Clark, 'Engendering Relief: Women, Ablebodiedness, and the New Poor Law in Early Victorian England' *Journal of Women's History* 11:4 (2000): 107–30; L.F. Cody, 'The Politics of Illegitimacy in an Age of Reform: Women, Reproduction, and Political Economy in England's New Poor Law of 1834', *Journal of Women's History* 11:4 (2000): 131–56; M. Levine-Clark, 'The Gendered Economy of Family

poor relief was available only to those physically unable to work, the ideological tension over whether or not women ought to be self-supporting was somewhat removed from the question since able-bodied unmarried women were held to the same standards as men. Conflicting interpretations of Settlement Law regarding women who were not explicitly included in it opened wide avenues for inspectors to argue that an undesirable pauper did not belong to their parish.

In the McMurrich-Cousland case, there were a large number of parishes that Inspector Brown could consider for the family's settlement. Cousland's first husband, James Hutton, was born in Eastwood, Renfrewshire. The couple (Hutton and Cousland) obtained a residential settlement in Bonhill in August 1843, and two of their three children were born in that parish. Peter McMurrich, Cousland's second partner, was born in Cardross – where he was first married and his son John was born – and they migrated into the town of Paisley in 1843. He lived on Oakshaw Street in Paisley Burgh Parish for two years, during which he and Cousland joined forces. In February or March 1845 they moved to Gauze Street in Abbey Parish, where they lived until May 1849. Then they moved back into Paisley Burgh Parish on Moncrieff Street (only a block or two from the poor house and Inspector Brown's home) until McMurrich's death in September 1850.[25] Shifting between the two Paisley parishes, they had not gained a residential settlement in either. Cousland and McMurrich's three girls were born in the town (one in Abbey and two in the Burgh parish) and would have birth settlements there when they reached adulthood. Finally, Cousland and her oldest child were born in Denny, Stirlingshire.

Each of the six parishes could have responsibility for some or all of the family. Inspector Brown wrote to the inspectors of Cardross and Bonhill shortly after Cousland applied.[26] Bonhill, which had reimbursed Abbey for support given in 1847–8, admitted that the Hutton children had a settlement there due to their father's residential settlement and because

Liability: Intergenerational Relationships and Poor Law Relief in England's Black Country, 1871–1911', *Journal of British Studies* 45:1 (2006): 72–89.

25 Statement 4402.

26 'Arbitration Cases', 184.

they had previously admitted liability.[27] Cardross admitted liability for McMurrich and his son John, but also reported the nature of McMurrich and Cousland's relationship and refused any support for Cousland or her children. In the eyes of the poor law McMurrich and Cousland were not in fact a family, but only cohabiting adults with no legal relationship. When Inspector Brown realised that Cousland was legally Hutton's widow (not McMurrich's), he wrote again to Bonhill, asking that Cousland be added to their role as Hutton's relict.

That parish agreed again to an obligation for James Hutton's children, but refused support for his widow, citing the case of *Crieff* v *Foulis Wester*. This case determined in 1842 (before the passage of the New Poor Law) that a widow could acquire (and thus by implication lose) a residential settlement after her husband's death, and that the resulting settlement would derive to her minor children. The Lord Ordinary in that case argued that a widowed mother, 'whose industry benefits the parish she resorts to', should have a settlement in her own right.[28] Cousland had been absent from Bonhill for more than four years and a day, thus under the principle of *Crieff* v *Foulis Wester* had lost the residential settlement in that parish. Yet in this case only the widow's settlement was affected, while the parish was still willing to support the children.[29]

When Inspector Brown determined that McMurrich and Cousland were not married, it became evident that the children in the household would have different settlements among them. Illegitimate children derived their settlement from their mother; if Cousland had a residential settlement

27 Archibald and Ann Hutton would have birth settlements in Bonhill when they forisfamiliated, but this admission was explicitly based on their father's settlement. 'Arbitration Cases', 185.

28 *Crieff* v *Little Dunkeld and Monzievaird*, 19 July 1842, *The Scottish Jurist: Reports of Cases Decided in the Supreme Courts of Scotland and in the House of Lords on Appeal from Scotland, &c., &c*, by W.H. Dunbar, et al., vol. XIV (Edinburgh: M. Andersen & Co., 1842), 610–16.

29 Throughout this case it is clear not only that parishes drew different conclusions about how the Law of Settlement should be applied but also had differing levels of concern for absolute accuracy. A sub-plot in the tale was an incident when Abbey parish mistakenly charged Bonhill for support of the whole family, received the payment, and later had to reimburse the error. 'Arbitration Cases', 184.

in Bonhill in her own right, the relief Bonhill provided in 1848 was sufficient to maintain that settlement in spite of her relocation to Paisley and Bonhill would be responsible for the younger (McMurrich) children as well as the Huttons. Debate over this point may have been the subject of the seven letters Brown wrote to the Bonhill inspector in 1850 and 1851.[30] Bonhill finally agreed to take the case to arbitration in October 1851, only a few days before 14-month-old Jean, the youngest McMurrich child, died.[31] No other parish agreed to participate in arbitration with Paisley and Bonhill, however, and the correspondence was suspended. Without an infant in the house Cousland was no longer considered 'disabled', but in consideration of the large family of children too young to work they were kept on Paisley's roll of outdoor poor at 14/- per month.[32]

A decision from the Court of Session a year later threw new doubt onto the McMurrich children's claim against Bonhill. Since 1845, Scottish courts had found that even very young fatherless children had birth settlements that were obligated to support them in case their parents could not. The 1851 case of *Barbour* v *Adamson* confirmed that children in a single family with no father present could have settlements split between different parishes. In this case, the parishes of Glasgow City and Lochwinnoch, Renfrewshire, contested over the support of a family after the father was transported for theft. Of his five children, only the two youngest were born in Glasgow. The Sheriff's Court that first heard the case determined that Lochwinnoch, the parish of the father's settlement, was responsible for the entire family. On appeal, the Court of Session declared that Glasgow City must support the children born there, and that the other children were settled on the parishes of their births.[33] The explanation given for this was that children were a part of their father's family and their need for relief was wrapped

30 'Arbitration Cases', 185. Only the dates, not the contents, of these letters have survived.

31 No cause of death was given.

32 HCP Relief Committee, vol. 7–27, 16 March 1852.

33 *Adamson* v *Barbour*, 30 May 1853; *Reports of Scotch Appeals and Writs of Error, Together with Peerage, Divorce, and Practice Cases in the House of Lords*, vol. I (Edinburgh, 1855), 376–84. Also *Adamson* v *Barbour*, 30 May 1853, *Reports of Cases*, vol. II, 86–91.

up in his. When the father was absent, whether due to death, desertion, enlistment or transportation, he was no longer available to be the conduit through which relief flowed to the children. Abandoned and orphaned children became paupers in their own rights, with settlement in their own birth parishes. Since the Hutton/McMurrich children were neither abandoned nor orphaned, this principle was not at first applied to their case.

However, in November 1852 the case of *Hay* v *Scott* built on *Barbour* v *Adamson* to conclude that a widow's derivative settlement from her late husband did not in turn derive to subsequent children born out of wedlock; such children would also be settled on the parish of their own birth.[34] These two cases worked to split up responsibility for the Cousland/Hutton/McMurrich family among various parishes. Even if Bonhill was Cousland's settlement, it was not responsible for her McMurrich children. Instead, each parish of the children's birth was liable for them. Paisley Burgh was thus the parish of settlement for 7-year-old Margaret McMurrich, and Abbey would be responsible for 5-year-old Grace. Bonhill admitted settlement for the three Hutton children, and John McMurrich continued to be supported by his own and his father's birthplace, Cardross.

The settlements were only of theoretical importance, because James Brown took no new action. Paisley parish continued to carry the family on their roll. Cousland had taken several calico printers in as lodgers to the family's two-roomed flat, and all three of her boys were tearing (quite likely for the lodgers), so even before Jean's death the parish aliment was supplemental rather than the family's only resource.[35]

34 *Hay* v *Scott*, 23 Nov. 1852, *Reports of Cases decided in the Court of Session, Teind Court, Court of Exchequer, Court of Justiciary and in The House of Lords*, from 12 Nov. 1852 to 20 July 1853, vol. II (Edinburgh, 1853), 36–8.

35 The *Poor Law Magazine* report maintained that the children of the family 'continued in receipt of relief' from Paisley throughout the duration of the 1850s. Details regarding the size and frequency of payments have not been identified. 'Arbitration Cases', 184. Information about the lodgers and employment from *Census of Great Britain* 1851, Paisley Middle Church Enumeration District 12, 16. Size of the flat determined from *Census of Scotland* 1881, Paisley (Middle Church) Enumeration District 56, 3.

Paisley was offered a hope of relief from the expense when, in 1853, a bombshell decision created shockwaves across the Scottish poor law system. Inspector Ebenezer Adamson of Glasgow City parish carried an appeal of his case against Lochwinnoch to the House of Lords as *Adamson* v *Barbour*, insisting that his parish was not responsible for the children of a transported father whose settlement was elsewhere, even if they had been born in his parish. This appeal moved the decision about derivative settlements in the Scottish poor law out of Scotland, to be decided by justices more familiar with English precedent.

The Lord Chancellor, Baron Cranworth, declared in the May 1853 decision on *Adamson* v *Barbour* that derivative settlements – whether in England or Scotland – were not created by statute law. From the start of the poor law, however, in accordance with the principles of coverture, '[I]t was assumed that the wife must be with her husband, that children must remain with their father; and that any settlement gained by him was gained, not for himself alone, but for all his family.'[36] Cranworth believed this principle applied to a birth settlement as well as a residential one, drew on precedent from both England and Scotland to support his position, and concluded,

> by the law of Scotland … legitimate children during nonage are to be considered as so far identified with their father, that it is to <u>his</u> place of settlement, however constituted that they are to look for relief when they are so circumstanced as to be entitled to relief at all. And I came to this conclusion because any other interpretation of the laws of settlement would or might lead to a harsh and violent severance of the domestic tie.[37]

The *Adamson* v *Barbour* decision, based on a fear of family separation through removal, thus established in 1853 a new policy that an entire pauper family must have one settlement, based on the male head of the household. In Paisley, for the Cousland/McMurrich family, it meant that the McMurrich children and their mother (not to mention her Hutton children) should not have different settlements. Without willingness to

36 *Adamson* v *Barbour*, *Reports of Scotch Appeals*, 378.
37 *Adamson* v *Barbour*, *Reports of Scotch Appeals*, 382–3, emphasis in original.

cooperate from other parishes, however, Brown seems not to have pursued any new action in the immediate wake of *Adamson* v *Barbour*.

Nevertheless, the case unleashed a flood of poor law decisions from the Scottish courts in the years that followed that ultimately had bearing on Cousland's case in Paisley. The first, *Gibson* v *Murray*, in June 1854, explicitly addressed the question of widows' settlements and how they would transfer to children. In the case, a widow's late husband, born in England, had no settlement in Scotland. The decision in *Adamson* v *Barbour* prohibited the children of the union from being settled in the Scottish parish of their own birth. The question became, could a married woman somehow retain a birth settlement in Scotland if her husband did not provide her with a derived one?[38]

The justices of the Second Division of the Court of Session revisited some arguments from *Crieff* v *Foulis Wester*, including the idea that the death of a husband dissolved an entire family, which was then possibly reconstituted as a new family with the widowed mother as its head, from whom settlement could flow.[39] One of the justices considering *Gibson*, Lord Curriehill, argued against this idea by pointing out the legal disabilities a widow still suffered,

> The death of a father leaving children in pupillarity has not the effect of transferring to their surviving mother the rights and powers of a father. She is not their guardian, and cannot interfere in the management of their affairs. She does not succeed to them in the event of their death without issue. The law does not view her residence as their home; and their tutors, if they have any, regulate their education, and fix their place of residence. And although, while they are under seven years of age, the law generally prefers the widowed mother's claim to the custody of the persons of the fatherless children, yet this is only to secure for them a continuance of maternal care during their tenderest years. Even then she cannot insist upon continuing that charge, if she enter into a second marriage, or do anything which unfits her for the charge. … The position of pauper children, therefore, in reference to their mother, is not materially altered by the death of their father; and I can see no principle for

38 *Gibson* v *Murray*, 13 June 1854; *The Scottish Jurist: Reports of Cases Decided in the Supreme Courts of Scotland, and in The House of Lords on Appeal from Scotland*, vol. XXVI (Edinburgh, 1854), 489–93.

39 *Gibson* v *Murray*, 490.

> holding that event has, *per se*, and instantly, the effect of depriving them of the settlement, whatever it may be, which previously belonged to them.[40]

The Lord Justice-Clerk agreed with Curriehill, admitting, 'it seems to me to be entirely repugnant to the leading principle of the relation of marriage formed between the spouses, to hold that the maiden settlement of the wife can be the settlement of the children of the marriage'.[41] The justices' assumption regarding marriage in this case was that women had an inherent disability in the relationship and could not function as male-substitutes in the absence of their husbands. Their opinions in the case did not hold sway, however. *Gibson* v *Murray* ultimately concluded that without an identifiable Scottish settlement for a father, even legitimate children could derive a settlement from their mother.

A case decided only a few days later, *Hay* v *Thomson and Manson*, set a precedent of female dependence that was to be immensely significant for Elizabeth Cousland. The case concerned a widow without a residential settlement either from her husband or acquired after his death. The court determined quite readily that marriage united man and wife to the extent that she took on his birthplace, and it was held 'that the parish of the husband's and not of the wife's birth, is liable for the relief of the pauper widow'.[42] In arguments the Lord Ordinary imagined a family very similar to Cousland's, with multiple young children born in different parishes (there were in fact no children involved in the *Hay* v *Thomson and Manson* case). He described the havoc that would arise from dissolving a derivative settlement at death and assigning those children to their own birth parishes, while the widow was settled into her own birth parish. He summarised, 'This would lead to that very separation of the family, and to those evils which are to be avoided in the case of the children, by holding them derivatively settled in their father's birth parish.'[43] While women were acknowledged to be able to affect their own settlement in the years after they were widowed, the *Barbour* bugaboo of divided families ensured that

40 *Gibson* v *Murray*, 491.
41 *Gibson* v *Murray*, 492.
42 *Hay* v *Thomson and Manson*, 23 June 1854; *The Scottish Jurist*, vol. XXVI, 541.
43 *Hay* v *Thomson and Manson*, 23 June 1854; *The Scottish Jurist*, vol. XXVI, 542.

at the moment of her husband's death any woman (with or without children) was identified by her relationships as wife and mother rather than her individual experiences.

Six months after the *Gibson* v *Murray* and *Hay* v *Thomson and Manson* decisions, and shortly after the youngest Hutton child turned twelve, James Shaw Brown was pulled into the debate over widows' settlements. His neighbor Inspector, Robert Robertson of Abbey Parish, insisted that Paisley Burgh was responsible for the settlement of Cornelia Kerr Boyd, the English-born widow of Matthew Boyd. The late Mr Boyd had been born in Renfrew parish and moved to Paisley to ultimately become Provost of the Burgh. After his death his widow returned to her native England for a number of years, came back to settle in Abbey Parish in 1848, and fell into poverty. Abbey Parish, certain that the widow was not their responsibility, brought the Inspectors of both Paisley and Renfrew parishes into the Renfrewshire Sheriff's Court. The sheriff, unable to arrive at a satisfactory conclusion, pushed the case upward to the Court of Session where it was heard in December 1854. At both levels the claim against Paisley was quickly dismissed as neither the widow nor her husband had lived long enough in the Burgh Parish to acquire a residential settlement. The question was, could this respectable Englishwoman be banished to her own birthplace, or had she acquired her husband's birth settlement along with her marriage vows? The sheriff-substitute hesitantly determined that she had.

> He has formed his opinion from the consideration that the relations of a wife to her husband are much more intimate than those of children to a father; and he grounds it on the assumption that the wife has not <u>acquired</u> this settlement since her husband's death, but has only <u>retained</u> that which she actually possessed during his life. He thinks that on her marriage she acquired all the rights of personal <u>status</u> which her husband had, and that this right of settlement by birth was one of them.[44]

At the Court of Session the Lord President – the highest justice in the nation – was much more confident in confirming the sheriff's decision by referring to both *Hay* v *Scott* and *Hay* v *Thomson and Manson* to

44 *Robertson* v *Brown and Stewart* 12 Dec. 1854; *The Scottish Jurist: Reports of Cases Decided in the Supreme Courts of Scotland, and in The House of Lords on Appeal from Scotland*, vol. XXVII (Edinburgh, 1855), 59, emphasis in original.

declare, '[I]t is now a settled point that the widow takes the benefit of the husband's settlement whether residential or birth.'[45] Lord Ivory, who was also hearing the case, came to a similar conclusion but added the caveat, 'The doctrine of the union of marriage I could not carry the length the Lord Ordinary has done. It is dissolved at death, and we cannot, by supposing what might have happened, get out of the difficulty.'[46] In spite of this hesitation regarding the duration of the marriage bond, the Court reaffirmed the principle that an impoverished widow in last resort relied on her husband's birth settlement, not her own. Her own personal history was erased by marriage.

These decisions diminished the effect of women's experiences on their legal status, contrary to the trend toward women's economic autonomy that was reflected in Inspector Brown's own family life. Women in nineteenth-century Scotland, as Lord Curriehill detailed in *Gibson* v *Murray*, had the same legal disadvantages as elsewhere in Britain and across Europe, but men in Scotland clearly had personal experience with women who were capable and independent. Eleanor Gordon and Gwyneth Nair found in Glasgow,

> Women's money supported family firms; women were major investors in enterprises like the railways. Some women ran successful small (or occasionally large) businesses. Women owned property; they employed lawyers and accountants; they administered large estates. … The middle-class women of Victorian Glasgow were by no means without money, control of money, and the power that goes with it.[47]

Middle-class Scotsmen like Brown and members of the parochial board realised the expediency and propriety of *femme covert* during marriage, but all evidence suggests that many of them also accepted the idea of women with a legal and economic identity that was independent of a husband or father. *Adamson* v *Barbour*, which the Lord Justice-Clerk hearing *Gibson* v *Murray* denounced as 'introducing a new [English] rule into the

45 *Robertson* v *Brown and Stewart*, 61.

46 *Robertson* v *Brown and Stewart*, 61.

47 E. Gordon and G. Nair, 'The Economic Role of Middle-Class Women in Victorian Glasgow', *Women's History Review* 9:4 (2000): 810. It is quite probable that men elsewhere in Britain and across Europe had similar experiences with women.

law of Scotland' and as being based on expediency that unsettled all legal principles, disrupted the Scottish inspectors' understanding of the legal landscape they inhabited.[48] It united as a single unit families that were previously treated as related-but-divisible individuals.

Reviving Cousland's Case

Inspector Brown's actions regarding Elizabeth Cousland modeled the process preferred by the Society of Poor Law Inspectors. Support for the family was clearly in contest, but Brown did not move the case into court. Instead, Cousland received the relief she needed from Paisley and the inspector pursued new avenues for their relief as cases made them apparent. His active interest in the Cousland case revived in late 1856, spurred by two factors. First, the case of *Hay* v *Thomson and Beattie* (May 1856) settled definitively that an illegitimate child took the settlement of its mother, no matter how that settlement was obtained.[49] For Brown, this was a new opportunity to find support from outside Paisley for the McMurrich children. Secondly, it is possible that he saw further expenses for Paisley from the family on the horizon. In early 1857, Cousland had a new partner.[50]

Inspector Brown began to focus on establishing Cousland's settlement in light of the decisions since *Adamson* v *Barbour*. He looked with new interest at birth settlements for Cousland's first husband, James Hutton, and in February 1857 for the first time also considered Cousland's own birth

48 *Gibson* v *Murray*, 492.

49 *Hay* v *Thomson, Laing, and Others, The Scottish Jurist: Reports of Cases Decided in the Supreme Courts of Scotland, and in the House of Lords in Appeal from Scotland*, vol. 28 by G. Fordyce, et al. (Edinburgh: M. Anderson, 1856), 191–7. John Hay was the Poor Law Inspector for the City of Edinburgh Parish and – from the frequency with which his name appears in court cases – was not as reluctant as Inspector Brown to bring cases into court.

50 Statement 4402. Cousland's romantic history is deduced from the birth of her child in October 1857.

parish, Denny, as potentially liable for her support. If Hutton's residential settlement in Bonhill was not admitted, perhaps one of the two birth settlements had been revived. Denny's inspector confirmed that Cousland was born in his parish, but refused any reimbursement to Paisley on the grounds that the widow must rely on her late husband's settlement. James Hutton had been born in Eastwood, Renfrewshire, and Brown also wrote to that parish's inspector, who refused payment with no explanation.[51]

At the same time, Paisley was embroiled in another case that had a bearing on Cousland's position. Though reluctant to carry cases into court, Inspector Brown did regularly seek judicial opinion regarding knotty cases with his fellow inspectors to determine proper settlement. The second-ever issue of *The Poor Law Magazine* included an opinion rendered by Sheriff Bell of the Lanarkshire Sheriff's Court on a case contested between Inspector Brown, Robert Robertson of Abbey Parish, and Ebenezer Adamson of Glasgow City.

The Inspectors agreed on the following order of events in this case: The pauper was born Margaret Lochhead in Abbey Parish in 1808. At 18 years old she married Charles Lang, a lifelong resident of Paisley Burgh Parish. She moved into a residence with him in that parish, obtaining with her marriage a derivative settlement in Paisley Burgh. Lang died in 1835 and his widow returned to Abbey Parish, but retained the settlement in Paisley.[52] If she had remained a widow and lost all residential settlements, her settlement of last resort would have been in Paisley, based on her husband's birth there.

However, it was difficult to survive as a widow in nineteenth-century Scotland and she was still a young woman. In 1838 she married Andrew Brown. Brown was Irish by birth, immigrating at age 8 with his parents to Scotland in 1817. He resided in Abbey parish with his family, securing a residential settlement that derived to Margaret with their marriage. The couple did not stay in Paisley to maintain the residential settlement, however. Just a year after their marriage they removed to Glasgow, after which

51 'Arbitration Cases', *Poor Law Magazine* 3, 185.

52 This and all other details of Margaret Lochhead Brown's case come from Mr Sheriff Bell, 'Opinion', *Poor Law Magazine* 1 (October 1858): 94–100. I've referred to Mrs Brown by her given name primarily to avoid confusion with Inspector Brown in the narrative.

Andrew almost immediately enlisted in the 64th regiment of Foot. When they were out of Paisley for four years and one day the settlement in Paisley was lost. Because Andrew Brown was an immigrant, the loss of a residential settlement meant that he and his family could be removed to Ireland if they applied for relief before another settlement was secured.

Andrew Brown was sent abroad soon after he enlisted and did not return to Scotland in his lifetime, dying at sea between Bombay and Chatham in 1853. Margaret, unsupported by her husband for fifteen years, found work as a fringer and winder, living in a series of lodgings in Glasgow City parish. She was usually able to support herself, but for a month in 1847 and three weeks in 1850 she was ill and applied to the City Parish for temporary relief, which was granted. Her final illness (diagnosed only by her primary symptom, dropsy), began less than a month after her husband's death in 1853 and rendered her unable to work. In May 1854, then 46 years old, she returned to Paisley Burgh, where she was supported by her relatives. She became either too ill or too expensive for those relatives to maintain and applied for relief from Paisley on 6 February 1855. Inspector Brown was certain that Margaret Brown was a deserving pauper, but one who did not properly belong to Paisley Burgh Parish. He suggested to Ebenezer Adamson that Glasgow City ought to support Mrs Brown 'in respect of a residential settlement'. Glasgow refused to admit the pauper, 'and subsequently a claim was made on Abbey, the parish of the pauper's birth, which was also refused'.[53]

In both these applications to Glasgow City Parish and to Abbey, Inspector Brown was claiming a settlement for Margaret in her own right, rather than relying on the derivative settlements from either of her late husbands. He claimed that, first, 'a married woman whose husband is a foreigner and has no settlement in Scotland, may acquire a settlement for herself by her own residence, apart from her husband during his lifetime'.[54] From this reasoning, Glasgow City Parish should have reimbursed Paisley for Margaret's costs based on her many years of residence there, in spite of her concurrent marriage to a husband who did not have a Glasgow City

53 Bell, 'Opinion', 95.

54 This argument was based on *Thomson* v *Knox*, 28 June 1850. Bell, 'Opinion', 95–6.

settlement. Secondly, he argued, 'if there is no residential settlement open to the pauper, the parish of her own birth is primarily liable'.[55] Under this argument, Abbey Parish was responsible for Margaret because of her birth there, just as it would have been for a male pauper.

The Glaswegian inspector, Adamson, maintained his perspective that a family settlement derived inevitably from a male head and countered with an interpretation that in fact a woman could not obtain a residential settlement of her own while apart from her living husband. He continued that soldiers were exempt from residency requirements because their absence was compulsory. Andrew Brown, therefore, in spite of his fifteen-year absence, had never lost his residential settlement in Abbey Parish. Margaret Brown, in Adamson's estimation, had her settlement in Abbey Parish because it derived from her late second husband, not through her own birth.[56]

Robert Robertson, Abbey Parish's inspector, brought in a point the Paisley inspector had neglected to consider: that Margaret had been married twice. Robertson agreed with Brown that a married woman could acquire a settlement apart from her husband, in the peculiar circumstance of marriage to an immigrant and subsequent abandonment, and he also maintained that enlistment was itself a voluntary act, therefore Andrew Brown's absence was not involuntary and he had relinquished his Abbey settlement while in India. However, Robertson then brought to bear cases from the early 1850s, including *Hay* v *Scott*, *Adamson* v *Barbour* and *Hay* v *Thomson*, culminating in the 1854 *Robertson* v *Stewart and Brown* decision regarding Cornelia Kerr Boyd. These cases maintained that a widow reverted to her husband's birth settlement, and Inspector Roberson added the claim that if a second husband had no birth settlement then the first husband's settlement should apply. Thus, he argued that death and even remarriage did not necessarily sever the bond of a derivative settlement. Robertson allowed, therefore, that Margaret as a deserted wife may have acquired a residential settlement in Glasgow City Parish in her own right (that point would have to be settled by Sheriff Bell, the arbitrator), but she had lost both potential settlements in Abbey: her own birth settlement

55 He based this argument on *Hay* v *Skene*, 13 June 1850. Bell, 'Opinion', 96.

56 Bell, 'Opinion', 96.

through the act of marriage, and her second husband's residential settlement due to his long absence from the parish. Her first derivative settlement, in Paisley, had to be seriously considered.

Sheriff Bell, on hearing all sides, did not fully agree with any of the positions. He thought it was possible that an abandoned married woman could obtain her own residential settlement – the point was as yet undetermined by law and would continue to plague the courts for the rest of the century – but Margaret Brown had not in fact gained such a settlement due to her repeated illnesses.[57] When she drew casual relief in 1847 and 1850, she interrupted her progress toward earning a residential settlement in Glasgow, regardless of whether or not that settlement was possible.

The question of which of her husbands' birth settlement should apply (given that Margaret had certainly not gained a residential settlement of her own) was more easily settled in Bell's mind. Andrew Brown had voluntarily abandoned his family through enlisting, he maintained, and thus lost his residential settlement in Scotland. Similarly, Margaret had voluntarily surrendered the derivative settlement gained from her first husband when she remarried. Robertson's theory that she could revert to a first husband's settlement Bell found invalid. This would mean that Margaret, Scottish born, should be tied to her second late husband's birth settlement in Ireland. In addition to the potential injustice of removing a native Scotswoman to another nation, there was no hope of reclaiming Paisley's costs from an Irish parish. If at all possible, a properly Scottish settlement had to be found for the widow. Thus, Bell pronounced that the law did not in fact *end* a woman's own personal settlement at marriage: it only *suspended* it. When or if she no longer had a derivative or residential settlement, her own birth settlement would again become active. The Sheriff's final decision was that Abbey Parish had to bear the cost of care for Margaret Brown because of her birth there.

Bell delivered his opinion in his chambers on 15 September 1858. When he did, Elizabeth Cousland was tending to her seventh child, a boy named

57 Between 1875 and 1902 there were six (often contradictory) Supreme Court decisions on the issue of settlement for deserted wives in Scotland. *The Scots Digest of the Cases Decided in the Supreme Courts of Scotland, 1873 to 1904*, vol. II (Edinburgh, 1905), 1562–3.

John McFarlane. She still was not married, and the infant's father, also named John McFarlane, had died soon after his son's birth in October 1857.[58] Armed with Bell's decision that a widow could fall on her own birth settlement, Inspector Brown reinvigorated his quest for a proper settlement for Cousland's brood. Perhaps convinced that he would not persuade any individual parish to agree unilaterally to responsibility for the family, he began attempting to arrange an extra-judicial settlement similar to the one regarding Margaret Brown. He obtained agreement from the inspectors of Cardross, Bonhill, and Eastwood to participate in an arbitration overseen by the MP for Greenock and author of *Treaties on the Scottish Poor Law*, Alexander Murray Dunlop.[59] Denny's parochial board twice refused to join with the other parishes. Even when directly requested by Dunlop to do so in early May 1860, they 'instruct[ed] the Inspector to refuse to join, or to have anything to do with this arrangement, or arbitration'.[60] At last, the other four parishes agreed to move forward without Denny's cooperation.

The inspector for Cardross likely had little fear going into the arbitration that Cousland's settlement would be found to be in his parish. Cardross had already admitted liability for Peter McMurrich and had paid support as needed for McMurrich's one son born in wedlock. Dunlop concluded that because McMurrich and Cousland were not legally married, neither the mother nor the children had gained a derivative settlement from the father's parish. While McMurrich had provided financial and presumably emotional support to Cousland and her children, that relationship did nothing to alter her legal status. Without a marriage, other social and biological relationships had no effect on settlement.[61]

Dunlop had to be more nuanced in his analysis of Bonhill's position. Cousland and her husband Hutton had held a residential settlement there, and two of their three children were born in the parish. Dunlop maintained that the derivative settlements enjoyed by children were separate

58 Statement 4402.

59 J. Foster, *Members of Parliament, Scotland, 1857–82*, 2nd edn (London, 1882), 116.

60 Denny Parochial Board Minutes, 10 Jan. 1859, 14 May 1860, Falkirk Archives A821.00/02.

61 The development of this precedent was summarised in, 'On Birth Settlement', *Poor Law Magazine* 11 (Jan. 1869): 145–6.

from those granted to wives or widows and that Bonhill's admission of liability for the Hutton children in 1848 did not imply any responsibility for their mother, Hutton's widow, and therefore not for her subsequent children out of wedlock. Cousland's own residential settlement in Bonhill, gained in tandem with her first husband, was held to have lapsed due to her absence after 1844, as permitted in *Crieff* v *Foulis Wester*. The legitimate children of her marriage, however, continued to derive their settlement from their late father until they were old enough to be forisfamiliated. This decision, separating a woman from both her late husband's and her legitimate children's settlements, may have been simply legal contortions to prevent parishes having to pay for an irregular family's support. However, it was also a salvo in the argument regarding women's settlements and a challenge to the *Adamson* v *Barbour* principle of settling an entire family in the same parish.

With Cardross and Bonhill managed, Dunlop was left with only Eastwood to consider, which he disposed of in a sentence. Yet that sentence was dependent on a Supreme Court case that had been concluded only months earlier and overturned a half-decade of decisions since *Hay* v *Thomson*. From the arguments advanced in the *Robertson* v *Stewart and Brown* and Margaret Lochhead Brown cases, both of which Paisley was involved with and which overlapped chronologically with Cousland's case, it was reasonable for Inspector Brown to expect that Hutton's birth parish, Eastwood, would be responsible for his widow. By the time Cousland's case came to arbitration, however, the legal landscape had changed. The case of *Prestonpans* v *Dunse*, heard before the Scottish Supreme Court in February 1860, determined, 'A widow who has lost a residential settlement possessed by her late husband at his death, and has not acquired another by her own residence or remarriage, has, on falling into poverty, her settlement in the parish of her own birth, and not in the parish of her deceased husband's birth.'[62]

The arguments in support of this decision were vehement regarding the capacity of women to affect and maintain their own settlements. They

62 *Prestonpans* v *Dunse*, 420–1; 'Arbitration Cases', 186.

included this statement from John Waite, Poor Law Inspector for the parish of Dunse, worth quoting at length:

> The pervading idea which forms the foundation of the whole argument for [linking a widow to her husband's birth settlement] is, a supposed identification of husband and wife, enduring even after the death of the husband.
>
> It is understood that this was, at one time, a doctrine of the law of Hindostan, but the defender must take leave to deny that it ever was a part of the law of Scotland. It is common enough to hear it said, that during the subsistence of a marriage, the personality of a wife is sunk in that of the husband, and the saying is undoubtedly true, in so far, at all events, as the law of settlement is concerned. But it is equally true, that on the husband's death, the *persona standi* of the widow again takes place. She becomes again a free woman, at least equally mistress of herself as before marriage, and equally capable of acquiring, or of losing a settlement. Why then should her future settlement be made to depend not upon her own acts, and upon facts connected with her own individual history, but upon vague and uncertain conjectures as to what would have been the settlement of her deceased husband if he had survived?[63]

It was argued in contrast that 'so long as [a pauper] remains a widow, and does not acquire for herself a new settlement, she is to be so identified with her late husband that her settlement is to be regulated in the same manner as if he were still alive and residing with her'.[64] The written arguments for both sides were laid before the whole court, who submitted six opinions between the thirteen justices.

The minority justices based their arguments by and large on the legally slippery term of settlement and what exactly was 'derived' to a wife and then a widow. Their assumption was that the woman's legal persona was extinguished by marriage: 'The right which she acquires through her marriage is a right to all the contingent rights that belong to him'.[65] They thus developed interpretations of what 'would have come into operation had <u>he</u> been the pauper', and statements such as, 'the widow is, derivatively just the husband surviving'.[66] They were concerned with the settlement of any

63 *Prestonpans* v *Dunse*, 424.
64 *Prestonpans* v *Dunse*, 430.
65 *Prestonpans* v *Dunse*, 459.
66 *Prestonpans* v *Dunse*, 459 (emphasis in original), 468.

children (although there were none in the case), raising again the spectre of *Adamson* v *Barbour* and the fear of separated families.[67]

The majority opinions, in contrast, focused on the meaning and duration of the marriage bond, arguing that while a wife did assume her husband's persona during marriage, as Lord Curriehill wrote, 'the dissolution of the marriage by her husband's death restores her to a position as distinct and independent as that of an unmarried person. She is once more unmarried when the marriage tie has been dissolved'.[68] A widow's settlement might change 'not because of anything which her husband might have done if he had lived, but because of what this woman did'.[69]

Although it was a narrow 7–6 decision, the Court's conclusion reflected an understanding of even poor women as fully capable and responsible for their own affairs. This interpretation was readily embraced by Mr Dunlop, who immediately excused Cousland's late husband's birth settlement, Eastwood, from liability for the widow. 'The claim against Eastwood can no longer be maintained, since the decision by the whole Court in the case of *Prestonpans* and *Dunse*.'[70] He declared finally, 'I am therefore of opinion that the claim of the Inspector of Paisley cannot be sustained against any of the three parishes.'[71] Because Paisley had agreed to abide by the arbitrator's decision and was the original parish to recognise the family's need for relief, Paisley alone was responsible for the expense of supporting the pauper and her children. Following the conclusion of the arbitration, James Shaw Brown was authorised by the Relief Committee to consult with the Paisley Parochial Board's law agents concerning pursuing Denny for reimbursement of the funds expended on Cousland and her family.[72] There is no record of the outcome, if any, of this consultation.

Inspector Brown may have been willing to let the Cousland case drop because she was no longer in need of relief. Her last child, the McFarlane

67 *Prestonpans* v *Dunse*, 468–9.
68 *Prestonpans* v *Dunse*, 462.
69 *Prestonpans* v *Dunse*, 463–4.
70 'Arbitration Cases, 186.
71 'Arbitration Cases', 186.
72 HCP Relief Committee, vol. 7–28, 15 March 1861.

boy, was born in a two-roomed flat on Cotton Street in Abbey Parish. The census of 1861 showed her calling herself Elizabeth McMurray and that she and her three teenage daughters were all employed in the town's mills. Ten years later she remained in Abbey and was married, still with her youngest son and raising a grandchild.[73] Though her husband was unemployed, she was working as a winder, her son was a message boy, and her 7-year-old grandchild attended school. In spite of her near-decade as a pauper in Paisley while she had a young family and no male partner, she had come through without being removed, incarcerated, or separated from her children. She died in 1883 of probable heart disease.[74]

Over the decade while Elizabeth Cousland was on Paisley's roll, legal interpretation shifted to fit social expectations for women in families. It was reasonable in 1850 for Inspector Brown to pursue the parishes in which both her late husband and the father of her younger children had settlements, and to virtually ignore Cousland's own birthplace. A decade later, the legal precedent existed to conclusively deny her any settlement based on her relationships and instead cast her onto her own history. The case was complicated not only by Cousland's irregular marriage status but by the changing legal landscape against which it was played out and the disparity between English and Scottish interpretations of coverture and settlement. Poor law inspectors considering her case were able to bounce potential responsibility for her around almost endlessly. Unlike the case of support for the able-bodied unemployed, which was so large-scale and potentially expensive that it sparked wide-ranging inquiries and opinions, the question of widows' settlements was a niche concern. In the absence of any meaningfully centralised administrative structure, every case had to be considered individually, at the local level, with decisions based on the inspectors' own individual interpretation of the law and subsequent court decisions, seasoned by their preconceptions about the proper structure of society. Complicated families were common, but the need of those families for relief was rare enough that they could be argued individually, gradually

73 Census of Scotland, Abbey Parish, 1861 (Census 1861 559/01 016/00 013), 1871 (Census 1871 559/01 001/00 017); White, J – Cousland, Elizabeth (Statutory Marriages 559/01 014) 1865, *ScotlandsPeople*.

74 Elizabeth White (Statutory Deaths 573/00 0772) *ScotlandsPeople.*

building precedent and regularity of practice rather than requiring urgent and sweeping conclusions. These smaller cases highlight parochial expectations for autonomy. At no point did the parishes involved turn to the Board of Supervision for advice; they pursued their cases, appeals, and abided by decisions as individual entities. Regular correspondence among inspectors, discussion of cases in meetings of various regional Poor Law Inspectors' Societies, and decisions published in *The Poor Law Magazine* drew inspectors toward consensus so that fewer and fewer cases were brought to court. It was not an efficient system, but by prioritising local decision making it fostered a set of best practices that reflected Scottish understanding and ultimately Scottish ownership of the system. When, in the mid-1860s, the Board of Supervision did begin to require more uniformity across the system, the practices imposed were founded on the nearly two decades of informal national consensus-building that came before.

The principle of local control with mild centralised supervision was effective and readily accepted in Paisley. The parochial board there generally tried to abide by the advice and recommendations that came from the Board of Supervision, realising that the recommendations often came from consolidation of best practices from around the nation (to which Paisley themselves contributed). Over the course of the 1850s Paisley adjusted their own regulations and practices, including major alterations to their poor house premises, to align themselves with the Board of Supervision's suggestions. They took up these alterations at their own pace, with moderate urgency, and delayed or side-stepped recommendations that did not fit their administrative, physical or financial capacity.[75] They used the same tactics when a newly formed governing body began to display genuine centralised power in the later 1850s. Unlike the Poor Law, the Lunacy Act for Scotland passed in 1857 vested executive power in a central organising body, the General Board of Commissioners in Lunacy for Scotland. All

75 Inspector Brown's dispensation to use his preferred schedule is one case of this mild resistance; a five-month negotiation in 1850 over the adoption of poor house rules was another. HCP Poorhouse Committee, vol. 7–27, 3 April 1850; 8 May 1850; 11 Sept. 1850.

institutions that cared for the mentally ill or disabled, including asylums connected with parochial poor houses, were required to follow their mandates. The final decade and a half of Inspector Brown's career was spent negotiating between the demands of the Scottish Lunacy Board and the Paisley Parochial Board's conflicting conviction that such matters were best left under local control.

CHAPTER 6

The Case of the Crowded Asylum: A Contest for Local Control: 1858–1876

While Inspector Brown was spending long days working on behalf of Paisley's poor, his wife Elizabeth was working at keeping their respectable home. Married at age 33 after twelve years as the hospital matron, she must have brought significant management skills of her own to the task of housekeeping. The Browns' late marriage meant that their two sons, David and John (born while Elizabeth was still matron) were their only children. When the boys were school-aged, Elizabeth's elderly father joined the household, living with them until his death in 1862. There was usually a live-in maid, and there was undoubtedly frequent communication and cooperation with the Misses Brown, James Shaw's sisters who lived in the same building.[1] David and John Brown were promising to continue the family's economic progress. As a teenager David trained for a career in the law, while John wavered between the law and following his namesake uncle into medicine.[2]

In the 1870s, John's waverings took a more serious turn. He began to show signs of mental illness in his early twenties, which his father attributed to intemperance but also included symptoms of depression, self-harm and delusions that he was somehow under his brother's control.[3] First examined

1 09/11/1847 Brown, James Shaw (O.P.R. Marriages 573/02 0040 0257 Paisley Middle); 1861 Brown, James S. (Census 573/36/11); 1862 Baird, John (Statutory Registers Deaths 573/3 178), *ScotlandsPeople.*

2 1871 Census of Scotland, 3 Back Sneddon Paisley Middle Parish. This nearly-illegible page has not been catalogued on *ScotlandsPeople*. This census shows John as a general law clerk; later documents record he was a medical student.

3 Notices of Admissions MC2_181 24605 John Brown, obtained courtesy of Scottish Indexes.

for treatment around New Year's 1874, John was committed at the Crichton Royal Asylum in April and spent the rest of his life in institutions. John Brown's illness must have brought home with terrible urgency an issue that consumed his father's and the parochial board's attention for more than a decade, that of adequate provision for the Burgh's 'lunatic paupers'. Brown was able to pay for his son's treatment at the Royal Asylum, but the questions of how people of unsound mind should be treated and housed were relevant regardless of economic status.

From well before the start of the New Poor Law, caring for this vulnerable population was taken seriously in Paisley Burgh Parish. As early as 1825, the hospital kept separate wards for inmates suffering from mental debility and by 1840 hired a separate 'Keeper' for their management.[4] The Act confirmed the parochial boards' obligation to obtain treatment when 'any poor person who shall have become chargeable ... is declared or known to be insane or fatuous ... in an asylum or establishment legally authorised to receive lunatic patients'.[5] Shortly before the *Lunacy Act (Scotland)* was passed in 1857 the parochial board in Paisley constructed an entirely new building to house the mentally ill, creating a separate institution within the poor house.[6] At the national level, a process was underway of dividing care and bureaucratic oversight for public health and treatment of the insane from care for pauperism.[7] After the Lunacy Act passed, the Paisley Parochial Board struggled to keep the care for these paupers under their own control, resisting the appearance of centralised oversight even as they accepted rules set by a national board.

The treatment of the destitute mentally ill has received more historical attention than other areas of the poor law in Scotland, perhaps because of the crossover interest in the history of psychiatry.[8] Lauren Farquharson,

4 R. Brown, *History of Paisley: From the Roman period Down to 1884*, vol. II (Paisley: J & J Cook, 1886), 466; HCP Poorhouse Committee, vol. 7–27, 19 Oct. 1849.

5 *Poor Law (Scotland) Act*, Sec. 59.

6 HCP Poorhouse Committee, vol. 7–27, 7 March 1853.

7 I. Levitt, *Poverty & Welfare in Scotland 1890–1948* (Edinburgh: Edinburgh University Press, 1988), 18.

8 See, for example, J Andrews, *'They're in the Trade ... of Lunacy, They 'cannot interfere' They Say' The Scottish Lunacy Commissions and Lunacy Reform in Nineteenth-Century Scotland* (London: Wellcome Institute for the History of

in particular, examined the complexities arising from overlapping bureaucracies of the New Poor Law and medical care on a national scale. Paisley's experience was not unique, although they maintained themselves in a 'limbo-land between Scottish Poor and Lunacy jurisdiction' longer than most.[9] Farquharson's study revealed at a national level the contest for control of institutions. Paisley's poor law records over the same period do not contradict her conclusions but complement them by revealing the extended debate within the parochial board itself over whether to retain or surrender control of their asylum.

The poor law records in Paisley today do not hold the same extensive records of asylum inmates as they do applicants for relief. Although the poor law provided for the care of the mentally ill or disabled when their families could not, pauper lunatics were wrapped into a system of medical care, not merely poor relief. It seems sensational and unseemly to delve into the patients' stories, as they do not illuminate in any meaningful way the question of this book. Mental illness or debility was generally accepted as a disability for the purposes of poor relief, and sufferers were accepted as indoor paupers when needed for either treatment or due to destitution. Thus the affected poor people of Paisley and their treatment are largely absent from this chapter, which focuses instead on the establishment and management of the physical institution.

A centralised system of care for the mentally ill in Scotland was first attempted in 1815. The *Act to Regulate Madhouses in Scotland* required the construction of six District Asylums in Scotland and provided that curably insane paupers should be transferred away from hospitals like Paisley's and into asylums for treatment, in order to ensure that those who could be were cured by modern medicine. Institutions and individuals who were not asylums but did care for incurable lunatics were required to pay for a license to do so and accept a regime of regular inspections. In spite of

Medicine Occasional Publication no. 8, 1998); P. Bartlett and David Wright, eds, *Outside the Walls of the Asylum: The History of Care in the Community 1750–2000* (Cambridge: Cambridge University Press, 1999); and L. Farquharson, 'A "Scottish Poor Law of Lunacy"? Poor Law, Lunacy Law and Scotland's Parochial Asylums', *History of Psychiatry* 28:1 (2017): 15–28.

9 Farquharson 'Scottish Poor Law of Lunacy', 16.

several subsequent acts, the oversight of these institutions was limited.[10] The 1845 Poor Law Amendment Act then intertwined care for mentally ill/disabled people with poor relief (as did the English poor law). The Board of Supervision was empowered by section 59 of the Act to ensure that removals of the 'insane and fatuous' to appropriate institutions took place. On the other hand, the very next section of the New Poor Law, which defined appropriate inhabitants of the poor houses, included 'poor Persons who from Weakness or Facility of Mind … are unable or unfit to take charge of their own affairs'.[11] There was no clear line between the fatuous and the weak of mind, and it is evident that there were always some lunatics in the Paisley Poorhouse. The raw number of mentally ill people they cared for rose over the course of decades, more likely due to an increased awareness of the potential for psychiatric treatment and capacity in the poor house than to an actual increase in mental illness. From 1851, when the asylum was simply separate wards within the main poor house, to 1871, when the parish was actively working on the expansion of their asylum, applications for relief spurred by mental illness or intemperance nearly tripled as a proportion of all applicants.[12]

Then as now, mental illness was often linked with destitution. In some communities, the poor house/infirmary/town hospital was the only institution able to provide any sort of appropriate shelter and care for a person who could not be cared for at home. Not all mentally ill or disabled people were under control of the poor law, but poor people did suffer such disabilities, and even a moderately well-off family could find the expense of caring for a mentally disabled family member in an asylum overwhelming. When pauper lunatics were committed to royal asylums, the parishes in which they had settlements were obligated to pay for their board. Substantially-sized parishes, like Paisley, found it more economical to accommodate and treat these cases within their own institutions. They could then, in turn, take patients and charge boarding fees from surrounding parishes. This practice was regarded with great suspicion by both the Board of Supervision

10 Andrews, '*Scottish Lunacy Commissioners*', 2–3.
11 *Poor Law (Scotland)*, Sec. 60.
12 See Table I, page 71.

and the Lunacy Inquiry of 1855–7 as being intended to save money rather than for the best interest of the patients.[13]

Paisley's parochial board, whether for reasons of economy or humanity, were insistent on the propriety of their treatment of their insane and fatuous poor. They dated their asylum to 1827, and since then the sheriff and medical men had inspected it regularly and approved it for the purpose.[14] Immediately after the New Poor Law Act was passed the board had, at the insistence of the sheriff, reduced and restricted the number of boarding patients admitted, in order to control crowding in the institution.[15] Since at least 1840 a specialised staff member supervised this class of inmate in the poor house. The board specified in 1849 that 'Keeper' was actually a post for two people, a 'properly qualified person' and his wife, 'without any family incumberance', so that both male and female patients would have appropriate attendance.[16] When, in early 1850, the Board of Supervision suggested that the parochial board needed to purchase licenses through the sheriff to care for the insane and fatuous at a cost of 10/6 per patient, the Poorhouse Committee took aim at the very premise of the request. While the Board of Supervision stated, 'This Board considers it very doubtful. Whether a Poor House could be held to be a public Hospital',[17] the Committee remarked, 'It seems to be very evident to the committee that the Paisley Town Hospital must be held as coming within the designation Public Hospital and such that it is as much entitled as any institution can be to the benefit of exemption from the tax in question.'[18] Considering the licenses unnecessary, they refused to apply. It was – unsurprisingly – not the end of the conflict.

13 Farquharson, 'Scottish Poor Law of Lunacy', 18.
14 HCP Poorhouse Committee, vol. 7–18, 30 June 1858.
15 HCP Parochial Board, vol. 7–19, 3 July 1846.
16 HCP Poorhouse Committee, vol. 7–27, 19 Oct. 1849. It is notable that the poor house matron Elizabeth Baird Brown was already mother to an infant and was perhaps more encumbered than desirable.
17 HCP Poorhouse Committee, vol. 7–27, 1 Feb. 1850.
18 HCP Poorhouse Committee, vol. 7–27, 3 April 1850.

Regulating Paisley's Asylum before the Lunacy Act

The Board of Supervision's suggestion regarding the license was part of the larger move toward centralised administration and regularisation of practice across Scotland. Poorhouse management was an early target. When the Poor Law Act was passed fewer than two dozen of Scotland's 880 parishes were operating hospitals and similar institutions, which made rationalisation of them a much easier premise than universal tasks like record keeping.[19] The board collected poor house regulations from all of the parishes already operating them across Scotland. They found so many of the regulations inadequate that they issued their own seventy-two individual rules which they expected would be adopted.[20] Upon close examination of these new regulations, the Paisley Poorhouse Committee actually found little to argue with. Only eight of the rules were not already practiced in Paisley's establishment. Of these, four had to do with the limited space in the House.

Proper management, according to the Board of Supervision, required complete physical separation of different categories of inmates, and the restriction of inmates from using the sleeping wards during the day. The Poorhouse Committee noted their opinion that the regulations were meant for much larger institutions than theirs. The poor house could readily house two hundred paupers in its original configuration, but there was not enough space or the necessary architecture to fully separate the thirty or so mentally ill paupers from the rest of the population. Inmates of all conditions might mingle in the one enclosed airing ground, and the sexes shared a single dining room. It was impossible to provide separate dayrooms and dormitories, as the two spaces were one and the same. After some struggle over an appropriate response, the parochial board dispatched the chairman of the board, the inspector, and two board members to seek clarification about

19 D. Englander, *Poverty and Poor Law Reform in Nineteenth-Century Britain, 1834–1914* (London: Addison Wesley Longman, 1998), 53.

20 *Fifth Annual Report of the Board of Supervision for the Relief of the Poor in Scotland* (Edinburgh, 1850), iv.

just how strictly the parish was expected to adhere to the rules outlined by the central body in all matters of poor house management, including the status of their lunatic wards.[21]

Sir John McNeill met with the group, but he was not particularly sympathetic. He justified the insistence on the full separation of the sexes (for both lunatic and sane paupers) by pointing out the separation was an unpleasantness that did not in fact reduce the material quality of life for inmates, thus served as a test of poverty that could discourage people from applying for admission to the house when it was not their true last resort. The Paisley delegation was not particularly successful in gaining exceptions to the Board of Supervision's rules, although McNeill expressed understanding that infrastructure changes could not be implemented immediately. However, there was good news regarding the lunatic department. 'In reply to a remark made by Mr Farquharson, Sir John and Mr Smyth the Secretary explained that after hearing the opinion of Sheriff Robertson, the Board of Supervision was satisfied that the Paisley Hospital comes within the description of public Hospitals … and is therefore exempted from the liability of taking out annual licenses for the Patients in the asylum.'[22]

Meanwhile, Abbey Parish had responded to the New Poor Law's exhortation to construct a poor house for every parish or union of parishes by actually building a new institution along approved lines in the area of the parish called Riccartsbar, about a mile from the town. The Abbey poor house was completed in 1849, with an adjoining asylum opened in 1851. That year Sheriff Robertson, who had previously reported that the Paisley institution provided adequate care to be considered a public hospital, began to hedge on his conclusion. He acknowledged recent improvements in Paisley that were brought about mainly by a reduction in the number of asylum patients in recent years (from 35 in 1849–50 down to 28).[23] 'At the same time [he had] never ceased to feel that the fundament [sic] objections to the

21 HCP Poorhouse Committee, vol. 7–27, 8 May 1850.

22 HCP Parochial Board, vol. 7–19, 11 July 1850.

23 *Fifth Annual Report of the Board of Supervision for the Relief of the Poor in Scotland* (Edinburgh: Murray and Gibb, 1850), 103; *Sixth Annual Report of the Board of Supervision for the Relief of the Poor in Scotland* (Edinburgh: Murray and Gibb, 1851), 99.

establishment are of such a nature as do not admit of being obviated, nor to hope that circumstances might arise admitting of its removal to a more desirable locality'. He went on, 'it has been impossible for me therefore to witness the amount of excellent unoccupied accommodation in the new establishment of Abbey parish without anxiously wishing that an arrangement could be made between the two parochial boards'. Barring the combination of the two asylums into one (housed in the Abbey building) he suggested moving just one sex of patients from Paisley to the new asylum. This solution suggests the genuine problem with Paisley was not the size, but the awkward ability of inmates there to mingle with the opposite sex.[24]

The Poorhouse Committee sharply rejected these options.[25] Moving the patients would cost Paisley £400 in board charges and (perhaps more importantly) would be a blow to the Burgh's pride. 'It is the highest degree desirable that a poor house designed to meet the wants of so large a Parish as Paisley should possess an Insane Department', the Committee declared.[26] To save these outcomes, they recommended less profound changes. First, they proposed taking only particular categories of lunatics, namely, 'Idiots and Incurables' and 'Those milder forms of insanity which arise from temporary causes, such as intemperance, puerperal illness &c., and for the recovery of which nothing more may be required than a brief seclusion and safe custody'.[27] Patients who might be violent or curable with more intensive treatment, they proposed secondly, would be sent for treatment to a public asylum. Finally – and most significantly – they proposed extensive renovations to turn the lunatic wards of the poor house into an acceptable asylum with a full division of the patients by sex.

From this point the parochial board began investing in expanding their facilities for both sane and insane paupers, not necessarily to improve the quality of care, but rather to comply with the national philosophy of indoor relief or treatment, which was to find a line between compassionate care for those in need and deterring potential freeloaders. While maintaining their main building on New Sneddon and Hospital Lane, within the decade the

24 HCP Poorhouse Committee, vol. 7–27, 28 Oct. 1851.
25 HCP Poorhouse Committee, vol. 7–27, 27 Nov. 1851.
26 HCP Poorhouse Committee, vol. 7–27, 27 Nov. 1851.
27 HCP Poorhouse Committee, vol. 7–27, 27 Nov. 1851.

poor house complex expanded to fill the entire length of Hospital Lane between New Sneddon and Back Sneddon Streets (see Illustration 2). Entire new blocks were constructed to provide dedicated housing for the mentally ill, as well as a large dining hall, dayrooms, laundry, and a nursery for the regular poor.

This plan required expanding the footprint of the House and asylum buildings. Inspector Brown, on instructions from the board, negotiated the purchase of adjacent properties, and the final plans for the expansion were approved by mid-September 1852.[28] Construction began with all due haste; within a few months notation was made that oatcakes had been removed from the asylum dietary due to 'the removal of the baking apparatus caused by the improvements now in progress'.[29] The new buildings were ready to receive patients in the middle of June 1854. By the time the ordnance survey of Paisley was produced in 1858 the complex had expanded to fill half of the block, with fully segregated yards and airing grounds for inmates and patients.

28 HCP Poorhouse Committee, vol. 7–27, 11 Sept. 1852.

29 HCP Poorhouse Committee, vol. 7–27, 23 Feb. 1852.

Illustration 2: Original and Expanded Poor House Complex: 1839 and 1858

1839 Plan of Paisley and Its Environs; Courtesy of ScotlandsPeople. *The Paisley Poorhouse is the chair-shaped block of buildings near the centre of the image.*

Town Plan of Paisley, Surveyed 1858 Ordnance Survey Large-Scale Scottish Town Plans; Courtesy of National Library of Scotland

The Lunacy Act (Scotland) 1857

The renovations to the lunatic wards completed in 1854 were carried out at the urging of the Board of Supervision, empowered by Section 60 to provide for the pauper lunatics. Very shortly thereafter, though, Westminster was stirred up by the American reformer Dorothea Dix to form a committee to formally inquire into the condition of lunatics all across Scotland.[30] The Lunacy Commission, largely hand-picked by Dix, confirmed her impression that provision for the insane in the nation was inadequate. Lunacy Commissioner James Coxe wrote to her in 1855, 'the whole system requires remodelling'.[31] The result of the inquiry was the introduction of the Lunacy Act (Scotland) in 1857, mandating just such a remodeling.

The Paisley Parochial Board, along with many of the other parishes with asylum wards, resisted the passage of the Lunacy Act. In a petition to Parliament opposing the Bill, the Paisley board noted, 'that your Petitioners consider the creation of a new Board for Lunacy, with the proposed complex and costly machinery to be entirely unnecessary and that the extraordinary powers with which the Bill invests the Commissioners are highly impolitic and inexpedient'.[32] They proposed instead that clarification of duties and powers of the existing bureaucracy – notably the Board of Supervision – would remedy the concerns that gave rise to the Lunacy Inquiry. Though joined in their opposition by other parishes, Paisley was particularly resistant to compliance with the new order.[33] Given the physical improvements they had recently undertaken, it is not surprising that they were unwilling to turn their inmates over to an entirely different institution. These local protests, however, were ineffectual against the reforming zeal of Parliament. MP William Baxter, who represented the Montrose Burghs, dismissed their concerns, just days after the Paisley petition was dispatched,

30 D. Gollaher, *Voice for the Mad: The Life of Dorothea Dix* (New York: The Free Press, 1995), 350–67.

31 Quoted in Gollaher, *Voice for the Mad*, 356.

32 HCP Committee on the Lunacy Bill, 7–28, 6 July 1857.

33 Farquharson, 'Scottish Poor Law of Lunacy', 22.

saying 'he greatly regretted that any portion of the people of Scotland, in their dread of centralisation or of increased taxation, should have shown an inclination to treat lightly the evils which had been exposed by the [Lunacy] Commissioners'.[34]

Most of the debate in Parliament was between Scottish Members, most expressing the same skepticism as Paisley's Parochial Board. The much-respected President of the Board of Supervision, Sir John McNeill, had refused the opportunity to wrap control of asylums into the poor law in 1849.[35] Though some Members strenuously argued for keeping pauper lunatics under the purview of the parochial boards and poor law inspectors, the final Act gave the newly-created General Board of Commissioners in Lunacy for Scotland (SLB) power to oversee care for all lunatics in Scotland, both institutionalised and in private care.[36] Not only was it centralised, the SLB also had significant powers of enforcement that the Board of Supervision lacked.[37] It 'was empowered to oversee the creation of district asylums' that would replace the patchwork of parish poor houses, private care and other solutions.[38] There was significant overlap and tension between the two national boards over how individuals could be identified as lunatics, how and where they could be housed, and who was responsible for their supervision.[39] This overlap left confusion over the status of Paisley's asylum. In June 1858 the Poorhouse Committee instructed Inspector Brown to write to the Scottish Lunacy Board asking what system of licenses, if any, the new law required for public asylums like Paisley's. To their disappointment, the board secretary replied, 'the lunatic wards of poor houses are not asylums under the Lunacy Act at all. The whole question regarding

34 Hansards, 'House of Commons Sitting of Thursday, 9 July 1857', 1169.
35 Hansards, 9 July 1857, 1185.
36 Contemporaries and scholars have given this board a variety of shortened names. For purposes of clarity I have adopted 'Scottish Lunacy Board' or SLB or simply the Lunacy Board, although the Paisley records more often called it the General Board or General Lunacy Board.
37 Farquharson, 'Scottish Poor Law of Lunacy', 15.
38 Farquharson, 'Scottish Poor Law of Lunacy', 20.
39 Farquharson, 'Scottish Poor Law of Lunacy', 20–1.

them is still under consideration and the Parochial Board of Paisley will be communicated with as soon as the Board are prepared to act.'[40]

While the Board of Supervision was prickly in defense of their prerogative and past treatment of pauper lunatics, the Lunacy Board was quickly successful in establishing authority over treatment of and conditions for the inmates of Paisley's asylum. In September 1859, an Amended Lunacy Act granted official permission for asylums associated with parochial poor houses – like Paisley's – to house and treat mentally unsound paupers. The parochial board had already shown itself willing to follow reasonable suggestions regarding their establishment, and this Act clarified the Scottish Lunacy Board's power to conduct semi-annual inspections of asylums and issue (or withhold) licenses. Paisley's Parochial Board did resist surrendering nominal control of their asylum and its inmates, but they also proved willing to go to great lengths to accommodate the Lunacy Commissioners' concerns. Those concerns were centred on the physical facilities, even as the care and treatment of inmates was praised.

The few years following the Lunacy Act's passage saw gradual improvement of the asylum's comforts. After the 1859 amendment was passed, the Poorhouse Committee took up Lunacy Commissioner Coxe's inspection report from the previous March and voted to recommend,

> 1) That the walks of the asylum male & female airing grounds be laid with pavement, 2) that for the convenience of the male patients an additional water closet be constructed at the south east corner adjoining the door entering into the day room.[41]

The next month, when another Commissioner conducted a new inspection, the Poorhouse Committee 'were gratified with the favourable terms of the report, and of the Commissioner's approval of the efforts made by the Board to promote the welfare of the insane'. They put off for another time, however, discussion of adding another water closet to the female department.[42]

40 HCP Poorhouse Committee, vol. 7–28, 30 June 1858.
41 HCP Poorhouse Committee, vol. 7–28, 9 Sept. 1859.
42 HCP Poorhouse Committee, vol. 7–28, 26 Oct. 1859.

From the perspective of the parochial board, an acceptable balance had been achieved. When Commissioner Coxe again inspected in November 1860, he found numerous cases of lunatics recovering and ample accommodation available. He remarked, 'that he found all the patients well and warmly clothed, clean in person, and tidy in dress', and that 'a gradual improvement has been taking place in internal arrangements'.[43] His concern was that the asylum should be a place of refuge and comfort, and he recommended more furniture like individual washstands and additional chairs in the dayrooms. The lack of extensive grounds was seen as the institution's greatest shortcoming. While the Board of Supervision had no concerns regarding mentally healthy paupers being housed in the centre of the town (they were after all disabled by definition), the Lunacy Commission recommended extensive outdoor exercise for the mentally ill. The Superintendent of the asylum sometimes sent patients outside the walls for exercise, 'but from the situation of the House in the middle of the Town', he could not send every patient on such excursions.[44] Lastly, Coxe noted that of the forty-three patients in the asylum when he visited, about sixteen were paupers belonging to other parishes, for whom Paisley was paid. Keeping these paupers from outside the parish supplemented the rates and provided the efficiencies of scale necessary to make the entire asylum enterprise possible.

Two years later, Lunacy Commissioner Coxe once again found all Paisley's asylum patients to be 'healthy, clean, well clothed and free from excitement'.[45] Nevertheless he repeated his complaint regarding the asylum's confined location and recommended the Burgh partner with Abbey to provide jointly for their patients in Abbey's more rural location. In rejecting the idea, Paisley's objections were almost entirely financial. They pointed to the over £3,000 price tag for the 1854 expansion and stated the buildings would be useless for the regular poor house. They did not believe Abbey could afford the necessary expansion to hold Burgh patients, nor that Abbey would agree to joint management of the institution. Only the fourth point of their argument was to defend their own premises, including

43 HCP Poorhouse Committee, vol. 7–28, 28 Dec. 1860.

44 HCP Poorhouse Committee, vol. 7–28, 28 Dec. 1860.

45 HCP Poorhouse Committee, vol. 7–28, 13 Jan. 1863.

the observation that most of their patients came from manufacturing occupations and were better served by work in the asylum's loomshop than they would be in the field labour Abbey patients were encouraged to undertake. As they had in 1839 they argued, '[m]ere field labour … is evidently inferior to weaving which besides supplying moderate exercise for the body, also calls into operation the mental faculties and accustoms the patient to sober thought.' Defending their town's noble craft, the board expressed a willingness to expand both the loomshop and, when they were able to acquire adjacent properties, the too-small airing grounds.[46]

Warming to their theme, the Burgh board cast doubt on their neighbor's care for inmates, comparing admission, recovery, and mortality statistics to demonstrate that while the Burgh establishment was smaller (averaging 42.88 patients compared to Abbey's 72.4), they had a far better rate of recovery (80.146 percent to Abbey's 48.350 percent). 'These figures present a remarkable contrast and indicate a decided superiority of the Burgh over the Abbey Asylum.' Furthermore, the smaller size of the Burgh asylum lent it 'a more quiet and domestic aspect' and more personal attendance. Finally, the board reasserted the high quality of the Burgh asylum, pointing to their past reports to show 'that it is not only superior to the Abbey Asylum, but also equal to any other in Scotland'.[47]

Pushed to Expand

No amount of efficiency and care, though, could give the Paisley asylum the fresh air, exercise, and pastoral vistas that were increasingly seen as vital to the treatment of mental disorders.[48] In the decades since the

46 HCP Poorhouse Committee, vol. 7–28, 13 Jan. 1863.
47 HCP Poorhouse Committee, vol. 7–28, 13 Jan. 1863.
48 See for instance Clare Hickman, 'Cheerful Prospects and Tranquil Restoration: The Visual Experience of landscape as part of the therapeutic regime of the British asylum, 1800–60', *History of Psychiatry* 20:4 (2009): 425–41; Steven Cherry and Roger Munting, '"Exercise is the Thing"? Sport and the Asylum c. 1850–1950', *The International Journal of the History of Sport* 22:1 (2005): 42–58; Kim A. Ross, 'The

hospital was first built – and more so since the passage of the New Poor Law – Paisley had grown around the Sneddon, most notably with the construction of the Gilmour Street Station and rail line that still dominates the district today. At least one train an hour departed the station throughout the day, with concomitant noise, rumble and soot.[49] Pushed by the Lunacy Commissioners' inspections and reports, the parochial board repeatedly invested in their asylum to bring it up to standards. In addition to extending buildings and the all-important airing courts, in 1863 they purchased six acres of land in nearby Nethercommon, just outside the burgh boundary to the north. This land, with a kitchen garden and piggery established, was supposed to provide the patients who were able to get there with the fresh air and healthful exercise prescribed.

In spite of Paisley's willingness to meet the demands of both boards to which they answered, it became clear in the mid-1860s that the entire county of Renfrew had a pauper lunatic problem – or, rather, that pauper lunatics in Renfrewshire were a particular problem for the national oversight envisaged by the Lunacy Act. That Act mandated a national system of District Asylums, which would be directed and overseen by District Boards of Lunacy; permitting poor house asylums to continue in operation had been intended as a stopgap on the way to this system. In this design, there was room for precisely one District Asylum in Renfrewshire.[50] Renfrewshire was over-provided with asylum beds per capita, divided among three parish poor houses – two of which were in Paisley. Neither Abbey nor Paisley Burgh was prepared to give up control of the patients in their care or the significant investments they had made in institutions. Between them, Abbey and Paisley had enough beds for the 'Upper Ward' (the eastern two-thirds) of Renfrewshire, and Paisley also boarded in some patients from other counties. In 1862, a new Lunacy Amendment Act (Scotland) granted Paisley and similar institutions within poor houses official status as 'Parochial

Locational History of Scotland's District Lunatic Asylums, 1857–1913', PhD Thesis in Geographical & Earth Sciences, University of Glasgow 2014. 191–5.

49 *Watson's Commercial Directory and General Advertiser for 1862–3* (Paisley: Paisley Herald, 1862), Appendix, p. 32. Only one of the four railways in the directory included a passenger schedule.

50 Ross, 'Locational History', 176.

Asylums', which granted them the right to (or acknowledged the reality that they did) house and treat both curable and incurable patients and made them beholden to both the Board of Supervision and the Scottish Lunacy Board.[51] The Lunacy Board began to urge the consolidation of asylums in the Renfrewshire District, especially focusing on a combination of the Abbey and Paisley Burgh establishments.[52]

The simple existence of beds was not enough to satisfy the Lunacy Board, and they had a winning card courtesy of the Lunacy Act: as the license-issuers they granted permission to every institution proposing to care for more than one mentally unsound person, and could withhold those licenses and issue fines for unsanctioned operations. They could direct District Boards unilaterally to erect District Asylums and mandate the treatment of all or some patients in a region at those institutions. The cost of these new asylums would be raised by assessing the ratepayers of the area served. It was a nightmare to Paisley's Parochial Board to think that after all their effort they could still be assessed for a new building over which they would have no control. Even worse, perhaps, was the idea that Abbey, with their asylum situated on a lush rural property that met with the SLB's approval, would not also have to pay.[53]

The original Lunacy Act provided for the possibility that counties or parishes could not or would not acquiesce to the District Asylum system. Section 59 of that Act provided that public asylums under certain conditions would 'be equivalent to a District Asylum for pauper lunatics according to the meaning of this act', but later amendments did not satisfactorily acknowledge the equivalence of Paisley's asylum.[54] The 1862 Amendment explicitly permitted licensing poor house lunatic wards 'for the reception … of such pauper lunatics only who are not dangerous, and do not require curative treatment', attempting to force the dangerous and curable patients into the medical asylum system.[55] In spite of pressure from Paisley and other Scottish parishes, no clear definition of 'asylum' to include

51 Farquarson, 'Scottish Poor Law of Lunacy', 23.
52 HCP Poorhouse Committee, vol. 7–28, 13 Jan. 1863.
53 HCP Poorhouse Committee, vol. 7–28, 13 Jan. 1863.
54 *Lunacy (Scotland) Act*, 1858 sec. 59.
55 *Lunacy (Scotland) Act*, 1862 sec. 3; Farquharson, 'Scottish Poor Law of Lunacy', 23.

poor house lunatic wards was included in the amendment.[56] Highlighting the special nature of their own establishment, it became the goal of the Paisley Parochial Board to maintain their own parochial asylum within the larger District system. They were convinced that local control would result in a less expensive institution for their already-burdened ratepayers and insisted, 'the Burgh Asylum from its opening down to the present time [January 1863] has fully answered all the practical purposes of an institution for the insane in respect both of safe custody and proper treatment.'[57] The trouble was, the Paisley Asylum did not meet the standards set by the Lunacy Board, and in spite of Paisley's willingness to take in boarding patients from other parishes, the lower ward of Renfrewshire (the district surrounding Greenock) was unprovided for.

In an attempt to resolve the impasse, the District Asylum Board for Renfrewshire (a local body empowered by the Lunacy Act and overseen by the Scottish Lunacy Board) facilitated a July 1864 meeting in Paisley's County Hall between representatives of the Burgh, Abbey, and Greenock parishes with a deputation from the SLB. At the end of the meeting, Greenock and Abbey had both agreed to changes to their asylums prescribed by the Lunacy Commissioners (similar to the changes Paisley was already undertaking) and in return, 'the deputation would not be disposed to recommend the General Board to insist on any change being made in the existing system'.[58] In other words, if the lunatic paupers of Renfrew were getting treated under the conditions the Scottish Lunacy Board found essential, that board would not insist on a centralised institution.

With immediate pressure relieved, Paisley's asylum retained its license, but the planned improvements were slow, stymied by delays in acquiring neighbouring land.[59] Commissioner Coxe's inspection of the asylum in April 1867 seemed satisfactory, but the SLB was still watching the bigger picture in Renfrewshire. On 22 March, they had written to Inspector Brown with an ominous message for the parochial board:

56 HCP Poorhouse Committee, vol. 7–28, 2 May 1863.
57 HCP Poorhouse Committee, vol. 7–28, 13 Jan. 1863.
58 HCP Poorhouse Committee, vol. 7–28, 25 July 1864.
59 HCP Poorhouse Committee, vol. 7–28, 6 July 1866; 25 Sept. 1866; 16 April 1867.

> Sir, the Board have, for some time, had under consideration arrangements connected with the accommodation of the Pauper Lunatics of the County of Renfrew, and as a part of these, it is their intention to restrict the Burgh Parochial Asylum to the reception of patients belonging to its own parish. Under such altered circumstances, I am instructed to enquire whether the Parochial Board would wish a continuance of the license, or would they prefer to enter into an agreement with an existing institution for the accommodation of the lunatics of the Parish.[60]

It was easier for the Lunacy Board to withdraw their permission for Paisley to accept (and treat) patients from outside the Burgh than to debate the asylum status of the parochial institution, and it could accomplish the same goal of closing the wards. Since generally a third of Paisley's asylum patients were from outside the parish, these boarders were essential for income to maintain the institution.[61]

Faced with this threat, the Paisley board immediately appointed a deputation including Provost Hugh M'Farlane, Parochial Board Chairman Robert Dalziel, and two more members of the board as well as Inspector Brown to meet with the Lunacy Board and 'endeavour to obtain their sanction to a renewal of the existing license'.[62] The deputation laid out all their arguments regarding the efficiency and care given to patients in the Paisley Asylum, while pointing out the unusually high rates already paid in the Burgh to demonstrate that the 'Managers in seeking to maintain their present position have not been influenced by any wish to keep down the local rates'.[63] The Lunacy Board was unmoved, declaring, 'That if the Parochial Board were in the position of applying for the first time for such a license as they now sought, the Board of Lunacy, looking at the situation of the building amidst a dense population, confined within so narrow limits, with no view beyond a square of dead walls and a bit of blue sky overhead, such application would not be entertained for a moment. … The Managers [of Paisley Asylum] may therefore expect that the present license will be

60 HCP Poorhouse Committee, vol. 7–28, 16 April 1867.

61 HCP Poorhouse Committee, vol. 7–28, 8 May 1867.

62 HCP Poorhouse Committee, vol. 7–28, 16 April 1867; *Watson's Directory for Paisley, Renfrew, Johnstone, Elderslie, Linwood, Quarrelton, Thornhill, Balaclava, and Inkerman, for the Year 1867–8* (Paisley: Paisley Herald, 1867), Appendix 18.

63 HCP Poorhouse Committee, vol. 7–28, 8 May 1867.

restricted accordingly as soon as the county shall have made the necessary provisions by the erection of a District Asylum.'[64]

In spite of the negative tone, the Poorhouse Committee latched on to the proviso, 'as soon as the county shall have', and launched into plans for expanding the asylum grounds. Their expectations for a continuance of their license while the eventuality of a District Asylum hovered were dashed the next month, when they were curtly informed, 'after the expiration of the present license to the Burgh poor house, the license will be restricted to patients belonging to the Parish'.[65]

It appeared, however, that Paisley was not the only parish shocked by SLB's ultimatum over boarding patients. About six weeks after declaring the asylum's license would be restricted, the Lunacy Board reversed course, admitting, 'So great has been the pressure for accommodation that the Board think it is right to inform you that it is probable that they will at 1st January reconsider their decision & continue the license on the same terms as formerly.'[66] The source of some of this pressure became evident a year later, when the SLB presented a new notice, 'Having had under consideration the whole circumstances affecting the Burgh Parochial Asylum and the District of Renfrew', they planned to restrict the Paisley license 'as soon as the District Asylums of Stirling and Ayr are opened, and to withdraw the license entirely whenever the Asylum for the District of Renfrew shall be opened'.[67]

Deciding to Build

Paisley was not the only parish facing such pressure. Barony, Govan, and Greenock, with similar licenses from the Lunacy Board, were similarly urged to improve their facilities, and Greenock's license was actually

64 HCP Poorhouse Committee, vol. 7–28, 8 May 1867.
65 HCP Poorhouse Committee, vol. 7–28, 19 June 1867.
66 HCP Poorhouse Committee, vol. 7–29, 3 Sept. 1867, quoting a letter written 22 July.
67 HCP Poorhouse Committee, vol. 7–29, 11 June 1868.

revoked.[68] To compound Inspector Brown's headaches, in the middle of 1867 conditions in the Paisley poor house proper were abruptly, urgently, found wanting. A regular inspection from the Board of Supervision found 'itch patients' (a scabies-like infestation) mingled with other probationary inmates in a quarantine ward, and women with children unacceptably housed with women who were without families. The Board of Supervision inspector wrote, 'This House, as the board is aware, has insuperable defects, but notwithstanding these the management is so good that an inspection of it always affords me satisfaction. I trust however that the day is not distant when the Parochial Board will provide, for their excellent officials, a house more worthy of them.'[69] Faced with condemnation on both sides of their facility, the Poorhouse Committee delayed any consideration of what further alterations to make for the ordinary paupers until the situation with the asylum was resolved, although they did designate a separate space for itch patients.

Along with the conviction that mentally ill people must have access to outdoor space, the prevailing beliefs about treatment of paupers was toward greater confinement or – in the preferred language of the time – classification.[70] What began with a division of sexes and removal of most children from the poor house became more rigid, until the single gate communicating between male and female airing grounds was bricked up and the sexes were entirely separate. In the later 1860s inspectors from the Board of Supervision wanted to see further divisions, particularly between the 'worthy' and 'unworthy' inmates of each sex. They believed the very presence of the unmarried mothers with nursing babes would contaminate or offend the married or otherwise more respectable paupers. Similarly, poor men determined to be degenerate should be separated from those who convinced the inspector or Governor of the House that they

68 Farquharson, 'Scottish Poor Law of Lunacy', 24.

69 HCP Poorhouse Committee, vol. 7–28, 19 June 1867.

70 Classification was of course a widespread obsession of the Victorians, whether it concerned the poor, species, or rooms of the house. J. Flanders, *Inside the Victorian Home: A Portrait of Domestic Life in Victorian England* (London: W.W. Norton, 2003), 31.

were morally uncorrupted even in the face of destitution. As described in Chapter 3, moral judgments to even make such a division were unusual in the records Paisley kept. It is not clear how poor house inmates were assigned to wards within the house, and regardless of sleeping quarters they were obliged to mingle in the dining halls, workrooms and day rooms. No matter how well managed, the Board of Supervision found the mixing itself offensive, while the Lunacy Board condemned both the buildings and the parochial (rather than medical) management.[71] Though the poor house complex now took up most of the block, it was too small to satisfy either of its national masters.

Throughout 1867 and 1868 the Paisley board continued attempting to make their cramped quarters acceptable. While they did their best to expand and update their facilities, they were also on the lookout for suitably rural and accessible land that they could use for expanding or building a new asylum.[72] Simultaneously they returned to considering cooperation with Abbey Parish, whether through a full union as provided for in the New Poor Law, through joint ownership of the Abbey poor house and asylum (which did meet Lunacy Board standards), by sharing only Abbey's poor house and acquiring part of Abbey's property to build a separate asylum for the Burgh, or through Abbey taking all of Paisley's indoor paupers as boarders, thus opening the poor house space for residents of the asylum.[73] Abbey's board agreed to a meeting to consider the proposals but found two large objections. First, the Burgh's poor rate was higher than Abbey's by about 25 percent, translating to a 6 shilling per year difference for a £10 rental. 'The Abbey Committee wished to be informed in what way this difference was to be met and what compensation they were to receive in return for the increase of poor rates necessarily resulting from combination.'[74] Secondly, any proposal that included taking Paisley's paupers into Abbey's buildings would itself require substantial expansion of Abbey's facilities, with all the attendant costs. Confronted (and somewhat put out) by these

71 HCP Poorhouse Committee, vol. 7–29, 23 March 1871; Farquharson 'Scottish Poor Law of Lunacy', 24.

72 HCP Poorhouse Committee, vol. 7–29, 16 April 1870.

73 HCP Poorhouse Committee, vol. 7–29, 15 June 1870.

74 HCP Poorhouse Committee, vol. 7–29, 12 July 1870.

objections, the Paisley Poorhouse Committee resolved to abandon the idea of combination and began to calculate how they would provide on their own for the deficiencies of their buildings.[75] By the end of July 1870, the parochial board was exploring whether the Board of Supervision and the Lunacy Board would agree to the construction of a new asylum building physically removed from the poor house followed by conversion of the empty asylum space into expanded wards for the ordinary indoor poor.

This general plan gained approval by all the supervising bodies, but it proved harder than expected to carry out.[76] The outlying property they had purchased at Nethercommon was too small to satisfy the needs of an asylum, and adjoining land was priced out of reach. For a few months the project was at a standstill – so much so that the Lunacy Board wrote in December to learn what, if any, progress had been made.[77] With this spur to action the Poorhouse Committee made a quick recommendation to the parochial board that a new asylum must be built. The board responded after their usual New Years' holiday by empaneling a special committee to examine the question.[78] Board Chair James Millar and Provost David Murray were both included on this subcommittee, along with Richard Watson, Robert Cochran and John Fisher (all of whom were Town Baillies as well as members of the board) and board members James Barclay, Robert Richardson, and former Chair R.F. Dalziel. Between them these men represented all four of the board's standing committees, carried significant institutional memory of the poor law in the burgh, and had a clear grasp of the town's overall finances as well.[79]

The Special Committee's first act was to turn a research assignment over to Inspector Brown. In just over a fortnight, Brown assembled information to let him estimate the cost of new District Asylums with all furnishings (£130/per bed) and that the cost for Paisley to erect their own new parochial asylum would be £71 per bed. With these encouraging numbers, and

75 HCP Poorhouse Committee, vol. 7–29, 12 July 1870.
76 HCP Poorhouse Committee, vol. 7–29, 5 July 1870.
77 HCP Poorhouse Committee, vol. 7–29, 31 Aug. 1870; 26 Dec. 1870.
78 HCP Special Committee on New Asylum, vol. 7–29, 31 Jan. 1871.
79 *Watson's Directory for Paisley for the Year 1870–1* (Paisley: Paisley Herald, 1870), 193, 214.

recognising that the costs would be borne by Paisley ratepayers regardless of whether the asylum was built by the parochial board or the District Board of Lunacy, the Special Committee entertained a resolution,

> moved by Mr Millar, seconded by Mr Dalziel and carried, 1st that it is desirable that lunatics as well as other classes of our Poor should remain as at present under our own immediate care. 2nd that the Lunacy commissioners have certified our present Asylum to be unfit for mental treatment in consequence of confined situation and the want of means of classification and outdoor employment and recreation. 3rd that the premises now occupied by the Asylum are necessary to bring the poor house accommodation into conformity with the orders of the Board of Supervision. 4th that in these circumstances it is advisable that early steps be taken by the Board to provide a new Parochial Asylum of suitable dimensions and on the most economical plan.[80]

The committee was convinced of this necessity, but time had run out for bringing the issue back to the parochial board.

In February 1871 a new board was elected and neither Chairman Millar or Mr Dalziel were returned. Past Provost Robert Brown, manufacturer of patent machine-made bricks, drain pipes and tiles, took the chair and shifted the balance of opinion on the parochial board to oppose a new building.[81] Before the April board meeting in 1871 they insisted on a new overture about potential combination with Abbey. The idea was rejected by the Lunacy Board, who replied to Inspector Brown's inquiry on the matter, 'in the opinion of the Commission there is no prospect whatsoever of a combination being effected between Abbey and Burgh parishes, and that any attempt for this purpose can have no result but loss of time'. They continued that '[s]eeing the unwillingness of the Parochial Board to undertake themselves the necessary steps for proper accommodation of their pauper lunatics …' there was space available in the Lunacy-Board-approved District Asylum of Argyll & Bute. They suggested Paisley immediately begin arranging to send the patients in their asylum to the institution in Lochgilphead.[82]

80 HCP Special Committee on New Asylum, vol. 7–29, 16 Feb. 1871.
81 *Watson's Directory for Paisley for the Year 1871–2* (Paisley: Paisley Herald, 1871), 219.
82 HCP Parochial Board, vol. 7–19, 26 April 1871.

Heedless of this strong direction, Paisley's Parochial Board instituted a new Special Committee to examine asylum accommodation, which shared only one member (James Barclay) with the previous year's version. Along with Chairman Brown and Mr Barclay, new board members Stewart Clark, Alexander Miller, Archibald Hutchison and John Brown (no apparent relation to the inspector) made up the new committee, whose first order of business was to again explore some kind of union with Abbey.[83] A preliminary meeting was held to lay the groundwork. At this joint meeting Chairman Brown 'went into at considerable length a number of statistics in reference to the position of the two parishes, and stated his views regarding the different modes of combination proposed, but called the attention of the meeting more particularly to a combination for Poor house and Lunatic purposes only' (leaving the rest of the poors' management separate).[84]

The Lunacy Board, however, had lost patience. Following Dr Coxe's Spring inspection of the asylum the SLB wrote to Governor McKenzie of the Paisley Parochial Asylum regarding the Commissioner's report, directing 'very special attention to his condemnation of the house as unfit to serve its present purpose. … The provision of suitable accommodation for the lunatics of the Parish is in the opinion of the [Lunacy Board] a thing which can no longer be justifiably delayed.'[85] Further, the board made it clear to a new in-person deputation from Paisley that they intended to direct the construction of a new District Asylum for Renfrewshire.[86] Paisley Burgh could expect to be assessed for their share of the cost of the District Asylum even if they were sending all of their own mental patients to the Abbey Asylum or built their own asylum for the Burgh. In such a case the Scottish Lunacy Board would nevertheless require the patients to be sent to the District Asylum. The only path away from a District Asylum they grudgingly offered was if Paisley were to build a new asylum large enough to accommodate the need for the entire upper ward of Renfrewshire aside from what was already met by

83 HCP Special Committee on Asylum Accommodation, vol. 7–29, 4, 11 May 1871.
84 HCP Special Committee on New Asylum, vol. 7–29, 23 June 1871.
85 HCP Parochial Board, vol. 7–19, 28 June 1871.
86 HCP Special Committee on Asylum Accommodation, vol. 7–29, 5 July 1871.

Abbey *and* if the Town of Greenock would do the same for the needs of the whole lower ward.[87]

Pushed into this corner, the Special Committee reluctantly abandoned the thought of combining with Abbey and requested from Inspector Brown the previous year's data on the incidence, cure rate, and cost of care for asylum inhabitants across Scotland, in Renfrewshire generally, and in the three existing parochial asylums in Renfrewshire. Once again, the comparison showed, contrary to the Lunacy Board's assertion, that a Paisley Parochial Asylum, even new built, would be less expensive and more effective than a District Asylum. Not only did they estimate a cost of maintenance half that of a District Asylum, but they predicted a cure rate at least 10 percent higher. Nevertheless the Special Committee was deeply worried that any investment in a parochial asylum, whether for Paisley's needs only or designed to accommodate the whole upper ward, would be wasted if the Lunacy Board went ahead with the District Asylum plan.

The Special Committee's final report argued against a new asylum, in part because they expected the Lunacy Board would nevertheless go ahead with the construction of a District Asylum and Paisley's investment would be lost.

> The same objections will apply with still greater force to the Burgh erecting an asylum for their own lunatics and for those of the other parishes in the upper ward of the County not already accommodated. The Committee are decidedly of opinion that it is not the duty of the Burgh of Paisley, already assessed with taxation to build an asylum to accommodate the lunatics in other parishes, as that should be done by the owners of property in these parishes. … There is no other safe procedure left to the Burgh Board, but to inform the Board of Lunacy and the District Board, [that] they would prefer an Asylum to be erected which should accommodate all the Lunatics in the County. … The committee are also further of opinion that the District Board should … purchase the Abbey Asylum and grounds and … have such accommodation erected to the present buildings as [to] make them in every way suitable to be an asylum for the whole county and thus place this difficult and vexed question upon a safe and consequently a permanent position.[88]

87 HCP Special Committee on Asylum Accommodation, vol. 7–29, 11 July 1871.
88 HCP Special Committee on Asylum Accommodation, vol. 7–29, 11 July 1871.

Four of the six committee members met to review and draft the report on 11 July, and the following week five members met to review and confirm it. Two members, James Barclay and Alexander Miller, opposed the conclusion and recorded their dissent.

The disagreement on the committee was then played out in the full parochial board. John Brown, who had missed the two meetings regarding the report, added his dissent to Barclay and Miller's, leaving the Special Committee deadlocked over a recommendation. Meanwhile, the board was notified that the District Lunacy Board had received firm instructions to begin erecting a District Asylum since neither Paisley nor Greenock had taken satisfactory steps to meet requirements. The dissenters on the special committee took the floor to present their points in opposition to the official committee report. While agreeing with some points of the committee report – such as the impracticality of any sort of union with Abbey – they argued in favor of a parochial asylum over the larger District Asylum, pointing to Inspector Brown's statistics on cures and postulating that the reason was the more intimate nature of the parochial asylum. 'The change is not so repulsive, as in large, probably distant asylums, where they are apt to suffer from feelings of isolation amidst a crowd of strangers. … They are near home, more or less acquainted with the managers, and within convenient reach of interchange of visits with their relatives.'[89] Finally they spoke in favor of the system of management for a parochial asylum, in which the supervisor was an employee of the body elected specifically to care for the poor and the ratepayers, rather than (as they suspected) leaving day-to-day care to a medical supervisor who had no obligation to the ratepayers of a district. The dissenters' arguments were effective enough that the parochial board authorised a meeting between Burgh and Greenock representatives to discuss a plan to best provide for all of Renfrewshire's pauper lunatics without centralising to a District Asylum.[90]

A month later, it was revealed at the parochial board meeting that the District Board of Lunacy had itself 'remonstrate[d] in the strongest terms against the introduction of a District Asylum into this county'.[91]

89 HCP Parochial Board, vol. 7–19, 26 July 1871.
90 HCP Parochial Board, vol. 7–19, 26 July 1871.
91 HCP Parochial Board, vol. 7–19, 30 Aug. 1871.

Greenock had stated their intention to sell their existing (inadequate) asylum and build a new one. The District Board recommended a union of Paisley Burgh and Abbey to cover the needs of Renfrewshire's upper ward. With this united opposition from Renfrewshire, the SLB relented with great skepticism, writing, 'Although the Commissioners have ceased to attach much weight to such representations [from Greenock], they are still willing in their anxiety to … postpone action for a limited time.'[92]

After this report was presented to the parochial board, the dissenters on the Special Committee, represented by John Brown and Alexander Miller, put forward their proposal to build a new parochial asylum, noting in particular that 'the mode by which the lunatic poor of this parish have been provided for under the immediate care of this Board, from 1752 down to the present day [putting aside the inconvenient fact the board was first constituted in 1846], has operated successfully and proved equally advantageous to the patients and the rate payers'.[93] The idea of keeping fiscal and medical control in the local body won the day. A new special committee was empaneled with Mr John Brown at its head and met that same day to begin work on the new asylum.[94] They began negotiation with the Lunacy Board, which included ensuring Greenock would continue to receive patients from the lower ward even if their plans for a new asylum were delayed. The Lunacy Board, though still preferring a District Asylum, agreed. At last in January 1872 Greenock 'definitely resolved to build for themselves a new Parochial asylum' and purchased the land to do so.[95] Days later the SLB gave their conceptual approval to a new Paisley Parochial Asylum and began discussing locations. Paisley was to provide enough beds to 'accommodate the patients of those parishes of the Upper Ward which are unprovided for in the Abbey Asylum'.[96] All thought of combining the two parishes in

92 HCP Parochial Board, vol. 7–19, 20 Sept. 1871.

93 HCP Parochial Board, vol. 7–19, 20 Sept. 1871.

94 HCP Special Committee appointed by the Board at their meeting of this date to carry into effect the resolution of the Board as to Asylum Accommodation, vol. 7–29, 20 Sept. 1871.

95 HCP Special Committee on Asylum Accommodation, vol. 7–29, 15 Jan. 1872; *PHRA* 6 Jan. 1872: 4.

96 HCP Special Committee on Asylum Accommodation, vol. 7–29, 24 Jan. 1872.

Paisley seemed to be past. The new special committee began investigating possible parcels of land and examining plans of model institutions.[97]

The Asylum and Local Control

The men of the Paisley Parochial Board were deeply invested in the asylum question, as evidenced by the many times it returned to their agenda. Some of their interest was clearly a question of finances; elected by the ratepayers, they were exquisitely sensitive to the costs of care. The impact on town rates meant the asylum also became a political question; in 1871 and again in 1872 men stood for the board precisely to vote in support of or against the plan. Yet there was also a sense of local, professional pride and duty of care to the people of Paisley that is evident in these arguments. While board members watched and bargained over the cost of food, repairs, and salaries connected to their institutions, they expressed at least as much pride over their care for the poor as they did for their fiscal responsibility, pride that extended to the parish's treatment of the mentally ill.

When the Paisley Asylum was first being critically examined by Commissioner Coxe and the Lunacy Act was a newsworthy sensation, *The Scotsman* raked Paisley with the crossfire of an attack against the poor law generally, extracting from the Lunacy Commissioner's report a horrific tale of mistreatment of a disabled girl in Falkland and continuing, 'a similar case was lately brought to light in Paisley. Only last year [1860] it was found that a young woman was kept in a cage in the backroom of a small shop in that town in a state of absolute nudity.'[98] The paper maintained it was a fear of the exorbitant cost of placing their daughter in care that brought the Paisley couple to imprison her at home. Inspector Brown was so incensed at the aspersion cast against his office that he – after consultation with the

97 HCP Special Committee on Asylum Accommodation, vol. 7–29, 31 Jan. 1872.

98 *The Scotsman* 31 Dec. 1861: 1 via *The British Newspaper Archive*.

parochial board – wrote twice to the paper's editor seeking to correct the record, finally inducing the father of the patient to write his own version of the facts exonerating the Paisley poor law authorities of any role in his daughter's experience or decision regarding her care.

For the *Poor Law Magazine*, which printed excerpts of the exchange, the case provided a chance to rail against the Lunacy Act.[99] For Inspector Brown, however, the goal was to defend his own and Paisley's reputation. As recorded after Inspector Brown presented the kerfuffle to the board, 'it was thereafter remitted to the Relief Committee to take any further steps in this matter which may seem to be necessary in vindication of the Board.'[100]

Whenever given the opportunity, the parochial board defended their treatment of both the poor and asylum inmates, including when they expended more than the minimum required by the poor law. Inmates of the asylum were treated to an annual 'soiree' featuring fruits and music at the New Year, and the board was at pains to point out that the diet provided to inmates of their House exceeded the government dietary tables in nutritional value.[101] They noted that regarding the asylum, the cost per inmate exceeded that in comparable institutions.[102] While these luxuries may not have been appreciated or even evident to the inmates or their families, they do add weight to the board's contention that they were genuinely concerned both with maintaining local control over a small institution as well as with the perceived excessive cost of a District Asylum.

Yet neither local pride nor the parochial board vote in favor of the new construction was enough to convince opponents of the project, and these men saw an opening in the unwinding of the calendar. By the time the Lunacy Board approved Paisley's plan for a new asylum the parochial board's 1871 term was near expiring. At the 31 January board meeting Provost David Murray threw the brakes on the Special Committee's actions, challenging their ability to purchase land and claiming that 'negotiations with

99 'How Stories about Lunatics are Got Up', *The Poor Law Magazine for Scotland* IV (Feb. 1862): 273–80.

100 HCP Parochial Board, vol. 7–19, 15 Jan. 1862.

101 HCP Poorhouse Committee, vol. 7–27, 6 June 1854.

102 HCP Poorhouse Committee, vol. 7–29, 6 May 1867.

the Abbey Board are not exhausted'.[103] Provost Murray's desire not to encumber the burgh with a new and expensive institution is understandable in the context of his focus as Provost on ending the economic disability Paisley had been under since the 1843 bankruptcy. After first serving as Provost in the immediate aftermath of the disaster and implementation of the New Poor Law, he was called back to serve a second time as Provost in 1869. Determined to bring the Town out of trusteeship, he was evidently reluctant to build a new, expensive hospital that would lay more obligations on the ratepayers.[104]

The Special Committee horrified, dispatched their chair (John Brown), Inspector Brown, and a sheaf of meeting minutes as evidence to seek advice in Edinburgh. They asked the Board of Supervision, in particular, if the parochial board was empowered to set aside the activities of a committee acting under their charge, specifically empowered to carry out those actions.[105] The Board of Supervision determined on a technicality that the parochial board had been within its rights to stop the land purchase, because the committee itself had asked the parochial board to sanction the action. They were not prepared to comment, though, on whether the whole process of constructing a new asylum could be stopped. That would have to be settled by the Scottish Lunacy Board.

When visited in their turn, the Lunacy Board was far less phlegmatic. In response to Inspector Brown's explanation of the situation the board secretary's clerk wrote, 'I was directed to say that they learned with surprise that the Parochial Board of Paisley had resiled from an arrangement which they had led the Board [SLB] to regard as conclusively settled'. Pointing out that Greenock had now acquired the land for their new asylum, the Lunacy Board told Paisley's board that they had only three options (none of which was the status quo): to go ahead with building their own new asylum; to accept that a District Asylum would be built complete with

103 HCP Parochial Board, vol. 7–19, 31 Jan. 1872.

104 J. C. Murray, *Memoir of David Murray, Late Provost of Paisley, with Sketches of Local History in His Time* (Paisley: Alexander Gardner, 1881), 107–8. Paisley was finally relieved of its debts with the passage of the Paisley Burgh and Navigation Act later in 1872.

105 HCP Special Committee on New Asylum, vol. 7–29, 9 Feb. 1872.

the additional assessment that would bring; or convince Greenock to expand their asylum plans sufficiently to take Paisley and the Upper Ward's patients who were not provided for by Abbey.[106] Finally, the Lunacy Board stated they would not now approve any plan to expand the Abbey Asylum to accommodate Paisley patients.

The Special Committee, no doubt gleeful at this repudiation of Murray's roadblock, arranged for the publication of the issue in the local press and began an active campaign to return a pro-asylum block to the board.[107] In an open letter to the ratepayers in Paisley they struck back at rumors of waste and luxury, asserting, 'a PLAIN and INEXPENSIVE building is all that is contemplated, and though it will fall to the Burgh to borrow the money needed for the erection, the adjoining parishes will pay their full share of the cost in the weekly charge made for their boarders'. After summarising the cost estimates and dismissing the option of combination with Abbey, they concluded with an appeal for local care as 'the most comfortable for the patients, and the most efficient in its curative properties; as well as most convenient for the patients being visited by their friends'.[108] The pro-asylum faction won seats and John Brown himself was called to the Board Chair in spite of a tradition of two-year terms that would have seen the anti-asylum Robert Brown retain the Chair. David Murray, who retained his ex-officio seat, immediately took the lead in opposing the new parochial institution.

Murray brought his decades of civil government experience into the first meeting about the asylum, determined to have his way through obstructionism if not through arguments. After opposing the election of a Chair based on his stance on a single issue, Murray attempted to delay action on Brown's preferred motion – to move forward with the new asylum – by insisting that the board could take up no business before their standing rules of order for the year had been adopted. The power of the pro-asylum group was reinforced when they backed their Chair in delaying the adoption of the rules. Murray's faction further delayed the approval of committee minutes

106 HCP Special Committee on New Asylum, vol. 7–29, 9 Feb. 1872.

107 HCP Special Committee on New Asylum, vol. 7–29, 9 Feb. 1872; 'Asylum Accommodation for Paisley', *PHRA*, 17 Feb. 1872: 4.

108 *PHRA*, 17 Feb. 1872: 5.

from the interim session, proposing instead to nullify any actions taken by any committee (only the Special Committee on the New Asylum had any such action) since the board had adjourned in January. After a roll-call vote, the minutes were accepted. Then the Provost refused to acquiesce to the decision for a new asylum. He refused to believe that a parochial asylum would be less expensive than a District Asylum, offering his own estimate in the £10,000–£12,000 range. He then again brought up the suggestion to form a union with Abbey. Although this proposal had been made and rejected several times in the past decade, in 1872 there was more than a whisper of possibility that it would happen regardless of the other parish's objections, because Parliament was again considering revision to the poor law in Scotland.[109]

Since 1869 a new Parliamentary Committee had been examining the workings of the poor law in Scotland. The MP from Ayr, Mr Edward Craufurd, was particularly driven by the pursuit of inefficiencies in the administration of the poor law.[110] The bill he first brought forward in 1869 and was still attempting to pass in 1872 included a provision that parishes like Abbey and Paisley, which split a significant community between them, would be fully combined for the purposes of poor relief.[111] Provost Murray and his faction proposed that no action on Paisley's asylum should go forward while Craufurd's bill was pending. This action, like the one before it, was voted down by a resounding majority of the board. The necessary committee on the new asylum was immediately empaneled – but their first action was to write to the Scottish Lunacy Board to ask for a delay on implementing their plans until after the second reading of Craufurd's bill (when it would be clear if the bill would be passed).[112] Thus the Special Committee on the New Asylum did not meet again until the Poor Law Amendment bill was withdrawn at the end of the Parliamentary session without a second reading.

The start-and-stop process of the asylum shows a crucial shortcoming of the civil government model in Victorian Scotland. In addition to navigating local political factions, the poor law managers were beholden to

109 *PHRA* 9 March 1872: 4.

110 'The Poor Law Bill (From the Courant)', *The Poor Law Magazine and Parochial Journal* 4 (1876): 233.

111 Hansards 'House of Commons Sitting of Tuesday, 13 February 1872.'

112 HCP Special Committee on Asylum Accommodation, vol. 7–29, 27 March 1872.

two separate (and potentially rival) supervisory boards and the supreme, distant legislative body. Even when the Board of Supervision and the SLB agreed on a course of action, the entire project was frozen for months as the locality waited to learn if their playing field would shift. The combination of jealousy over local control and the potential futility of such control in the face of a distant Parliament worked to undermine the desired efficiency of action.

Asylum Construction

In August 1872, more than five years after the Lunacy Board's ultimatum, Paisley Parochial Board finally purchased a 25-acre lot at Riccartsbar, adjoining the Abbey poor house/asylum property, for the construction of their own parochial asylum. In addition to being an expansive rural setting, the location was chosen precisely to leave open the possibility of a future union of the parishes' institutions. The price for the land alone was £5,000, which was the whole amount Inspector Brown had estimated for land and building, including furniture, eighteen months earlier. On 25 November, Inspector Brown presented the Board of Supervision-approved plans for the new asylum to the Asylum Committee. As Chairman Brown had promised, it was to be plain, sturdily made without frills, and the building alone was estimated to cost £8,500, bringing the total cost with land to £11,400 – a purported £56 per bed less than a District Asylum.[113]

When Inspector Brown returned home from this meeting, he came to a house in turmoil. Elizabeth was suffering with typhoid fever, a disease all too common in the crowded, dirty Sneddon. She died the next day. There must have been a palpable gap in the family that James Shaw had left to her running. It was 23-year-old David Brown, not his father, who signed the death record certifying he had been present at the time.[114] Younger

113 HCP Asylum Committee, vol. 7–29, 25 Nov. 1872.

114 1872 Brown, Elizabeth (Statutory Deaths 573/867), *ScotlandsPeople*.

brother John may have already been exhibiting worrying signs of mental illness, perhaps self-medicating with the alcohol his father would initially blame for his troubles. Undoubtedly the Misses Brown rallied around to care for their brother and his family, but Elizabeth's steady hand could not be easily or quickly replaced.

In recognition of the inspector's bereavement, the parochial board delayed their regular meeting for a week.[115] When the delayed meeting was convened, Provost Murray and his faction made a last attempt to derail the project. Although the land was purchased, a donation of stone from the Earl of Glasgow's Foxbar quarries had been secured, and an £8,000 bank loan was arranged, the faction voted against approval of the Asylum Committee's actions.[116] Someone calling themselves 'A Burgh Ratepayer' published a personal attack on John Brown, claiming the Chairman, 'who is using such great and arbitrary efforts to get the Burgh involved in apparently something like an expenditure of £20,000, only pays annually £1 13s. 8. of poor rates in the Burgh'.[117] Two weeks later, in the parochial board meeting that happened to fall on Christmas Eve, Robert Brown and Provost Murray presented two separate amendments to stop the asylum proceedings and combine with Abbey. Both failed. The next month Murray again protested the plans, offering formal documentation of his dissent and the reasons for it. Although the board was at the end of its session, they appointed a special committee, headed by James Barclay, to formally give the majority's response to the Provost.

Murray covered no new ground. Again, he pointed to the likelihood that Abbey and Paisley would be forced into combination through future legislation, and objected to the idea that a stand-alone parochial asylum could be run any more economically than a District Asylum. The responding board members pointed out the convenient location of the Riccartsbar site if a combination was carried out. They roundly rejected the idea that anything had been done in haste, given the half-decade delay since the Paisley Asylum had been pronounced unfit. They defended the economy of

115 HCP Parochial Board, vol. 7–19, 27 Nov. 1872.
116 HCP Special Committee on New Asylum, vol. 7–29, 9 Dec. 1872.
117 *PHRA* 7 Dec. 1872: 4.

their plans as bid to cost £110 per bed (a savings of £60 on average District Asylum costs, though a 40 percent increase over original estimates), and cited the support their plan had from the Lunacy Board and the Board of Supervision. In countering a point about what supposed control parishes sending boarding patients to the asylum might have, the board maintained, 'It is a distinctive and important feature of the new asylum that subject to the rules of the General Board [SLB] it is under our own exclusive management and control.'[118]

The dissenting faction again made the asylum an issue in the parochial board election of 1873, including a public meeting that resolved to support candidates opposed to the asylum.[119] In spite of this apparent public support, none of the dissenters were returned to the parochial board for the next session.[120] Of his faction, only Provost Murray continued on the board by virtue of his position. Following this last attempt to derail the project, the construction of the asylum went forward relatively smoothly.

By April 1874 it was clear that the cost of the asylum was going to far exceed Inspector Brown's estimates, as a surge of inflation had hit Britain since the project began.[121] There were also troubles in the management of the poor house, not only with its size but with a lice outbreak in the women's ward.[122] Inspector Brown must have felt these blows to his professional reputation, but in the same months he had much greater concerns at home. His son John's mental state had deteriorated since the New Year, being both 'restless and depressed' and refusing to eat 'on the ground that it injures others'.[123] Although he maintained John's troubles were caused by intemperance, he used his professional knowledge to get his son into the best possible treatment when it became clear he needed medical intervention. On April 7 he conveyed the young man to Dumfries, where he was examined by the sheriff and two doctors, then committed as a private patient in the Crichton Royal Institution. There is no indication why John

118 HCP Special Committee on New Asylum, vol. 7–29, 6 Feb. 1873.
119 *PHRA* 15 Feb. 1873: 1.
120 *Watson's Directory for Paisley* 1873–1874: 212.
121 HCP Poorhouse Committee, vol. 7–29, April 1874.
122 HCP Poorhouse Committee, vol. 7–29, 4 March 1874.
123 John Brown, Notice of Admission, 11 April 1874.

was treated at Crichton instead of the much-closer Gartnavel Royal Asylum in Glasgow. The Dumfries asylum was newer and founded with an intent to humanely treat its patients (including a therapeutic art program), but by the 1870s there was little to choose between the hospitals.[124] Perhaps Inspector Brown wanted his son in the more peaceful setting outside the city, or perhaps he was placing an embarrassment outside the circle of his professional acquaintance.

The medical men at Crichton did not share James Shaw Brown's opinion that John's illness was caused by drink. They described delusions, 'when he eats he says it causes pain to others ... by inflicting wounds upon himself destroys his brother's influence over him', and certified he was of unsound mind.[125] He remained at Crichton for fourteen years and was institutionalised for the rest of his life. While Inspector Brown was adjusting the Paisley Asylum design and contract to remove the clock and belfry that had become an unaffordable luxury, he must have been imagining his younger son in the dreary place.[126]

Meanwhile, the Board of Supervision's displeasure with the poor house proper became increasingly strident, going so far in March 1876 as to propose a wholly new building in order to obtain proper classification. The parochial board rejected that idea as unsustainable after the costs for the new asylum. The Board of Supervision had no real power to force the Paisley board into action – no licenses to withhold or legal jurisdiction over inmates – and the poor house remained where it was, shifting paupers to fill the vacated asylum space.

Then, in April 1876, as the finishing touches were being put on the asylum and its rules formally accepted, what had been Inspector Brown's creeping frailty became sudden illness.

> He left his last meeting complaining much of weakness, and he was never again on the street in life. Congestion of the lungs, supervening upon an acute bronchial attack,

124 M. Park, *Art in Madness: Dr W.A.F. Browne's Collection of Patient Art at Crichton Royal Institution, Dumfries* (Dumfries: Dumfries and Galloway Health Board, 2010).

125 John Brown, Notice of Admission, 11 April 1874.

126 HCP Poorhouse and Asylum Committee, vol. 7–29, 24 March 1874.

> soon proved fatal to his enfeebled system; and thus his frequently expressed desire, that he should be able for his work until his last, was fulfilled.[127]

Inspector Brown did not see the ceremonial opening of the new asylum. He did not know (though surely he had a suspicion) that the final tally for constructing and furnishing the asylum was over £21,000 – more than three times his original estimate and more even than the scare comparisons offered by the opponents of the new building. This fact was carefully recorded in the massive *History of Paisley from Roman Times to the Present* that former Provost and Board Chairman Robert Brown wrote in his retirement. A firm member of the asylum dissenting faction, Brown devoted a full page of his 500-page opus to the asylum controversy, including his own role in delaying the project and the bitterly triumphant grand total.[128]

The parochial asylum, at least in terms of start-up costs, was no more economical for ratepayers than a District Asylum would have been. But by insisting on it the parochial board had successfully insisted on the primacy of local control over the national institutions of the poor law and the Lunacy Act. The victory was frankly in name only; by 1892 the parochial board's standing orders gave as the charge for the Asylum Committee, 'The proceedings of this committee shall continue to be conducted and regulated by the special Rules and Regulations for its guidance sanctioned by the General Board of Lunacy.'[129] The asylum was at long last combined with the Abbey establishment after the Paisley Poorhouse on New Sneddon was closed in 1896 and it officially became a District Asylum in 1909.[130] Yet the form of the thing was important. Since the Burgh of Paisley had taken charge of poor relief in 1839 the managers had shown a belief that they, not legislators or paid bureaucrats, knew how best to manage care for the disadvantaged in their community. It was not a belief they surrendered easily.

127 *PHRA* 13 May 1876: 1.

128 R. Brown, *History of Paisley: From the Roman Period Down to 1884*, vol. II (Paisley: J & J Cook, 1886), 467–8.

129 *Paisley Parochial Board Standing Orders*, 1892, 8. Bound into HCP Parochial Board, vol. 7–19.

130 Farquharson, 'Scottish Poor Law of Lunacy', 25.

Epilogue: Inspector Brown's Legacy: The New Poor Law in Paisley after 1876

Death brought more public recognition to James Shaw Brown than he ever permitted in his life. The *Paisley Herald and Renfrewshire Advertiser* first published a short notice the Saturday after his death, concluding,

> Mr Brown had a good knowledge of poor law matters, being a thoughtful, prudent man, he conducted the complicated affairs of the board with other parishes with great success, and during his whole career scarcely ever lost a case when forced to go into court. In fact, it is no exaggeration to say that he had no superiors and few equals as an Inspector of the Poor in Scotland. He was likewise just and humane to the poor, and in all respects a model officer, whose loss the parochial board will not easily be able to supply.[1]

At a special meeting of the parochial board called to plot a course forward in Brown's absence, board member James Clark reflected,

> He had not had the privilege of the late Mr Brown's acquaintance so long as many of them but during its existence he had been enabled to adequately appreciate his great value and worth and was assured that his place would be most difficult indeed to fill up with one equally qualified for the performance of its many onerous duties. He had been informed by one of the most able solicitors that in matters of Poor Law few men could give an opinion so reliable as that of the late Mr Brown and his death was a loss to the country at large as well as to our own more particularly interested parish. It has been his privilege to visit during the past two years with the Committee and Mr Brown the children boarded throughout the country and he was deeply impressed with the care he always took in having them put under guardians who might be depended upon so that the children might in their early days have such a good example shewn to them as would mould their character in after life. In every sense of the word Mr Brown was a good man and his unexpected and sudden removal by death he deeply regretted whilst sincerely sympathising with his afflicted family.[2]

1 *PHRA* 8 April 1876: 4.
2 HCP Parochial Board Minutes, vol. 7–19, 11 April 1876.

Soon afterward *The Paisley Herald* reprinted in full the obituary written by Brown's fellow inspectors for *The Poor Law Magazine,*

> It is unnecessary, in this Magazine, to enlarge upon Mr Brown's capacity as an inspector. His knowledge of the Poor Law, as thorough as it was minute, was quite recognised, and highly esteemed by his brother inspectors. … In cases of disputed settlements, involving a construction and application of the statute, or of case-law, he was virtually the law-agent of his board; and, perhaps, there has not, hitherto, been any parish of similar extent in Scotland, which has been so rarely, and so successfully, engaged in litigation as the parish of Paisley. … Unambitious and diffident, Mr Brown was contented to remain … in a narrower sphere than that to which his education and faculties might have entitled him to aspire. … [A]lthough he was a man of considerable literary culture and of varied information, the exactness and extent of these were known only to intimate friends. But all who knew him, knew of his goodness of heart, and gentle courtesy.[3]

The Poor Law Magazine noted that Inspector Brown's death meant more than the passing of a respected colleague. After honoring his long service, they added: 'With him there has passed one of the few remaining official links between the former and the present methods of parochial administration.'[4] Inspector Brown's youth when he began his work with the poor law meant that at the end of his long career most of his colleagues had never known another system of relief. Memories of devastating want in the 1840s were fading from official memory, and both court decisions and reforming legislation from the later 1860s onward tended toward narrowing access to relief. A proliferation of new charitable organisations took on voluntary care for improving the lot of the poor whom they believed 'redeemable', and supporting a 'more discriminatory, more reformatory, and more rational' version of poor relief for Scotland. Brown's death is as good a moment as any to mark the 'end of the beginning' of the New Poor Law, when it was firmly set into the system of 'adequate but discriminatory relief' that was ultimately replaced by the postwar welfare state.[5]

3 'The Late Mr James Shaw Brown', *The Poor Law Magazine for Scotland* IV (May 1876): 240–1; *PHRA*, 13 May 1876: 1.

4 'The Late Mr James Shaw Brown', 241.

5 I. Levitt, *Poverty & Welfare in Scotland 1890–1948* (Edinburgh: Edinburgh University Press, 1988), 15, 7.

The transition was literally visible in the Paisley record. For four weeks following Inspector Brown's death his assistant, appointed Interim Inspector, kept the books as before. Immediately after the new inspector, promoted from a position as clerk in the Abbey poor house, took office the format of the minutes changed, refreshed for a new, modernised era when clarity was more important than conserving paper. One month later the asylum patients were transferred to the new building at Riccartsbar. The move out of the Sneddon asylum was the first concrete action to acknowledge that the century-old site was no longer suitable and the presence of the poor house so near the town centre was not desirable. By the end of the century the long-debated union with Abbey poor house took place and the old hospital was demolished.

Poor law administration offers a lens to see the dynamic social complexity in Paisley and similar Scottish communities as they coped with economic stress. As originally implemented the purpose of the Law was to ease want, and the leadership of the Burgh embraced that goal in the name of maintaining civic order. Yet the history at this perspective is messy, made up of conflicting goals and agendas both between the recipients of relief and its administrators and between the administrators themselves. Paisley was both conformist to centralised demands and an outlier, agitating for their own interests before ultimately complying with instruction from the centre (which had itself been shaped by communication with the periphery). Applicants for relief were both paupers and successful survivors of poverty, and the managers of the poor were both sympathetic and needed to make hard decisions about granting relief.

Paisley's inhabitants were not unified in their view or use of the poor law, and the same kind of variety existed across Scotland. There were clear and predictable differences between Scottish communities regarding how many financial and mental resources they would invest in the poor and how they might distribute these resources. Paisley illustrates one collection of circumstances, the sense of which can be inferred for every other parish in the nation. The nuance of compliance and resistance, disagreement, consensus, and petty revenge was repeated in every parish, each with its own unique outcome. The poor law was a pervasive element of every community as a threat or a promise, a safety net or a shameful descent (or both).

Like any community institution its development was a process of contest and argument, never simple compliance with a top-down mandate, and legislation did not magically reform behaviors or institutions. The pace of change was slow and erratic precisely because it involved so many individuals and levels of power with poorly defined relationships. Government is easily seen as a series of Parliamentary debates and acts that may or may not be effective. Probing into the effects at a local level shows the conflicting pressures on the men who had to implement the Law, an implementation that was neither easy nor necessarily welcome.

The poor law was not quite finished with James Shaw Brown and his family. As his health failed, Inspector Brown had established a trust that ensured lifetime care for his son John. James Shaw's brother, John, and elder son, David, were the primary trustees. In 1888 the money intended to support John mysteriously vanished, and he was brought back to Paisley to live with his aunts in the family building. The experiment in home care was not successful. John was recommitted in July, this time as a pauper lunatic in the Riccartsbar asylum.[6] Until his death in 1893 he was maintained there by poor rates, as none of his surviving relations were legally obligated to support his care.[7]

David Brown died in Edinburgh the day after his brother was committed in Riccartsbar, and following John's death the 3 Back Sneddon property transferred to David's childless widow and unmarried sister-in-law.[8] What had begun for the Brown family in 1815 with optimism and upward mobility for David Brown, blacksmith, ended with half a dozen women holding significant property while the male line expired. Nearly a century after the little family moved to the burgh, the blacksmith's last

6 John Brown, Notices of Admission MC2_352 24625, obtained courtesy of Scottish Indexes.

7 1893 Brown, John (Statutory registers Deaths 573/353), *ScotlandsPeople*.

8 1894 Brown, David (Wills and testaments Reference SC70/1/329. Edinburgh Sheriff Court Inventories) *ScotlandsPeople*. The coincidence of the loss of the money, John's recommitment, and David's near-simultaneous death is obviously tantalising, but is both beyond the scope of this work and apparently lost to time.

surviving daughter left legacies totaling more than £5,000 to a variety of institutions, relations and friends, including a £400 contribution to her kirk congregation for support of 'the deserving poor'.[9] The parochial institutions that had consumed her brother's life and housed her nephew were not recognised among her legatees.

9 1908 Brown, Ann (Reference SC58/45/16 Paisley Sheriff Court Wills) *ScotlandsPeople*.

Bibliography

Archival Sources

The Heritage Centre, Paisley @ OneRen

Committee Minute Books	Vol. 7–27; 7–28; 7–29
Town Hospital Minute Books	Vol 6–3; 6–4
Parochial Board Minute Book	Vol. 7–19
Statements of Cases	Vol. 11–6; 11–8; 11–12; 11–13; 11–16; 11–17
Town Council Minute Book	Vol 1–28

Newspapers

Glasgow Saturday Post
Paisley Herald and Renfrewshire Advertiser
Paisley Journal and Renfrewshire Gazette

Parliamentary Papers

Cockton Title	Parliament/Vol.
Legislation	
An Act for the Amendment and Better administration of the Laws relating to the Relief of the Poor in Scotland	1845
The Regulation of the Care and Treatment of Lunatics, and for the Provision, Maintenance, and Regulation of Lunatic Asylums in Scotland	1857

Cockton Title	Parliament/Vol.
An Act for the Amendment and better Administration of the Laws relating to the poor in England and Wales	1834

Papers and Reports

Papers relative to Internal State of Country, 1819	P.P. 1819–20 IV
Royal Com. on Handloom Weavers. Assistant Coms' Reports (on Scotland, etc.)	P.P. 1839 XLII
Royal Com. on Handloom Weavers, Assistant Coms'. Reports (on Scotland, etc.)	P.P. 1839 XLII
Coms. On Sanitary Condition of Labouring Population of Great Britain: Reports on Scotland	P.P. 1842 XXVII
Letter to Archbishop of Canterbury, May 1842, for Collection in Aid of Subscription for Relief of Working Classes in England and Scotland	P.P. 1842 XXXVII
Select Committee to inquire into Treatment of Unemployed and Destitute inhabitants of Paisley since 1841.	P.P. 1843 VII
Return of Number of Population and Amount of Poor Relief in each Parish of Scotland, 1836–41.	P.P. 1843 XLIX
Abstract Return Pursuant to Act for taking Account of Population of Great Britain (Enumeration Abstract 1841)	P.P. 1843 XXII
Royal Com. for Inquiring into Administration and Practical Operation of Poor Laws in Scotland: appendix Part I. (Minutes of Evidence, Edinburgh, Glasgow, Greenock, Paisley, Ayr and Kilmarnock)	P.P. 1844 XX
Royal Com. for inquiring into Administration and Practical Operation of Poor Laws in Scotland	P.P. 1844 XX
First Annual Report of the Board of Supervision for the Relief of the Poor in Scotland	P.P. 1847 XXVIII
Return of Population; Annual Value of Property rated to Poor; Expenditure for Relief of Poor; and Number of Paupers relieved in Scotland, 1851–2	P.P. 1854 LIX.
Select Committee on Operation of Poor Law (Scotland). Report, Proceedings, Minutes of Evidence, Appendix, Index	P.P. 1868–9 XI
Select Committee on Operation of Poor Law in Scotland: Report, Proceedings	P.P. 1871 XI

Cockton Title	Parliament/Vol.
Select Committee on Operation of Laws in United Kingdom Relating to Settlement and Irremovability of Paupers, with Special Reference to Removals to Ireland. Report, Proceedings, Minutes of Evidence, Appendix, Index	P.P. 1878–9 XII

Hansards

House of Lords Sessional Papers Third Series	Third series 1842 vol. 63
19th Century House of Commons Sessional Papers	Third series Vol. 64 1842
19 Century House of Commons Sessional Papers	Third Series vol. 76
19th Century House of Commons Sessional Papers	Third Series Vol. 82

Court Cases

Case	Court	Session/Year
Crieff v Foulis Wester (Crieff v Little Dunkeld and Monzievaird)	Court of Session, Second Division	19 July 1842
Adams v M'William and Thomson and M'Tear v Lindsay	Court of Session	27 Feb. 1849
Hay v Scott	Court of Session, Second Division	23 Nov. 1852
Adamson v Barbour	House of Lords	30 May 1853
Gibson v Murray	Court of Session, Second Division	13 June 1854
Hay v Thomson and Manson	Court of Session, Second Division	23 June 1854
Robertson v Brown and Stewart	Court of Session, First Division	12 Dec. 1854
Hay v Thomson and Beattie (Hay v Thomson, Laing, and Others)	Court of Session, First Division	6 February 1856
Meek v Hunter and Petrie	Supreme Court, Second Division	4 March 1859

Case	Court	Session/Year
Prestonpans v Dunse	Supreme Court, Whole Court	24 February 1860
Jack v *Isdale*	House of Lords	12 February 1866
John Welsh (Inspector of Poor for Parish of Kelton) v *John Lowden (Inspector of Poor for Parish of Urr)*	Court of Session	25 Oct. 1894

Other Archives: Manuscript Sources

Falkirk Archives, Denny Parochial Board Minutes

National Records of Scotland, Notices of Admission by the Superintendent of the Mental Institutions

Other Archives: Digitised Resources

National Records of Scotland via *ScotlandsPeople*, scotlandspeople.gov.uk

Plan of Paisley and its Environs, 1839

Sheriff's Court Records

Valuation Rolls

Vital Records

National Library of Scotland

Fowler's Commercial Directory of Renfrewshire, 1834–5

Fowler's Commercial Directory of Paisley, 1838–54

Watson's Commercial Directory and General Advertiser, 1862–84

Maps

Ordnance Survey, Paisley 1857, 25 inch, 1st edn

Ordnance Survey, Paisley 1867–8, Large-scale Town Plan

Wood, John. *Paisley* 1828

Published Sources

Alison, W.P. *Illustrations of the Scottish System of Management of the Poor*, Edinburgh, 1840.

Andrews, J. *'They're in the Trade … of Lunacy, they "cannot interfere" They Say': The Scottish Lunacy Commissions and Lunacy Reform in Nineteenth-Century Scotland*. London: Wellcome Institute for the History of Medicine Occasional Publication no. 8, 1998.

Baker, L. 'Survival Strategies of Widows in Dijon during the French Revolution'. *Women's Studies* 31 (2002): 53–65.

Bain, A. 'The Beginnings of Democratic control of Local Education in Scotland'. *Scottish Economic and Social History* 23:1 (2003): 7–25.

Baldwin, M.P. 'Subject to Empire: Married Women and the British Nationality and Status of Alien Act'. *Journal of British Studies* 40:4 (Oct. 2001): 522–56.

Barrie, D.G. 'Anglicization and Autonomy: Scottish policing, Governance and the State, 1833 to 1885'. *Law and History Review* 30:2 (May 2012): 449–94.

Bartlett, P. and D. Wright, eds. *Outside the Walls of the Asylum: The History of Care in the Community 1750–2000*. Cambridge: Cambridge University Press, 1999.

Blaikie, A. 'Nuclear Hardship or Variant Dependency? Households and the Scottish Poor Law'. *Continuity and Change* 17:2 (2002): 253–80.

Blaikie, A. 'Accounting for Poverty: Conflicting Constructions of Family Survival in Scotland, 1855–1925'. *Journal of Historical Sociology* 18:3 (Sept. 2005): 202–26.

Blaikie, A. *Illegitimacy, Sex, and Society: Northeast Scotland, 1750–1900*. Oxford: Clarendon Press, 1993.

Blair, M. *The Paisley Shawl and the Men Who Produced It: A Record of an Interesting Epoch in the History of the Town*. Paisley: Alexander Gardner, 1904.

Brown, R. *A History of Paisley from the Roman Period Down to 1884*. Paisley: J. & J. Cook, 1886.

Brundage, A. *The Making of the New Poor Law: The Politics of Inquiry, Enactment, and Implementation, 1832–9*. New Brunswick, NJ: Rutgers University Press, 1978.

Calomiris, C. and L. Schweikart, 'The Panic of 1857: Origins, Transmission, and Containment'. *Journal of Economic History* 51:4 (1991): 807–34.

Campey, L. *An Unstoppable Force: The Scottish Exodus to Canada*. Toronto: Natural Heritage Books, 2008.

Chalmers, T. *Christian and Economic Polity of a Nation with Special Reference to Large Towns*. Edinburgh: T. Constable, 1854.

Cherry, S. and R. Munting. '"Exercise is the Thing"? Sport and the Asylum c. 1850–1950'. *The International Journal of the History of Sport* 22:1 (2005): 42–58.

Clabburn, P. *Shawls: In Imitation of the Indian*. Haverfordwest: Shire Publications, 1981.

Clark, A. 'The New Poor Law and the Breadwinner Wage: Contrasting Assumptions'. *Journal of Social History* 34:2 (2000): 261–81.

Clark, S. *Paisley: A History*. Edinburgh: Mainstream Publishing, 1988.

Coats, A.W., ed. *Poverty in the Victorian Age Vol. IV, Scottish Poor Laws 1815–70*. Westmead, Hants: Gregg International Publishers, 1973.

Cody, L.F. 'The Politics of Illegitimacy in an Age of Reform: Women, Reproduction, and Political Economy in England's New Poor law of 1834'. *Journal of Women's History* 11:4 (2000): 131–56.

Cockburn, C. *The Local State: Management of Cities and People*. London: Pluto Press, 1977.

Cullen, M.J. *The Statistical Movement in Early Victorian Britain: The Foundations of Empirical Social Research*. New York: Barnes and Noble Books, 1975.

Devine, T.M. *The Scottish Nation: A History 1700–2000*. New York: Viking-Pengui, 1999.

Devine, T.M. *The Great Highland Famine: Hunger, Emigration and the Scottish Highlands in the Nineteenth Century*. Edinburgh: John Donald, 1988.

Dickson, A. and W. Speirs. 'Changes in Class Structure in Paisley, 1750–1845'. *Scottish Historical Review* 59:167 part 1 (April 1980): 54–72.

Dickson, T. and T. Clarke, 'Social Concern and Social Control in Nineteenth-Century Scotland: Paisley 1841–3'. *Scottish Historical Review* 65:179 part 1 (April 1986): 48–60.

Dunlop, A. *The Law of Scotland Regarding the Poor*. Edinburgh and London: W. Blackwood and Sons, 1854.

Englander, D. *Poverty and Poor Law Reform in Nineteenth-Century Britain, 1834–1914*. London and New York: Addison Wesley Longman, 1998.

Erikson, A. 'Coverture and Capitalism'. *History Workshop Journal* 59:1 (Spring 2005): 1–16.

Evans, E. *The Forging of the Modern State: Early Industrial Britain 1783–1870*. 3rd edn. London and New York: Longmans, 2001.

Farquharson. 'A "Scottish Poor Law of Lunacy"? Poor Law, Lunacy Law and Scotland's Parochial Asylums'. *History of Psychiatry* 28:1 (2017): 15–28.

Flanders, J. *Inside the Victorian Home: A Portrait of Domestic Life in Victorian England*. London: W.W. Norton, 2003.

Foster, J. *Members of Parliament, Scotland, 1857–82*. 2nd ed. London: Hazell, Watson, and Viney, 1882.

Fraser, W.H. and R.J. Morris, eds. *People and Society in Scotland 1830–1914*. Edinburgh: John Donald, 1990.

Gollaher, D. *Voice for the Mad: The Life of Dorothea Dix*. New York: The Free Press, 1995.

Goose, N. 'Workhouse Populations in the Mid- Nineteenth Century: The case of Hertfordshire'. *Local Population Studies* 52 (1999): 52–67.

Gordon, E. and G. Nair, *Public Lives: Women, Family, and Society in Victorian Britain*. New Haven: Yale University Press, 2003.

Gordon, E. and G. Nair, 'The Economic Role of Middle-Class Women in Victorian Glasgow'. *Women's History Review* 9:4 (2000): 791–814.

Gordon, W. *Mill Girls and Strangers: Single Women's Independent Migration in England, Scotland and the United States, 1850–81*. Albany: State University of New York Press, 2002.

Gordon, W. 'Destitute in December: Unmarried Scots Navigating Poverty in Paisley, 1861'. In *Single Life and the City 1200–1900*, J. De Groot, I. Devos and A. Schmidt, eds. New York: Palgrave Macmillan, 2015.

Gordon, W. 'The Demographics of Scottish Poverty: Paisley's Applications for Relief, 1861–71'. *Journal of Scottish Historical Studies* 30:1 (2010): 25–45.

Gordon, W. 'Seeking Relief on Love Street: Gender, Mobility and Pauperism in Mid-nineteenth Century Scotland'. In *Gender and Mobility in Scotland and Abroad*, S. Dy, E. Ewan and A. Glaze, eds. Guelph: University of Guelph, 2018.

Grierson, A. 'One-hundred Years of Scottish Local Government'. *Public Administration* 13:3 (1935): 230–41.

Griffin, B. 'Class, Gender, and Liberalism in Parliament, 1868–82: The Case of the Married Women's Property Acts'. *The Historical Journal* 46:1 (2003): 59–87.

Harley, J. 'Material Lives of the Poor and Their Strategic Use of the Workhouse During the Final Decades of the English Old Poor Law'. *Continuity and Change* 30:1 (2015): 71–103.

Harris, B. and C. McKean. *The Scottish Town in the Age of the Enlightenment 1740–1820*. Edinburgh: Edinburgh University Press, 2014.

Harris, B. 'Parsimony and Pauperism: Poor Relief in England, Scotland and Wales in the Nineteenth and Early Twentieth Centuries'. *Journal of Scottish Historical Studies* 39:1 (2019): 40–74.

Hassan, G. 'The Rise and Fall of Civil Society in Scotland'. *Scottish Review* 12 Aug. 2020.

Healey, J. '"By the Charitie of Good People": Poverty and Neighbourly Support in Seventeenth Century Lancashire'. *Family & Community History* 19:2 (2016): 83–94.

Henderson, W.O. 'The Cotton Famine in Scotland and the Relief of Distress, 1862–4'. *Scottish Historical Review* 30:110 part 2 (1951): 154–64.

Hickman, C. 'Cheerful Prospects and Tranquil Restoration: The Visual Experience of Landscape as Part of the Therapeutic Regime of the British Asylum, 1800–60'. *History of Psychiatry* 20:4 (2009): 425–41.

Hinde, A. 'The Population of Two Hampshire Workhouses, 1851–61'. *Local Population Studies* 61 (1998): 38–53.

Hughes, J.R.T. 'The Commercial Crisis of 1857'. *Oxford Economic Papers* new series 8:2 (1956): 194–222.

Huston, J. *The Panic of 1857 and the Coming of the Civil War*. Baton Rouge: Louisiana State University Press, 1987.

Hutchison, I.G.C. *Industry, Reform and Empire: Scotland, 1790–1880*. Edinburgh: Edinburgh University Press, 2020

J.W.C. *The Town of Paisley: Historical Sketch*. Paisley, 1878.

Johnston, R. '"Charity that Heals": The Scottish Labour Colony Association and Attitudes to the Able-bodied Unemployed in Glasgow, 1890–1914'. *Scottish Historical Review* LXXVII:1, no. 203 (1998): 77–95.

Jones, P. and S. King, eds. *Obligation, Entitlement, and Dispute Under the English Poor Laws*. Newcastle upon Tyne: Cambridge Scholars, 2015.

Keith, T. 'Municipal Elections in the Royal Burghs of Scotland: II. From the Union to the Passing of the Scottish Burgh Reform Bill in 1833'. *Scottish Historical Review* 1:51 (1916): 111–25.

King, S. and A. Tompkin, eds. *The Poor in England 1700–1850: An Economy of Makeshift*. Manchester: Manchester University Press, 2003.

Knox, W.W. *Hanging by a Thread: The Scottish Cotton Industry, c. 1850–1914*. Preston: Carnegie Publishing, 1995.

Lees, L. *The Solidarities of Strangers: The English Poor Laws and the People, 1700–1948*. Cambridge: Cambridge University Press, 1998.

Leneman, L. '"A Natural Foundation in Equity": Marriage and Divorce in Eighteenth and Nineteenth-Century Scotland'. *Scottish Economic & Social History* 20:2 (2000): 199–215.

Levine-Clark, M. 'Engendering Relief: Women, Ablebodiedness, and the New Poor law in Early Victorian England'. *Journal of Women's History* 11:4 (2000): 107–30.

Levine-Clark, M. 'The Gendered Economy of Family Liability: Intergenerational Relationships and Poor law Relief in England's Black Country, 1871–1911'. *Journal of British Studies* 45:1 (2006): 72–89.

Levitt, I. *Poverty and Welfare in Scotland 1800–1948*. Edinburgh: Edinburgh University Press, 1988.

MacDonald, H.J. 'Boarding-Out and the Scottish Poor Law, 1845–1914'. *Scottish Historical Review* 75:2, no. 200 (1996): 197–220.

MacKinnon, M. 'English Poor Law Policy and the Crusade Against Outrelief'. *Journal of Economic History* 47:3 (1987): 603–25.

Maltby, J. '"The Wife's Administration of the Earnings"? Working-class Women and Savings in the Mid-Nineteenth Century'. *Continuity and Change* 26:2 (2011): 187–217.

Marion, D.E. 'The British Civil Service: A Political Excavation and Review. *Administration and Society* 24:4 (1993): 470–87.

McKay, J. *The Kirk and the Kingdom: A Century of Tension in Scottish Social Theology, 1830–1929*. Edinburgh: Edinburgh University Press, 2012.

McKichan, F. 'A Burgh's Response to the Problems of Urban Growth: Stirling, 1780–1880'. *The Scottish Historical Review*, 57:163 part 1 (April 1978): 68–86.

Meredith, D. and D. Oxley, 'Blood and Bone: Body Mass, Gender and Health Inequality in 19th Century British Families'. *University of Oxford Discussion Papers in Economic and Social History* 118 (2013).

Middleton. C.R. 'The Emergence of Constitutional Bureaucracy in the British Foreign Office, 1782–1841'. *Public Administration* 53:4 (Winter 1975): 365–81.

Mitchison, R. *The Old Poor Law in Scotland: The Experience of Poverty, 1574–1845*. Edinburgh: Edinburgh University Press, 2000.

Monypenny, D. *Remarks on the Poor Laws and on the Method of Providing for the Poor in Scotland*. Edinburgh: T. Clark, 1834.

Morris, R.J. and G. Morton, 'Where was Nineteenth-Century Scotland?' *Scottish Historical Review* LXXIII:195 (April 1994): 89–99.

Morton, G. 'Civil Society, Municipal Government and the State: Enshrinement, Empowerment and Legitimacy, the Antecedents of the 1872 Education Act'. *Scottish Educational Studies* 4:2 (1972): 73–92.

Morton, G. and T. Griffiths, 'Closing the Door on Modern Scotland's Gilded Cage'. *Scottish Historical Review* 92:234 (April 2013): 103–14.

Muller, N. 'Deceit, Deservingness, and Destitution: Able-Bodied Widows and the New Poor Law'. *Journal of Victorian Culture* 26:1 (2021): 89–102.

Murray, J.C. *Memoir of David Murray, Late Provost of Paisley, with Sketches of Local History in His Time*. Paisley: Alexander Gardner, 1881.

Nicholls, G. *A History of the Scotch Poor Law, in Connexion with the Condition of the People*. London: John Murray, 1856.

O'Grada, C. and E. White. 'The Panics of 1854 and 1857: A View from the Emigrant Industrial Savings Bank'. *Journal of Economic History* 63:1 (2003): 213–40.

Park, M. *Art in Madness: Dr W.A.F. Browne's Collection of Patient Art at Crichton Royal Institution, Dumfries*. Dumfries: Dumfries and Galloway Health Board, 2010.

Parkhill, J. *The History of Paisley*. Paisley: Robert Stewart, 1857.

Paterson, A. 'The Poor Law in Nineteenth-Century Scotland'. In *The New Poor Law in the Nineteenth Century*, D. Fraser, ed. New York: St. Martin's Press, 1976.

Peters, L. 'Paisley and the Cotton Famine of 1862–3'. *Scottish Economic & Social History* 21:2 (2001): 121–39.

Raffe, A. '1707, 2007, and the Unionist Turn in Scottish History'. *The Historical Journal* 53:4 (Dec. 2010): 1071–83.

Ross, D. 'Savings Bank Depositors in a Crisis: Glasgow 1847 and 1857'. *Financial History Review* 20:2 (2013): 183–208.

Ross, K. 'The Locational History of Scotland's District Lunatic Asylums, 1857–1913', Unpublished Ph.D. Thesis in Geographical and Earth Sciences, University of Glasgow, 2014.

Sharpe, P. 'Survival Strategies and Stories: Poor Widows and Widowers in Early Industrial England'. In *Widowhood in Medieval and Early Modern Europe*, S. Cavallo and L. Warner, eds. Harlow: Routledge, 1999.

Smith, C. *Adam Ferguson and the Idea of Civil Society: Moral Science in the Scottish Enlightenment*. Edinburgh: Edinburgh University Press, 2020.

Smitley, M. *The Feminine Public Sphere: Middle-Class Women in Civic Life in Scotland, c. 1870–1914*. Manchester: Manchester University Press, 2009.

Smout, T.C., ed. *The Search for Wealth and Stability: Essays in Economic and Social History Presented to M.W. Flinn*. London: Macmillan, 1979.

Stevenson, J. 'Writing Scotland's History in the Twentieth Century: Thoughts from across the Border'. *Scottish Historical Review* 76:201 (April 1997): 103–14.

Tabili, L. 'Outsiders in the Land of Their Birth: Exogamy, Citizenship, and Identity in War and Peace'. *Journal of British Studies* 44:4 (Oct. 2005): 796–815.

Thane, P. 'Women and the Poor Law in Victorian and Edwardian England'. *History Workshop* 6 (1978): 30–51.

Whatley, C. *The Industrial Revolution in Scotland*. Cambridge: Cambridge University Press, 1997.

Williams, S. 'Earnings, Poor Relief and the Economy of Makeshifts: Bedfordshire in the Early Years of the New Poor Law'. *Rural History* 16:1 (2005): 21–52.

Index

Studies in the History and Culture of Scotland

Valentina Bold, General Editor

This series presents a new reading of Scottish culture, establishing how Scots, and non-Scots, experience this devolved nation. Within the context of a rapidly changing United Kingdom and Europe, Scotland is engaged in an ongoing process of self-definition. The series will deal with this process as well as with cultural phenomena, from debates about the relative value of Gaelic-based, Scots and Anglicised culture, to period-specific definitions of Scottish identity. Orally transmitted culture - from traditional narratives to songs, customs, beliefs and material culture - will be a key consideration, along with the reconstruction of historical periods in cultural texts (visual and musical as well as historical). Taken as a whole, the series will go some way towards achieving a new understanding of a country with potential for development into parallel treatments of locally based cultural phenomena. The series welcomes monographs as well as collected papers.

Vol. 1 Valentina Bold.
James Hogg: A Bard of Nature's Making. 376 pages. 2007.
ISBN 978-3-03910-897-8

Vol. 2 James Porter (ed.).
Defining Strains: The Musical Life of Scots In the Seventeenth Century. 386 pages. 2007.
ISBN 978-3-03910-948-7

Vol. 3 Aaron Kelly.
James Kelman: Politics and Aesthetics. 251 pages. 2013.
ISBN 978-3-03911-130-5

Vol. 4 Jonathan Murray.
Discomfort and Joy: The Cinema of Bill Forsyth. 270 pages. 2011.
ISBN 978-3-03911-391-0

Vol. 5 Jessica Aliaga Lavrijsen.
The Fiction of Brian McCabe and (Scottish) Identity. 309 pages. 2013.
ISBN 978-3-0343-0830-4

Vol. 6 Susan Buckham, Peter C. Jupp and Julie Rugg (eds).
Death in Modern Scotland, 1855–1955: Beliefs, Attitudes and Practices. 343 pages. 2016.
ISBN 978-3-0343-1821-1

Vol. 7 Sarah Neely.
Between Categories: The Films of Margaret Tait: Portraits, Poetry, Sound and Place. 334 pages. 2017.
ISBN 978-3-0343-1854-9

Vol. 8 Edward Corp.
Sir David Nairne: The Life of a Scottish Jacobite at the Court of the Exiled Stuarts. 534 pages. 2018.
ISBN 978-1-78707-934-2

Vol. 9 Peter C. Jupp and Hilary Grainger (eds).
Death in Scotland: Chapters From the Twelfth Century to the Twenty-First. 339 pages. 2019.
ISBN 978-1-78997-268-9

Vol. 10 Virginia Blankenhorn.
Tradition, Transmission, Transformation: Essays on Scottish Gaelic Poetry and Song. 550 pages. 2019.
ISBN 978-1-78874-552-9

Vol. 11 Elizabeth Ford.
The Flute in Scotland from the Sixteenth to the Eighteenth Century. 228 pages. 2020.
ISBN 978-1-78874-716-5

Vol. 12 David Manderson.
The Anti-hero's Journey: The Work and Life of Alan Sharp. 390 pages. 2023.
ISBN 978-1-78997-575-8

Vol. 13 Kathryn A. Burnett, Ray Burnett, Michael Danson (eds).
Scotland and Islandness: Explorations in Community, Economy and Culture. 276 pages. 2021.
ISBN 978-1-78997-377-8

Vol. 14 Wendy M. Gordon.
The Girl Who Lived on Her Clothes: The People of Paisley and the New Poor Law, 1839–1876. 232 pages. 2024.
ISBN 978-1-80079-990-5

www.ingramcontent.com/pod-product-compliance
Ingram Content Group UK Ltd.
Pitfield, Milton Keynes, MK11 3LW, UK
UKHW021058130926
8556IPUK00046B/1149

9 781800 799905